# CONTENTS

## PORK ................................................................ 37

## STEWS ...........................................................124

## VEGAN & VEGETARIAN ...............................................129

## DESSERTS & DRINKS ...................................................................................................... 142

## RECIPE INDEX .............................................................................................................. 146

# INTRODUCTION

Instant Pot is a magic pot which can transform a few, affordable ingredients into the most delicious dinner in the fastest and easiest way. If you are about to start using the Instant Pot that will be one of the best companion in your journey to a healthier and happier life. Even if you have a tight schedule, you can always find 5-10 minutes to prepare a bunch of ingredients and put them in the pot. You can steam the baby carrots, cook the lentils or produce the homemade yogurt from one single touch of the display. Instant Pot will make you love the world of food, so you will be more successful in sticking to your diet with way less efforts.

During the last century, the food industry provided us with too many options of tasty, but unhealthy processed foods full of artificial additives, colors, and preservatives. Long-term consumption of such products resulted in worsening health conditions of the population, so it's time to make a change. Home cooking can prevent the development of diabetes, stroke and heart failure, and it can also normalize blood pressure and cholesterol levels. Moreover, this magnificent cooking appliance can be used as a safe and effective tool for improving weight loss.

If you are reading this page, it means that you have already decided to start better eating habits and you chose the one of the healthies and fastest way to prepare the food - the Instant Pot pressure cooker. I congratulate you with the right choice to change your life for the better. This book contains 1000 recipes which will help you enjoy mouthwatering and healthy meals, everyday and for any occasion for the whole family and friends.

## Why The Instant Pot is Great to Have

Sometimes it's easier to buy ready-to-eat sausages in the supermarket or a quick cheesy burger at burger king. The combination of various unnatural additives, huge amounts of monosodium glutamate and sugar ruin the digestive system and affect some organs. Nothing bad will happen because of one or two "cheat meals", but repetetive consumption of processed foods over the course of months and years will affect you and your health.

The second thing you should do is to change your shopping behavior and buy fresh, organic and quality products so you can start cooking at home. I promise that you will find tons of mouthwatering recipes in this book which will excite you to cook and forget about the quick sugary snacks.

## One-Touch Cooking Modes of Instant Pot

Instant Pot Pressure Cooker is your best friend in the kitchen that will help you immensely to achieve freedom in your kitchen - quickly and effortlessly. Thanks to one-touch cooking modes, the Instant Pot saves a lot of time and energy, and rewards you with tasty and nutritious meals.

- **Soup/Broth**. This pre-set method is for cooking soups or broths.
- **Meat/Stew**. This mode will be useful for stewing almost all kind of vegetables including peas, zucchini, spinach and other leafy veggies along with some juicy beef or park stew meat
- **Beans/Chili**. Lentils and beans are healthy plant-based sources of protein, so this setting will help you cook them in the fastest and hassle-free way.
- **Poultry.** Chicken and turkey should be prepared under this cooking mode. The meat will cook itself becoming tender and juicy.
- **Rice.** While rice is not considered as a part of the 20 healthiest foods, yet you can still utilize this setting for cooking quinoa or other nutritious grains.

- **Multigrain**. Wholegrains are full of the fiber, micro and macro elements, so you must add them to your everyday meals. The Instant Pot significantly reduces the cooking time of whole grains in comparison to a standard oven.

- **Porridge.** Tasty and nutritive oatmeal is a great way to start your day. This mode will help you cook the perfect breakfast.

- **Steam**. Steaming is the safest and the most effective cooking method, since it maximizes the amount of antioxidants and fiber in the food.

- **Sauté.** This mode allows stir-frying, browning or searing veggies, meat, poultry of fish.

- **Yogurt.** The best option for a homemade low-fat yogurt. When cooked at home, the yogurt is a very healthy food, without any added sugars and preservatives.

- **Pressure cook/Manual mode** - this is the most important Instant Pot setting. You can use this function for any kind of food preparation and adjust the pressure and cooking time as needed.

- **Slow cook**. The Instant Pot can also function as a Slow cooker. If you have plenty of time before a dinner, this method will help you to prepare the most delicious and tasty stews.

- **Pressure Level**. Depending on the amount of ingredients and their properties, you can adjust higher or lower pressure level to ensure the best cooking results.

- **Delay start.** You have a busy day and don't want to spend morning time in the kitchen? No problem, just prepare the ingredients, throw them in the Pot and set it to start cooking in 8h. And the dinner will be ready just in time. This function is also handy for soaking beans/grains.

- **Keep warm.** This function keeps the food warm. No need to microwave the meal anymore.

**Note!** Some Instant Pot models may have slightly different functions or buttons. Always check the manufacturer's manual before using any setting on your pressure cooker.

# MORNING RECIPES

## Speedy Soft-Boiled Eggs

Serving Size: 4 | Total Time: 10 minutes

4 large eggs

Salt and pepper to taste

To the pressure cooker, add 1 cup of water and place a wire rack. Place eggs on it. Seal the lid, press Steam, and cook for 3 minutes on High Pressure. Do a quick release. Allow to cool in an ice bath. Peel the eggs and season with salt and pepper before serving.

## Spinach & Feta Pie with Cherry Tomatoes

Serving Size: 2 | Total Time: 35 minutes

4 eggs

Salt and pepper to taste

½ cup heavy cream

1 cup cherry tomatoes, halved

1 cup baby spinach

1 spring onion, chopped

¼ cup feta, crumbled

1 tbsp parsley, chopped

Grease a baking dish with cooking spray and add in the spinach and onion. In a bowl, whisk the eggs, heavy cream, salt, and pepper. Pour over the spinach and arrange the cherry tomato on top. Sprinkle with the feta. Add a cup of water to the Instant Pot and insert a trivet. Place the dish on the trivet. Seal the lid, press Manual, and cook on High pressure for 15 minutes. Release pressure naturally for 10 minutes. Scatter parsley to serve.

## Strawberry Jam

Serving Size: 6 | Total Time: 30 minutes

1 lb strawberries, chopped

1 cup sugar

½ lemon, juiced and zested

1 tbsp mint, chopped

Add the strawberries, sugar, lemon juice, and zest to the Instant Pot. Seal the lid, select manual, and cook for 2 minutes on High.

Release pressure naturally for 10 minutes. Open the lid and stir in chopped mint. Select Sauté and continue cooking until the jam thickens, about 10 minutes. Let to cool before serving.

## Ricotta & Potato Breakfast

Serving Size: 4 | Total Time: 25 minutes

2 tbsp olive oil

1 lb potatoes, chopped

5 eggs, whisked

1 cup ricotta, crumbled

½ tsp dried oregano

1 tsp dried onion flakes

Salt and pepper to taste

Warm the olive oil in your Instant Pot on Sauté.

Place the potatoes and cook for 3-4 minutes. Add in eggs, ricotta cheese, oregano, dried onion flakes, ¼ cup of water, salt, and pepper.

Seal the lid, select Manual, and cook for 10 minutes on High pressure.

Once ready, perform a quick pressure release and unlock the lid. Serve immediately.

## Light & Fruity Yogurt

Serving Size: 12 | Total Time: 24hr

¼ cup Greek yogurt containing active cultures

1 lb raspberries, mashed

1 cup sugar

3 tbsp gelatin

1 tbsp fresh orange juice

8 cups milk

In a bowl, add sugar and raspberries and stir well to dissolve the sugar. Let sit for 30 minutes at room temperature. Add in orange juice and gelatin and mix well until dissolved. Remove the mixture and place in a sealable container, close, and allow to sit for 12 hrs to 24 hrs at room temperature before placing in the fridge. Refrigerate for a maximum of 2 weeks.

Into the cooker, add milk, and close the lid. The steam vent should be set to Venting then to Sealing. Select Yogurt until "Boil" is showed on display. When complete, there will be a display of "Yogurt" on the screen.

Open the lid and using a food thermometer, ensure the milk temperature is at least 185°F. Transfer the steel pot to a wire rack and allow to cool for 30 minutes until the milk has reached 110°F.

In a bowl, mix ½ cup warm milk and yogurt. Transfer the mixture into the remaining warm milk and stir without having to scrape the steel pot's bottom. Take the steel pot back to the base of the pot and seal the lid. Select Yogurt and cook for 8 hrs. Allow the yogurt to chill in a refrigerator for 1-2 hrs. Transfer the chilled yogurt to a bowl and stir in fresh raspberry jam.

## Greek Yogurt with Honey & Walnuts

Serving Size: 10 | Total Time: 15hr

2 tbsp Greek yogurt
8 cups milk
¼ cup sugar honey
1 tsp vanilla extract
1 cup walnuts, chopped

Add the milk to your Instant Pot. Seal the lid and press Yogurt until the display shows "Boil". When the cooking cycle is over, the display will show Yogurt. Open the lid and check that milk temperature is at least 175°F. Get rid of the skin lying on the milk's surface. Let cool in an ice bath until it becomes warm to the touch.

In a bowl, mix one cup of milk and yogurt to make a smooth consistency. Mix the milk with yogurt mixture. Transfer to the pot and place on your Pressure cooker.

Seal the lid, press Yogurt, and adjust the timer to 9 hrs. Once cooking is complete, strain the yogurt into a bowl using a strainer with cheesecloth. Chill for 4 hours. Add in vanilla and honey and gently stir well. Spoon the yogurt into glass jars. Serve sprinkled with walnuts and enjoy.

# EGGS & VEGETABLES

## Cauliflower & Kale Curry

Serving Size: 4 | Total Time: 10 minutes

1 lb cauliflower florets

1 can coconut milk

½ tsp fresh ginger, grated

1 lb kale, chopped

2 tsp garam masala

1 cup tomato sauce

1cup vegetable broth

Salt and pepper to taste

Mix the cauliflower, coconut milk, kale, garam masala, tomato sauce, ginger, broth, salt, and pepper in your Instant Pot. Seal the lid, select Manual, and cook for 4 minutes on High pressure. When done, perform a quick pressure release and unlock the lid. Serve immediately.

## Parsnip & Cauliflower Mash

Serving Size: 4 | Total Time: 15 minutes

1 cauliflower, cut into florets

2 parsnips, chopped

Salt and pepper to taste

2 tbsp safflower oil

1 green onion, chopped

Pour 1 cup water into your Instant Pot and fit in a steamer basket. Place in the cauliflower and parsnips and seal the lid. Select Manual and cook for 3 minutes on High.

Once over, perform a quick pressure release and unlock the lid. Mash the cauliflower and parsnips with a potato masher and mix in salt, pepper, and safflower oil. Serve topped with green onion.

## Fall Vegetable Mash

Serving Size: 4 | Total Time: 25 minutes

1 lb pumpkin, cubed

¼ lb celeriac, cubed

1 parsnip, cubed

2 potatoes, cubed

½ tsp dried thyme

½ tsp dried rosemary

2 tbsp butter

1 tsp garlic powder

¼ cup milk

Salt to taste

Pour 1 cup of water into your Instant Pot and fit in a steamer basket. Place in pumpkin, celeriac, parsnip, and potatoes and seal the lid. Select Manual and cook for 12 minutes on High. Once ready, perform a quick pressure release and unlock the lid. Transfer the vegetable to a bowl and mash them with a potato mash. Mix in milk, butter, garlic powder, rosemary, thyme, and salt. Serve.

## Zucchini with Asparagus

Serving Size: 4 | Total Time: 15 minutes

1 lb asparagus, trimmed and chopped

2 tbsp olive oil

2 garlic cloves, minced

2 zucchinis, sliced

½ cup whipping cream

½ cup vegetable broth

Salt and pepper to taste

2 tbsp fresh dill, chopped

Warm the olive oil in your Instant Pot on Sauté. Place the garlic and cook for 2 minutes. Stir in zucchinis, asparagus, vegetable broth, salt, and pepper. Seal the lid, select Manual, and cook for 4 minutes on High pressure. When done, perform a quick pressure release and unlock the lid. Stir in whipping cream. Serve topped with dill.

## Mango & Pumpkin Porridge

Serving Size: 4 | Total Time: 20 minutes

1 lb pumpkin, chopped

1 mango, chopped

1 cup milk

2 tbsp cinnamon powder

2 tbsp maple syrup

2 tbsp walnuts, chopped

A pinch of salt

Mix the pumpkin, mango, cinnamon powder, maple syrup, milk, and salt in your Instant Pot. Seal the lid, select Manual, and cook for 12 minutes on High pressure. Once ready, perform a quick pressure release and unlock the lid. Serve topped with walnuts.

## Steamed Asparagus with Salsa Verde

Serving Size: 4 | Total Time: 15 minutes

1 lb asparagus, trimmed

1 tbsp onion, chopped

Salt and pepper to taste

2 tbsp parsley, chopped

4 anchovy fillets, chopped

2 tbsp extra-virgin olive oil

1 tbsp sherry vinegar

2 tsp capers, chopped

Pour 1 cup of water into your Instant Pot and fit in a trivet. Place the asparagus on the trivet. Season with salt and pepper. Seal the lid and cook for 2 minutes on Steam. Once ready, perform a quick pressure release. Add parsley, onion, sherry vinegar, olive oil, anchovies, and capers in a blender and process until everything is well mixed. Drizzle the asparagus with the sauce.

## Steamed Artichokes with Salsa Roquefort

Serving Size: 4 | Total Time: 25 minutes

1 lb artichokes, trimmed

1 lemon wedge

½ cup Roquefort cheese

1 cup heavy cream

Pour 1 cup of water into your Instant Pot and fit in a steamer basket. Place in artichokes and seal the lid. Select Manual and cook for 10 minutes on High pressure. When over, perform a quick pressure release. Remove artichokes to a plate to cool. Clean the pot and heat the heavy cream on Sauté. Add in the Roquefort cheese and stir constantly until the cheese melts, about 3-4 minutes.Pour the sauce over the artichokes and serve with lemon.

## Coconut Pumpkin Chili

Serving Size: 4 | Total Time: 20 minutes

½ lb pumpkin, chopped

2 cups tomatoes, diced

1 cup coconut milk

1 tsp red chili flakes

1 tbsp red curry paste

1 tsp cumin

1 tbsp chili powder

Salt and pepper to taste

2 tbsp cilantro, chopped

Mix the pumpkin, tomatoes, cumin, coconut milk, chili powder, curry paste, salt, pepper, and 2 cups of water in your Instant Pot and seal the lid. Select Manual and cook for 10 minutes on High pressure. Once ready, perform a quick pressure release and unlock the lid. Top with red chili flakes and cilantro and serve.

## Mascarpone Mashed Turnips

Serving Size: 4 | Total Time: 32 minutes

1 lb turnips, cubed

1 onion, chopped

½ tsp ground nutmeg

½ cup chicken stock

Salt and pepper to taste

¼ cup sour cream

2 tbsp mascarpone

Place the turnips, onion, and chicken stock in your Instant Pot and seal the lid. Select Manual and cook for 12 minutes on High. Once over, allow a natural release for 10 minutes and unlock the lid. Add in sour cream, nutmeg, and mascarpone and mash it using a potato masher until smooth. Sprinkle with salt and pepper.

## Tarragon Baby Carrots with Parsnips

Serving Size: 4 | Total Time: 25 minutes

1 tbsp olive oil

1 small onion, chopped

½ lb baby carrots, sliced

2 parsnips, sliced

1 tsp ground cumin

1 tsp lemon juice

Salt and pepper to taste

2 tbsp tarragon, chopped

Warm the olive oil in your Instant Pot on Sauté. Place the onion and cook for 3 minutes. Add in baby carrots, parsnips, cumin, and lemon juice and sauté for 1 more minute; season with salt and pepper.

Add in 1 cup of water and seal the lid. Select Manual and cook for 7 minutes on High pressure. When done, perform a quick pressure release and unlock the lid. Serve topped with tarragon.

## Carrot & Beet Medley

Serving Size: 4 | Total Time: 20 minutes

2 tbsp olive oil
2 shallots, chopped
1 lb carrots, sliced
2 beets, peeled and cubed
1 cup vegetable broth
1 tbsp caraway seeds
Salt and pepper to taste

Warm the olive oil in your Instant Pot on Sauté. Place the shallots and cook for 3 minutes. Stir in caraway seeds, carrots, beets, vegetable broth, salt, and pepper. Seal the lid, select Manual, and cook for 8 minutes on High pressure. Once ready, perform a quick pressure release and unlock the lid. Serve warm.

## Orange Glazed Carrots

Serving Size: 4 | Total Time: 25 minutes

1 tbsp butter
6 carrots, sliced diagonally
¼ tsp orange zest
½ cup orange juice
1 tbsp orange marmalade
Salt and black pepper to taste

Pour 1 cup of water into your Instant Pot and fit in a steamer basket. Place in the carrots and seal the lid. Select Manual and cook for 8 minutes on High. When done, perform a quick release. Remove carrots to a bowl. Clean the pot and melt in the butter on Sauté. Add in orange zest, orange juice, orange marmalade, salt, and pepper and stir to combine. Add in carrots and cook until they are caramelized and sticky, 5-8 minutes. Serve.

## Garlic Eggplants with Parmesan

Serving Size: 4 | Total Time: 20 minutes

2 tbsp olive oil
1 onion, chopped
3 garlic cloves, minced
1 lb eggplants, cubed
Salt and pepper to taste
1 cup tomato sauce
½ tsp dried oregano
¼ cup Parmesan, grated

Warm the olive oil in your Instant Pot on Sauté. Place the onion and garlic and cook for 3 minutes. Add in the eggplants, salt, pepper, tomato sauce, oregano, and ½ of water. Season with salt and pepper.

Seal the lid, select Manual, and cook for 8 minutes on High. Once ready, perform a quick pressure release and unlock the lid. Serve topped with Parmesan cheese.

## Yogurt Eggplant Dip

Serving Size: 4 | Total Time: 20 minutes

3 tbsp olive oil
3 eggplants, chopped
4 garlic cloves, sliced
Salt to taste
1 lemon, juiced
1 cup Greek yogurt
1 tsp ground cumin
1 cup vegetable broth
2 tbsp cilantro, chopped

Warm the olive oil in your Instant Pot on Sauté. Place the eggplants and cook for 3 minutes, stirring occasionally. Add in garlic and Sauté for another 30 seconds. Season with salt and pour in vegetable broth Seal the lid. Select Manual and cook for 6 minutes on High pressure. When over, perform a quick pressure release and unlock the lid. Transfer the mixture to a food processor and lemon juice, cumin, and yogurt and blend until smooth. Sprinkle with cilantro and serve.

## Spicy Okra & Eggplant Dish

Serving Size: 4 | Total Time: 25 minutes

2 tbsp olive oil
1 onion, chopped
2 garlic cloves, minced

2 eggplants, cubed
½ lb okra, tops removed
1 tsp ground coriander
½ tsp chili powder
½ cup diced tomatoes
¾ cup vegetable stock
Fresh scallions, chopped

Warm the olive oil in your Instant Pot on Sauté. Place the onion, garlic, okra, and eggplants and cook for 3-4 minutes, stirring often. Add in the coriander, chili powder, tomatoes, and vegetable stock. Seal the lid, select Manual, and cook for 8 minutes on High pressure. Once over, perform a quick pressure release and open the lid. Adjust the seasonings and serve topped with fresh scallions.

## Winter Root Vegetables with Feta

Serving Size: 4 | Total Time: 40 minutes
½ lb beets
½ lb carrots
1 tbsp olive oil
1 clove garlic, minced
2 tbsp parsley, chopped
Salt and pepper to taste
3 tbsp raspberry vinaigrette
½ cup feta, crumbled

Pour 1 cup of water into your Instant Pot and fit in a steamer basket. Place in the beets and carrots and seal the lid. Select Manual and cook for 12 minutes on High pressure. Mix the garlic, parsley, salt, pepper, and raspberry vinaigrette in a bowl.

When over, allow a natural release for 10 minutes. Peel and slice the vegetables. Arrange on a greased baking sheet, drizzle with olive oil, and season with salt and pepper. Place under a preheated broiler for 4-5 minutes. Add in the dressing and feta and toss to coat. Serve.

## Orange & Thyme Beet Wedges

Serving Size: 4 | Total Time: 25 minutes
1 lb beets
2 tbsp butter, melted
2 thyme sprigs

1 orange, juiced

Pour 1 cup of water into your Instant Pot and fit in a steamer basket. Place in the beets and seal the lid. Select Manual and cook for 12 minutes on High pressure. Once ready, perform a quick pressure release and unlock the lid. Remove the beets to a plate and let cool. Peel and cut into wedges. Clean the pot and melt the butter on Sauté. Add in the thyme sprigs and cook for 30-40 seconds. Pour in the orange juice and beets and stir for 2-3 minutes. Discard the thyme sprigs and serve.

## Butter-Braised Cabbage

Serving Size: 4 | Total Time: 30 minutes
4 tbsp butter
1 head cabbage, shredded
1 ½ cups vegetable broth
½ tsp red pepper flakes
½ tsp herbs de Provence
1 carrot, grated
2 tsp cornstarch

Melt the butter in your Instant Pot on Sauté. Add in the cabbage and 2-3 tbsp of the vegetable broth and cook for 6 minutes, stirring occasionally. Mix in carrots, herbs de Provence, and the remaining vegetable broth.

Seal the lid, select Manual, and cook for 6 minutes on High pressure. When done, perform a quick pressure release and unlock the lid. Remove the cabbage and carrot to a bowl with a slotted spoon.

Combine the cornstarch with some of the cooking liquid and pour it into the pot. Press Sauté and cook until the sauce thickens, about 3-4 minutes. Stir in red pepper flakes and pour over the cabbage. Serve warm.

## Mushroom & Bell Pepper Casserole

Serving Size: 4 | Total Time: 30 minutes

1 ½ cups cremini mushrooms, sliced

2 tbsp butter

1 onion, chopped

1 red bell pepper, sliced

½ cup heavy cream

½ cup chicken broth

½ cup crispy onions

Melt butter in your Instant Pot on Sauté. Place in onion, bell pepper, and mushrooms and cook for 3-4 minutes. Stir in heavy cream and chicken broth. Seal the lid, select Manual, and cook for 15 minutes on High pressure. Once over, perform a quick pressure release and unlock the lid. Serve topped with crispy onions.

## Curried Tofu with Vegetables

Serving Size: 4 | Total Time: 20 minutes

2 tbsp sesame oil

3 green onions, sliced

3 garlic cloves, minced

1 celery stalk, chopped

1 cup mushrooms, sliced

1 red bell pepper, chopped

¼ tsp curry powder

28 oz firm tofu, cubed

1 cup bbq sauce

1 tbsp sesame seeds, toasted

Warm the sesame oil in your Instant Pot on Sauté. Place the green onions, garlic celery, mushrooms, and bell pepper and cook for 3 minutes. Stir in salt and curry powder and cook for 2 more minutes.

Add in tofu, and bbq sauce, and ½ cup of water. Seal the lid, select Manual, and cook for 5 minutes on High. Once ready, perform a quick pressure release and unlock the lid. Serve warm topped with sesame seeds.

## Asparagus & Mushrooms with Bacon

Serving Size: 4 | Total Time: 30 minutes

1 lb asparagus, trimmed

6 oz bacon, chopped

1 clove garlic, minced

1 yellow onion, chopped

8 oz mushrooms, sliced

Salt and pepper to taste

1 tbsp balsamic vinegar

Place asparagus in your Instant Pot and pour in water. Seal the lid, select Manual, and cook for 3 minutes on High pressure. When ready, allow a natural release for 10 minutes and unlock the lid. Strain asparagus; set aside. Press Sauté on the pot and add bacon; cook for 1-2 minutes. Stir in garlic and onion and sauté for 2 minutes. Mix in mushrooms and cook until they are soft. Mix in cooked asparagus, salt, pepper, and balsamic vinegar and combine. Serve immediately.

## Green Vegetables with Tomatoes

Serving Size: 6 | Total Time: 15 minutes

1 tsp olive oil

1 clove garlic, minced

2 cups chopped tomatoes

½ cup vegetable stock

½ lb green beans, trimmed

½ cup green peas

½ lb asparagus, trimmed

Salt and pepper to taste

Warm the olive oil in your Instant Pot on Sauté. Place in garlic and cook for 30 seconds until fragrant. Stir in tomatoes. Pour in vegetable stock, green beans, green peas, and asparagus; season with salt, and pepper. Seal the lid, select Manual, and cook for 5 minutes on High pressure. When done, perform a quick pressure release.

## Yummy Vegetable Soup

Serving Size: 4 | Total Time: 25 minutes

2 tbsp olive oil

1 cup leeks, chopped

2 garlic cloves, minced

4 cups vegetable stock

1 carrot, diced

1 parsnip, diced

1 celery stalk, diced

1 cup mushrooms

1 cup broccoli florets
1 cup cauliflower florets
½ red bell pepper, diced
¼ head cabbage, chopped
½ cup green beans
2 tbsp nutritional yeast
Salt and pepper to taste
½ cup parsley, chopped

Heat oil on Sauté. Add in garlic and leeks and cook for 6 minutes until slightly browned. Add in stock, carrot, celery, broccoli, bell pepper, green beans, salt, nutritional yeast, cabbage, cauliflower, mushrooms, parsnip, and pepper. Seal the lid and cook on High Pressure for 6 minutes. Release pressure naturally. Stir in parsley to serve.

# POULTRY

## Country Chicken with Vegetables

Serving Size: 4 | Total Time: 30 minutes

4 boneless, skinless chicken thighs
1 cup quartered cremini mushrooms
Salt and pepper to taste
2 tbsp olive oil
2 chopped carrots
½ lb green peas
1 chopped onion
3 garlic cloves, smashed
1 tbsp tomato paste
10 cherry tomatoes, halved
½ cup pitted green olives
½ cup fresh basil, minced
¼ cup parsley, chopped

Sprinkle chicken thighs with salt and pepper. Warm the olive oil in your Instant Pot on Sauté and cook carrots, mushrooms, and onion for 5 minutes. Add in garlic and tomato paste and cook for another 30 seconds. Stir in cherry tomatoes, chicken thighs, and olives.

Pour in 1 cup of water. Seal the lid, select Manual, and cook for 10 minutes on High pressure. Once ready, perform a quick pressure release and unlock the lid. Select Sauté and mix in green peas; cook for 5 minutes. Serve topped with fresh basil and parsley.

## Saucy Chicken Marsala

Serving Size: 4 | Total Time: 30 minutes

4 chicken breasts
¼ cup ketchup
¾ cup Marsala wine
½ cup soy sauce
2 green onions, chopped

Place chicken breasts, 1 cup of water, ketchup, Marsala wine, and soy sauce in your Instant Pot and stir. Seal the lid and cook for 15 minutes on Manual.

When ready, perform a quick pressure release and unlock the lid. Simmer for 5 minutes on Sauté until the sauce thickens. Top with green onions and serve.

## Garlic Chicken

Serving Size: 4 | Total Time: 35 minutes

1 lb chicken breasts
Salt and pepper to taste
2 tbsp butter
1 cup chicken broth
2 garlic cloves, minced
2 tbsp tarragon, chopped

Place chicken breasts in your Instant Pot. Sprinkle with garlic, salt, and pepper. Pour in the chicken broth and butter. Seal the lid, select Manual, and cook for 15 minutes on High pressure.

When over, allow a natural release for 10 minutes and unlock the lid. Remove the chicken and shred it. Top with tarragon and serve.

## Herby Chicken with Peach Gravy

Serving Size: 4 | Total Time: 55 minutes

4 chicken breasts
¼ cup olive oil
1 cup onions, chopped
2 celery stalks, chopped
2 peaches, cut into chunks
½ tsp dried thyme
½ tsp dried sage
2 cups chicken stock
Salt and pepper to taste

Heat oil on Sauté in your Instant Pot and stir-fry the onions for 2-3 minutes until soft. Add celery stalks and peaches and cook for 5 minutes, stirring occasionally.

Rub the meat with salt, pepper, thyme, and sage. Add it to the pot along with the stock. Seal the lid and cook on High Pressure for 35 minutes. Do a quick release. Serve.

## Chicken Wings in Yogurt-Garlic Sauce

Serving Size: 6 | Total Time: 35 minutes
12 chicken wings
3 tbsp olive oil
Salt to taste
3 cups chicken broth
½ cup sour cream
1 cup yogurt
2 garlic cloves, minced

Heat oil on Sauté in your Instant Pot. Brown the wings for 6 minutes, turning once. Pour in broth, salt, and seal the lid. Cook on Poultry for 15 minutes on High. Do a natural release. Unlock the lid. In a bowl, mix sour cream, yogurt, salt, and garlic. Drizzle with yogurt sauce. Serve.

## Spinach Chicken Thighs

Serving Size: 4 | Total Time: 40 minutes
1 lb chicken thighs
1 lb spinach, chopped
2 garlic cloves, minced
½ cup soy sauce
½ cup white wine vinegar
2 bay leaves
Salt and pepper to taste

Combine garlic, soy sauce, vinegar, bay leaves, salt, and pepper in a bowl. Add in chicken thighs and toss to coat. Transfer to your Instant Pot. Seal the lid and cook for 15 minutes on Poultry. Once ready, allow a natural release for 10 minutes and unlock the lid. Discard bay leaves and mix in spinach. Cook on Sauté for 4-5 minutes until the spinach wilts. Serve right away.

## Thai Chicken

Serving Size: 4 | Total Time: 25 minutes
1 lb chicken thighs
1 cup lime juice
4 tbsp red curry paste
½ cup fish sauce
2 tbsp brown sugar
1 red chili pepper, sliced
2 tbsp olive oil
1 tsp ginger, grated
2 tbsp cilantro, chopped

Combine lime juice, red curry paste, fish sauce, olive oil, brown sugar, ginger, and cilantro in a bowl. Add in chicken thighs and toss to coat. Transfer to your Instant Pot and pour in 1 cup water.

Seal the lid, select Manual, and cook for 15 minutes on High. When done, perform a quick pressure release. Top with red chili slices and serve.

## Chicken Fricassee

Serving Size: 4 | Total Time: 40 minutes
4 chicken breasts
2 tbsp olive oil
1 onion, chopped
2 garlic cloves, minced
Salt and pepper to taste
½ cup dry white wine
½ cup chicken broth
¼ cup heavy cream
2 tbsp capers
1 bay leaf
2 tbsp tarragon, chopped

Warm the olive oil in your Instant Pot on Sauté. Sprinkle chicken with salt and pepper and place in the pot. Cook for 6 minutes on all sides. Add in onion and garlic and cook for 3 minutes. Pour in chicken broth, white wine, and bay leaf. Seal the lid, select Manual, and cook for 15 minutes on High pressure.

When ready, perform a quick pressure release. Remove bay leaf and put in heavy cream and capers. Stir for 2-3 minutes and cook in the residual heat until thoroughly warmed. Ladle into bowls, top with tarragon, and serve.

## Spring Onion Buffalo Wings

Serving Size: 6 | Total Time: 30 minutes

2 lb chicken wings, sectioned

2 spring onions, sliced diagonally

½ cup hot pepper sauce

1 tbsp Worcestershire sauce

3 tbsp butter

Sea salt to taste

2 tbsp sugar, light brown

Combine hot sauce, Worcestershire sauce, butter, salt, and brown sugar in a bowl and microwave for 20 seconds until the butter melts. Pour 1 cup of water into your Instant Pot and fit in a trivet. Place the chicken wings on the trivet and seal the lid. Select Manual and cook for 10 minutes on High pressure.

Once done, perform a quick pressure release and unlock the lid. Remove chicken wings to a baking dish and brush the top with marinade. Broil for 4-5 minutes, turn the wings and brush more marinade. Broil for 4-5 minutes more. Top with spring onions and serve.

## Curried Chicken with Mushrooms

Serving Size: 4 | Total Time: 25 minutes

1 cup shiitake mushrooms, sliced

1 cup white mushrooms, sliced

1 lb chicken breasts, cubed

2 tbsp olive oil

1 yellow onion, thinly sliced

1 tbsp curry paste

1 cup chicken stock

½ bunch cilantro, chopped

Warm the olive oil in your Instant Pot on Sauté. Add in the chicken breasts and cook for 2 minutes until browned. Stir in onion and mushrooms and cook for another 3 minutes. Mix curry paste and chicken stock in a bowl and pour into the pot. Seal the lid, select Manual, and cook for 15 minutes on High pressure. Once ready, perform a quick pressure release and unlock the lid. Serve topped with cilantro.

## Chili & Lemon Chicken Wings

Serving Size: 4 | Total Time: 20 minutes

1 lb chicken wings

2 tbsp olive oil

1 tbsp honey

1 lemon, zested and juiced

½ tsp garlic powder

½ tsp cayenne pepper

½ chili pepper, chopped

Salt and pepper to taste

1 ½ cups chicken broth

Combine olive oil, lemon zest, lemon juice, red chili pepper, honey, garlic powder, cayenne pepper, black pepper, and salt in a bowl. Brush chicken wings with the mixture on all sides. Place the chicken broth and chicken wings in your Instant Pot. Seal the lid, select Manual, and cook for 10 minutes on High pressure. When over, perform a quick pressure release. Serve warm.

## Sticky Chicken Wings

Serving Size: 6 | Total Time: 35 minutes + marinating time

2 lb chicken wings

3 tbsp light brown sugar

2 tbsp soy sauce

1 small lime, juiced

½ tsp sea salt

1 tsp five-spice powder

Combine soy sauce, lime juice, five-spice powder, brown sugar, and salt in a bowl. Place chicken wing and marinade in a resealable bag and shake it. Transfer to the fridge and let marinate for 30 minutes.

Pour 1/2 cup of water and marinate chicken wings with the juices in your Instant Pot. Seal the lid, select Manual, and cook for 15 minutes on High pressure. When done, allow a natural release for 10 minutes and unlock the lid. Cook on Sauté until the sauce thickens. Serve.

## Korean-Style Chicken

Serving Size: 6 | Total Time: 35 minutes

3 green onions, sliced diagonally
3 chicken breasts, halved
5 tbsp sweet chili sauce
5 tbsp sriracha sauce
1 tbsp grated ginger
4 garlic cloves
1 tbsp rice vinegar
2 tbsp sesame seeds
1 tbsp soy sauce
½ cup chicken stock

Combine chili sauce, sriracha sauce, ginger, garlic, vinegar, sesame seeds, soy sauce, and chicken stock in a bowl. Add in the chicken fillets and toss to coat. Transfer to your Instant Pot. Seal the lid, select Manual, and cook for 15 minutes on High pressure. Once ready, allow a natural release for 10 minutes and unlock the lid. Top with green onions and serve.

## Chicken & Pepper Cacciatore

Serving Size: 4 | Total Time: 50 minutes

4 chicken thighs, with the bone, skin removed
3 mixed bell peppers, cut into strips
2 tbsp olive oil
Salt and pepper to taste
2 garlic cloves, minced
1 diced onion
1 cup canned diced tomatoes
2 tbsp chopped rosemary
½ tsp oregano
10 black olives, pitted

Warm olive oil in your Instant Pot on Sauté. Sprinkle chicken with salt and pepper and cook in the pot for 2-3 minutes per side; reserve. Add bell pepper, garlic, and onion to the pot and cook for 5 minutes. Stir in tomatoes, oregano, and 1 cup water and return the chicken. Seal the lid, select Manual, and cook for 20 minutes on High pressure. When done, allow a natural release for 10 minutes and unlock the lid. Serve topped with black olives and rosemary.

## Spicy Honey Chicken

Serving Size: 4 | Total Time: 20 minutes

4 chicken drumsticks
5 tbsp soy sauce
2 tbsp honey
1 cup chicken broth
1 garlic clove, minced
2 tbsp hot chili sauce
2 tbsp cornstarch
1 lime, cut into wedges

Place soy sauce, honey, garlic, and chili sauce in your Instant Pot and stir. Add in chicken drumsticks and toss to coat. Pour in chicken broth and seal the lid. Select Manual and cook for 12 minutes on High pressure. Mix 2 tbsp of water and cornstarch in a bowl.

When over, perform a quick pressure release and unlock the lid. Add in the slurry and simmer on Sauté until the sauce thickens. Serve right away with lime wedges.

## Chicken & Tomato Curry

Serving Size: 4 | Total Time: 35 minutes

2 lb chicken breasts
16 oz canned coconut milk
1 lb tomatoes, chopped
1 tbsp tomato paste
2 garlic cloves, minced
1-inch piece ginger, grated
1 onion, chopped
2 tbsp red curry paste
1 tsp salt
2 tbsp cilantro, chopped

Place coconut milk, tomatoes, tomato paste, garlic cloves, ginger, onion, curry paste, salt, and cilantro in your Instant Pot and stir. Add in chicken and 1 cup of water and seal the lid and stir. Select Manual and cook for 15 minutes on High pressure. When over, allow a natural release for 10 minutes and unlock the lid. Top with cilantro and serve.

## Creamy Mascarpone Chicken

Serving Size: 4 | Total Time: 30 minutes

8 bacon slices, cooked and crumbled
1 lb chicken breasts
8 oz mascarpone cheese
1 tbsp Dijon mustard
1 tsp ranch seasoning
3 tbsp cornstarch
½ cup cheddar, shredded

Place the chicken breasts, mustard, and mascarpone cheese in your Instant Pot. Add in ranch seasoning and 1 cup of water. Seal the lid, select Manual, and cook for 15 minutes on High pressure. Once ready, perform a quick pressure release and unlock the lid. Remove the chicken and shred it. Add in cornstarch, shredded chicken, cheese, and bacon and cook for 3 minutes on Sauté. Lock the lid and let chill for a few minutes. Serve.

## Greek Chicken with Potatoes & Okra

Serving Size: 4 | Total Time: 45 minutes

2 lb chicken thighs, skinless and boneless
1 lb potatoes, peeled and cut into quarters
2 tbsp olive oil
¾ cup chicken stock
¼ lb okra, tops removed
¼ cup lemon juice
2 tbsp Greek seasoning
Salt and pepper to taste

Warm the olive oil in your Instant Pot on Sauté. Sprinkle chicken thighs with salt and pepper. Place in the pot and cook for 6 minutes on all sides. Combine chicken stock, lemon juice, and Greek seasoning in a bowl and pour over the chicken. Stir in potatoes, okra, salt, and pepper and seal the lid. Select Manual and cook for 15 minutes on High pressure. Once ready, allow a natural release for 10 minutes and unlock the lid. Serve warm.

## Harissa Chicken Thighs

Serving Size: 4 | Total Time: 25 minutes

2 lb boneless chicken thighs

2 tbsp harissa
¼ cup soy sauce
1 tbsp ketchup
2 tbsp olive oil
¼ cup honey
2 tsp garlic powder
2 cups cooked rice
Salt and pepper to taste

Place soy sauce, ketchup, olive oil, honey, garlic powder, harissa, pepper, and salt in your Instant Pot and stir. Add in chicken thighs and pour in 1 cup of water. Seal the lid, select Manual, and cook for 20 minutes on High pressure.Once done, perform a quick pressure release and unlock the lid. Serve with a bed of rice.

## Filipino-Style Chicken Congee

Serving Size: 6 | Total Time: 55 minutes

6 chicken drumsticks
1 cup Jasmine rice
1 tbsp fresh ginger, grated
1 tbsp fish sauce
4 green onions, chopped
3 hard-boiled eggs, halved

Place chicken, rice, 6 cups of water, fish sauce, and ginger in your Instant Pot and stir. Seal the lid, select Manual, and cook for 25 minutes on High pressure.

When done, allow a natural release for 10 minutes. Remove the chicken and shred it. Put shredded chicken back in the pot and cook for 10 minutes on Sauté. Top with eggs and green onions and serve.

## Famous Chicken Adobo

Serving Size: 4 | Total Time: 50 minutes

4 chicken thighs
Salt and pepper to taste
2 tbsp olive oil
¼ cup white vinegar
¼ cup soy sauce
1 tbsp honey
1 onion, chopped
2 garlic cloves, crushed
2 bay leaves

2 tbsp cilantro, chopped

Warm the olive oil in your Instant Pot on Sauté. Sprinkle chicken with salt and pepper. Place it in the pot and brown for 8 minutes on all sides. Stir in vinegar, soy sauce, honey, onion, garlic, bay leaves, 1 cup of water, and pepper. Seal the lid, select Manual, and cook for 20 minutes on High pressure.

Once done, perform a quick pressure release and unlock the lid. Simmer for 10 minutes on Sauté until the sauce thickens. Discard bay leaves and top with cilantro. Serve.

## Jamaican Chicken with Pineapple Sauce

Serving Size: 4 | Total Time: 40 minutes

1 lb chicken thighs
½ cup coconut cream
2 tbsp soy sauce
1 cup pineapple chunks
1 tsp Jamaican seasoning
1 tsp coriander seeds
¼ tsp salt
½ cup cilantro, chopped
1 tsp arrowroot starch

Place chicken thighs, coconut cream, soy sauce, Jamaican jerk seasoning, coriander seeds, and salt in your Instant Pot and stir. Pour in 1 cup of water and seal the lid; cook for 15 minutes on manual. Once over, allow a natural release for 10 minutes and unlock the lid.

Remove chicken to a bowl. Combine arrowroot starch and 1 tbsp of water in a cup and pour it into the pot. Add in pineapple chunks and cook for 4-5 minutes on Sauté. Top the chicken with cilantro and sauce. Serve.

## Buffalo Chicken with Blue Cheese Sauce

Serving Size: 4 | Total Time: 30 minutes

1 lb chicken breasts, cut into thin strips
2 tbsp olive oil
1 tsp paprika
1 yellow onion, chopped
½ cup celery, chopped
½ cup buffalo sauce
½ cup chicken stock
¼ cup blue cheese, crumbled

4 tbsp sour cream

Place the chicken breasts, olive oil, paprika, onion, celery, buffalo sauce, and chicken stock in your Instant Pot. Seal the lid, select Manual, and cook for 12 minutes on High. When ready, allow a natural release for 10 minutes and unlock the lid. In a bowl, combine the crumbled blue cheese and sour cream and add 1 cup of the cooking juice and stir. Pour into the pot. Serve right away.

## Homemade Chicken Puttanesca

Serving Size: 6 | Total Time: 45 minutes

6 chicken thighs, skin on
2 tbsp olive oil
2 anchovy fillets, chopped
14 oz canned diced tomatoes
2 garlic cloves, crushed
½ tsp red chili flakes
6 oz pitted black olives
1 tbsp capers
1 tbsp fresh basil, chopped
Salt and pepper to taste

Warm the olive oil in your Instant Pot on Sauté. Place in the chicken thighs skin side-down and brown for 4-6 minutes. Remove to a bowl. Place tomatoes, garlic, chili flakes, anchovy fillets, black olives, capers, fresh basil, salt and pepper into the pot. Pour in 1 cup of water.

Bring to a simmer. Add in back the chicken and seal the lid. Select Manual and cook for 20 minutes on High pressure. When ready, allow a natural release for 10 minutes and unlock the lid. Serve immediately.

## Sweet & Spicy BBQ Chicken

Serving Size: 4 | Total Time: 35 minutes

6 chicken drumsticks
1 tbsp olive oil
1 onion, chopped
1 tsp garlic, minced
1 jalapeño pepper, minced
½ cup sweet BBQ sauce
1 tbsp arrowroot

Warm the olive oil in your Instant Pot on Sauté. Add in the onion and cook for 3 minutes. Add in garlic and jalapeño pepper and cook for another minute. Stir in barbecue sauce and 1/2 cup of water. Put in chicken drumsticks and seal the lid. Select Manual and cook for 18 minutes on High pressure. When over, perform a quick pressure release and unlock the lid. Mix 2 tbsp of water and arrowroot and pour it into the pot. Cook for 5 minutes on Sauté until the liquid thickens. Top with sauce and serve.

## Fennel Chicken with Tomato Sauce

Serving Size: 4 | Total Time: 35 minutes
1 lb chicken breasts
½ cup chicken broth
Salt and pepper to taste
1 tbsp fennel seeds
2 tbsp olive oil
2 cups tomato-basil sauce
Place the chicken breasts, olive oil, chicken broth, fennel seeds, salt, and pepper in your Instant Pot. Seal the lid, select Manual, and cook for 20 minutes on High pressure. When done, perform a quick pressure release and unlock the lid. Shred the chicken and add in tomato sauce. Simmer for 5 minutes on Saute. Serve immediately.

## Chicken Gumbo

Serving Size: 4 | Total Time: 40 minutes
4 chicken thighs
1 onion, diced
2 garlic cloves, minced
2 sticks celery, finely diced
2 green peppers, diced
1 tsp Cajun seasoning
Salt and pepper to taste
2 tbsp olive oil
1 ½ cups tomato sauce
1 jalapeno, halved
2 tbsp sage, chopped
Warm the olive oil in your Instant Pot on Sauté. Place in chicken and cook for 4-6 minutes on all sides; reserve. Add in onion, garlic, celery, and green peppers and cook for 5 minutes. Stir in Cajun seasoning, tomato sauce, salt,

pepper, and 1 cup of water. Seal the lid, select Manual, and cook for 20 minutes on High pressure. When ready, perform a quick pressure release and unlock the lid. Top with sage and jalapeño pepper and serve.

## Sticky Teriyaki Chicken

Serving Size: 4 | Total Time: 30 minutes
1 lb chicken breasts
2/3 cup teriyaki sauce
1 tsp sesame seeds
½ cup chicken stock
Salt and pepper to taste
3 green onions, chopped
Set your Instant Pot to Sauté. Place in teriyaki sauce and simmer for 1 minute. Stir in chicken stock, salt, and pepper and seal the lid. Select Manual and cook for 12 minutes on High pressure. Once over, allow a natural release for 10 minutes and unlock the lid. Transfer the chicken to a plate and shred it. Remove 1/2 cup of cooking liquid. Put chicken back in the pot and stir in green onions. Top with sesame seeds and serve.

## Za'atar Chicken with Baby Potatoes

Serving Size: 4 | Total Time: 30 minutes
1 lb chicken thighs
½ lb baby potatoes, halved
2 tbsp olive oil
1 tbsp za'atar seasoning
1 garlic clove, minced
1 large onion, sliced
Salt and pepper to taste
Warm the olive oil in your Instant Pot on Sauté. Place in onion and garlic and cook for 2 minutes. Add in chicken thighs and cook for 4-6 minutes on both sides. Scatter with za´atar seasoning, salt, pepper, potatoes, and pour in 1 cup of water. Seal the lid, select Manual, and cook for 15 minutes on High pressure.
Once ready, perform a quick pressure release and unlock the lid. Remove the chicken and shred it. Put chicken back to the pot and toss to coat. Serve right away.

## Indian-Style Chicken

Serving Size: 6 | Total Time: 37 minutes + marinating time

6 chicken thighs, bone-in
½ cup Greek yogurt
1 tbsp curry paste
1 tbsp lemon juice
Salt and pepper to taste
1 tbsp fresh ginger, grated
2 tbsp cilantro, chopped

Combine yogurt, lemon juice, curry paste, salt, and pepper in a bowl. Add in chicken thighs and toss to coat. Let marinate in the fridge for 2 hours. Place the chicken, marinade, ginger, and 1 cup of water in your Instant Pot. Seal the lid, select Manual, and cook for 12 minutes on High pressure. When over, allow a natural release for 10 minutes and unlock the lid. Transfer to a baking tray and put under the broiler 3-5 minutes. Top with cilantro.

## Chicken with Chili & Lime

Serving Size: 4 | Total Time: 25 minutes

1 lb chicken breasts
¾ cup chicken broth
Juice and zest of 1 lime
1 red chili, chopped
1 tsp cumin
1 tsp onion powder
2 garlic cloves, minced
1 tsp mustard powder
1 bay leaf
Salt and pepper to taste

Place the chicken breasts, chicken broth, lime juice, lime zest, red chili, cumin, onion powder, garlic cloves, mustard powder, bay leaf, salt, and pepper in your Instant Pot. Seal the lid, select Manual, and cook for 10 minutes on High. When ready, allow a natural release. Remove chicken and shred it. Discard the bay leaf. Top the chicken with cooking juices and serve.

## Cuban Mojo Chicken Tortillas

Serving Size: 4 | Total Time: 80 minutes + marinating time

4 chicken breasts
2 tbsp olive oil
1 lime, juiced
1 grapefruit, juiced
4 garlic cloves, minced
1 tsp ground cumin
Salt and pepper to taste
2 tbsp chopped cilantro
4 tortillas
1 avocado, sliced
2 tbsp hot sauce

Combine olive oil, lime juice, grapefruit juice, garlic, cumin, cilantro, salt, and pepper in a bowl. Add in chicken breasts and let marinate covered for 30 minutes. Transfer chicken and marinade to your Instant Pot and pour in 1 cup of water. Seal the lid and cook for 20 minutes on Manual. Once done, allow a natural release for 10 minutes and unlock the lid. Remove the chicken and shred it, then add it back to the pot; stir. Divide the chicken between the tortillas and top with avocado slices and hot sauce. Serve right away.

## Creole Chicken with Rice

Serving Size: 4 | Total Time: 45 minutes

2 tbsp olive oil
1 onion, diced
3 garlic cloves, minced
1 lb chicken breasts, sliced
1 cup chicken broth
1 (14.5-oz) can tomato sauce
1 cup white rice, rinsed
1 bell pepper, chopped
2 tsp creole seasoning
1 tbsp hot sauce

Warm the olive oil in your Instant Pot on Sauté. Place in onion and garlic and cook until fragrant, about 3 minutes. Stir in chicken breasts, bell pepper, hot sauce, and creole seasoning. Cook for 3 more minutes. Mix in chicken broth, tomato sauce, and rice and seal the lid. Select Manual and cook for 20 minutes on High pressure. When ready, allow a natural release for 10 minutes and unlock the lid. Serve warm.

# Moroccan-Style Chicken

Serving Size: 4 | Total Time: 30 minutes

1 lb chicken thighs, skinless
2 tbsp vegetable oil
Salt and pepper to taste
3 garlic cloves, minced
1 large onion, chopped
¼ tsp cumin
½ cup chicken broth
12 dried apricots, sliced
1 lb canned tomatoes, diced
1 tbsp fresh ginger, grated
½ tsp cinnamon, ground
2 tbsp cilantro, chopped
2 tbsp flaked almonds

Warm the vegetable oil in your Instant Pot on Sauté. Sprinkle chicken thighs with salt and pepper and place in the pot along with garlic and onion. Cook for 5 minutes. Stir in chicken broth, apricots, tomatoes, fresh ginger, cumin, and cinnamon. Seal the lid, select Manual, and cook for 12 minutes on High pressure. Once ready, perform a quick pressure release and unlock the lid. Serve topped with cilantro and almonds.

# Chicken in Creamy Mushroom Sauce

Serving Size: 4 | Total Time: 50 minutes

1 lb chicken breasts
1 tbsp olive oil
1 cup mushrooms, sliced
1 large onion, chopped
2 garlic cloves, minced
1 cup chicken stock
Salt and pepper to taste
1 cup heavy cream
2 green onions, chopped

Warm the olive oil in your Instant Pot on Sauté. Place in mushrooms, onion, and garlic and cook for 4-5 minutes. Sprinkle chicken breasts with salt and pepper and place in the pot. Cook for 6-8 minutes on all sides. Add in chicken stock and stir. Seal the lid, select Manual, and cook for 12 minutes on High pressure.

Once done, allow a natural release for 10 minutes. Remove the chicken. Add the heavy cream to the cooker

and stir for 3 minutes on Sauté. Pour the sauce over the chicken, top with green onions, and serve warm.

# Peppered Chicken with Chunky Salsa

Serving Size: 4 | Total Time: 30 minutes

3 mixed-color peppers, cut into strips
1 lb chicken breasts
2 tbsp olive oil
2 jalapeño peppers, sliced
1 onion, sliced
Salt and pepper to taste
½ tsp oregano
½ tsp cumin
2 cups chunky salsa

Warm the olive oil in your Instant Pot on Sauté. Place in onion, peppers, and jalapeño peppers and sauté for 5 minutes. Sprinkle chicken breasts with salt and pepper and place them in the pot along with oregano, cumin, chunky salsa, and ½ cup of water. Seal the lid and cook for 15 minutes on Manual on High. When ready, perform a quick pressure release. Shred chicken before serving.

# Chicken & Bacon Cacciatore

Serving Size: 4 | Total Time: 45 minutes

2 cups canned tomatoes and juice, crushed
1 lb chicken drumsticks
4 oz bacon, chopped
1 red onion, chopped
1 cup chicken stock
1 garlic clove, minced
1 tsp oregano, dried
1 bay leaf
Salt to taste
1 roasted pepper, chopped
12 Kalamata olives, sliced

Set your Instant Pot to Sauté. Add in the bacon and cook for 5 minutes. Stir in onion and garlic and cook for 3 minutes. Pour in chicken stock, tomatoes, oregano, bay leaf, salt, and chicken. Seal the lid, select Manual, and cook for 15 minutes on High pressure. Once over, allow a natural release for 10 minutes and unlock the lid. Discard the bay leaf and mix in roasted pepper. Serve topped with olives.

## Lemon & Thyme Chicken

Serving Size: 6 | Total Time: 40 minutes

3 lb red potatoes, peeled and quartered

2 lb chicken thighs

2 tbsp olive oil

1 onion, chopped

2 garlic cloves, minced

2 tbsp thyme, chopped

¾ cup chicken broth

1 lemon, juiced and zested

Salt and pepper to taste

Warm the olive oil in your Instant Pot on Sauté. Place in the chicken thighs and brown for 2-3 minutes, stirring occasionally. Add in onion and garlic and cook for 3 minutes. Stir in chicken broth, lemon zest, lemon juice, potatoes, half of the thyme, salt, and pepper. Seal the lid and cook for 15 minutes on Poultry. Once ready, allow a natural release for 10 minutes and unlock the lid. Top with thyme and serve.

## Cumin Chicken with Capers

Serving Size: 4 | Total Time: 30 minutes

4 chicken breasts

½ cup butter

½ tsp cumin

Salt and pepper to taste

Juice of 1 lemon

1 cup chicken broth

½ cup capers

Melt butter in your Instant Pot on Sauté. Sprinkle chicken breasts with cumin, salt, and pepper and place in the pot. Cook for 7-8 minutes on all sides. Stir in lemon juice, chicken broth, and capers and seal the lid. Select Manual and cook for 10 minutes on High pressure. Once ready, allow a natural release for 5 minutes and unlock the lid.

## Feta Cheese Turkey Balls

Serving Size: 6 | Total Time: 35 minutes

1 onion, minced

½ cup plain bread crumbs

1/3 cup feta, crumbled

Salt and pepper to taste

½ tsp dried oregano

1 lb ground turkey

1 egg, lightly beaten

1 tbsp olive oil

1 carrot, minced

½ celery stalk, minced

3 cups tomato puree

2 cups water

In a mixing bowl, combine half the onion, oregano, turkey, salt, crumbs, pepper, and egg, and stir until everything is well incorporated. Heat oil on Sauté in your Instant Pot. Cook celery, remaining onion, and carrot for 5 minutes until soft. Pour in water and tomato puree. Adjust the seasonings. Roll the mixture into meatballs, and drop into the sauce. Seal the lid. Press Meat/Stew and cook on High Pressure for 5 minutes. Release the pressure naturally for 20 minutes. Serve topped with feta.

## Chicken with Port Wine Sauce

Serving Size: 6 | Total Time: 41 minutes

1 (3 lb) chicken, cut into pieces

2 tbsp olive oil

1 large onion, finely diced

1 cup mushrooms

¼ cup Port wine

Salt and pepper to taste

2 tbsp parsley, chopped

Warm olive oil in your IP on Sauté. Add in the chicken pieces and cook until the chicken is light brown, about 6-7 minutes; set aside. Add onion and mushrooms to the pot and sauté for 3-4 minutes. Deglaze with Port wine and pour in 1 cup of water. Season with salt and pepper and return the chicken. Seal the lid, select Manual, and cook for 20 minutes on High. Once ready, release pressure naturally. Sprinkle with parsley and serve.

## Turkey Cakes with Ginger Gravy

Serving Size: 4 | Total Time: 25 minutes

1 lb ground turkey
¼ cup breadcrumbs
¼ cup grated Parmesan
½ tsp garlic powder
2 green onions, chopped
Salt and pepper to taste
2 tbsp olive oil
2 cups tomatoes, diced
¼ cup chicken broth
GINGER SAUCE
4 tbsp soy sauce
2 tbsp canola oil
2 tbsp rice vinegar
1 garlic clove, minced
1 tsp ginger, grated
½ tbsp honey
¼ tsp black pepper
½ tbsp cornstarch

Combine turkey, breadcrumbs, green onions, garlic powder, salt, pepper, and Parmesan cheese in a bowl. Mix with your hands and shape meatballs out of the mixture. In another bowl, mix soy sauce, canola oil, rice vinegar, garlic clove, ginger, honey, pepper, and cornstarch. Warm the olive oil in your Instant Pot on Sauté.

Place in meatballs and cook for 4 minutes on all sides. Pour in ginger gravy, tomatoes, and chicken stock and seal the lid. Select Manual and cook for 10 minutes on High pressure. Once over, perform a quick pressure release and unlock the lid. Serve in individual bowls.

## Delicious Turkey Burgers

Serving Size: 4 | Total Time: 35 minutes

1 lb ground turkey
2 egg
1 tbsp flour
1 onion, finely chopped
Salt and pepper to taste
1 tbsp sour cream

In a bowl, add ground turkey, egg, flour, onion, salt, pepper, and sour cream and mix well. Form the mixture into patties. Line parchment paper over a baking dish and arrange the patties. Pour 1 cup of water into your Instant Pot. Lay the trivet and place the baking dish on top.

Seal the lid. Cook on Manual for 15 minutes on High. Release the pressure naturally for 10 minutes. Unlock the lid. Serve with lettuce and tomatoes.

## Rigatoni with Turkey & Tomato Sauce

Serving Size: 4 | Total Time: 30 minutes

2 tbsp canola oil
1 lb ground turkey
1 egg
¼ cup bread crumbs
2 cloves garlic, minced
1 tsp dried oregano
1 tsp cumin
1 tsp red pepper flakes
Salt and pepper to taste
3 cups tomato sauce
8 oz rigatoni
2 tbsp grated Grana Padano

In a bowl, combine turkey, crumbs, cumin, garlic, and egg. Season with oregano, salt, red pepper flakes, and pepper. Form the mixture into meatballs. Warm the oil on Sauté in your Instant Pot. Cook the meatballs for 3-4 minutes until browned on all sides; set aside.

Add rigatoni to the cooker and pour the tomato sauce over. Cover with water. Stir well. Throw in the meatballs. Seal the lid and cook for 4 minutes on High Pressure. Release the pressure quickly. Serve topped with cheese.

## Sunday Turkey Lettuce Wraps

Serving Size: 4 | Total Time: 35 minutes

¾ cup olive oil
4 cloves garlic, minced
3 tbsp maple syrup
2 tbsp pineapple juice
1 cup coconut milk
3 tbsp rice wine vinegar

3 tbsp soy sauce

1 tbsp Thai-style chili paste

1 lb turkey breast, boneless, cut into strips

1 lettuce, leaves separated

1/3 cup chopped peanuts

¼ cup chopped cilantro

In your Instant Pot, mix oil, garlic, rice wine vinegar, soy sauce, pineapple juice, maple syrup, coconut milk, and chili paste until smooth; add turkey strips and ensure they are submerged in the sauce. Seal the lid and cook on High Pressure for 12 minutes. Release the pressure quickly. Place the turkey at the center of each lettuce leaf. Top with cilantro and chopped peanuts.

## Homemade Turkey Pepperoni Pizza

Serving Size: 4 | Total Time: 25 minutes

1 cup fire-roasted tomatoes, diced

1 cup turkey pepperoni, chopped

1 pizza crust

1 tsp oregano

7 oz gouda cheese, grated

2 tbsp olive oil

Grease a baking pan with oil. Line some parchment paper and place the pizza crust in it. Spread the fire-roasted tomatoes over the pizza crust and sprinkle with oregano. Make a layer with cheese and top with pepperoni. Add a trivet to your Instant Pot and pour in 1 cup water. Seal the lid and cook for 15 minutes on High Pressure. Do a quick release. Remove the pizza and serve.

## Turkish-Style Roasted Turkey

Serving Size: 6 | Total Time: 70 minutes

2 lb boneless turkey breast, halved

2 garlic cloves, crushed

1 tsp dried basil

Salt and pepper to taste

3 whole cloves

½ cup soy sauce

½ cup lemon juice

¼ cup oil

3 cups chicken broth

Place the turkey in a Ziploc bag and add basil, cloves, soy sauce, oil, salt, pepper, and lemon juice. Pour in 1 cup of broth and seal. Shake and refrigerate for 30 minutes. Heat oil on Sauté in your Instant Pot. Cook the garlic for 2 minutes. Add in turkey and 2 tbsp of the marinade and the remaining broth. Seal the lid. Cook on Manual for 25 minutes on High. Release the pressure naturally. Serve.

## Spicy Turkey Casserole with Tomatoes

Serving Size: 4 | Total Time: 30 minutes

2 (14-oz) cans fire-roasted tomatoes

2 bell peppers, cut into thick strips

2 tbsp olive oil

½ sweet onion, diced

3 cloves garlic, minced

1 jalapeño pepper, minced

1 lb turkey breast, cubed

1 cup salsa

2 tsp chili powder

1 tsp ground cumin

Salt to taste

1 tbsp oregano, chopped

Warm oil on Sauté. Add in garlic, onion, and jalapeño and cook for 5 minutes until fragrant. Stir in turkey and cook for 5-6 minutes until browned. Add in salsa, tomatoes, bell peppers, and 1 ½ cups water. Season with salt, cumin, and chili powder. Seal the lid, press Manual, and cook for 10 minutes on High. Release the pressure quickly. Top with oregano and serve.

## Cranberry Turkey with Hazelnuts

Serving Size: 4 | Total Time: 40 minutes

1 lb turkey breasts, sliced

3 tbsp butter, softened

2 cups fresh cranberries

1 cup hazelnuts, chopped

1 cup red wine

1 tbsp rosemary, chopped

2 tbsp olive oil

2 tbsp orange zest

Salt and pepper to taste

Rub the turkey with oil and sprinkle with orange zest, salt, pepper, and rosemary. Melt butter in your Instant Pot on Sauté and brown turkey breast for 5-6 minutes. Pour in the wine, cranberries, and 1 cup of water. Seal the lid. Cook on High Pressure for 25 minutes. Do a quick release. Serve with chopped hazelnuts.

## Parsley & Lemon Turkey Risotto

Serving Size: 4 | Total Time: 40 minutes

2 boneless turkey breasts, cut into strips
2 lemons, zested and juiced
1 tbsp dried oregano
2 garlic cloves, minced
1 ½ tbsp olive oil
1 onion, diced
2 cups chicken broth
1 cup arborio rice, rinsed
Salt and pepper to taste
¼ cup chopped parsley
8 lemon slices

In a Ziploc bag, mix turkey, oregano, salt, garlic, juice and zest of two lemons. Marinate for 10 minutes. Warm oil on Sauté in your Instant Pot. Add onion and cook for 3 minutes. Stir in the rice and chicken broth and season with pepper and salt.

Empty the Ziploc having the chicken and marinade into the pot. Seal the lid and cook on High Pressure for 12 minutes. Release the pressure quickly. Garnish with lemon slices and parsley to serve.

## Sage Turkey & Red Wine Casserole

Serving Size: 4 | Total Time: 50 minutes

1 lb boneless turkey breast, cubed
1 onion, sliced
1 celery stalk, sliced
2 tbsp olive oil
1 carrot, diced
½ cup red wine
Salt and pepper to taste
1 cup chicken broth
1 tbsp tomato puree
2 tbsp sage, chopped

Warm olive oil in your IP on Sauté. Add in the turkey cubes and brown for 4-5 minutes, stirring occasionally; set aside. Add onion, celery, and carrot to the pot and sauté for 3-4 minutes. Stir in tomato puree, red wine, salt, and pepper and pour in chicken broth. Stir and return the turkey. Seal the lid, select Manual, and cook for 20 minutes on High. Once ready, release pressure naturally for 10 minutes. Unlock the lid, top with sage and serve.

## Spicy Ground Turkey Chili with Vegetables

Serving Size: 6 | Total Time: 60 minutes

1 tbsp olive oil
1 small onion, diced
2 garlic cloves, minced
1 lb ground turkey
2 bell peppers, chopped
6 potatoes, chopped
1 cup carrots, chopped
1 cup corn kernels, roasted
1 cup tomato puree
1 cup diced tomatoes
1 cup chicken broth
1 tbsp ground cumin
1 tbsp chili powder
Salt and pepper to taste

Warm oil on Sauté in your Instant Pot and stir-fry onion and garlic until soft for about 3 minutes. Stir in turkey and cook until thoroughly browned, about 5-6 minutes. Add the bell peppers, potatoes, carrots, corn, tomato puree, tomatoes, broth, cumin, chili powder, salt, and pepper, and stir to combine. Seal the lid and cook for 25 minutes on High Pressure. Do a quick release. Set to Sauté and cook uncovered for 15 more minutes. Serve.

## Turkey & Black Bean Chili

Serving Size: 6 | Total Time: 30 minutes

2 lb chopped turkey breast
1 ½ cups vegetable stock
2 (14-oz) cans black beans
2 garlic cloves, peeled
1 onion, diced
1 yellow bell pepper, diced
1 (7 oz) green chiles, diced
1 (14 oz) can diced tomatoes
1 tbsp hot sauce
½ tsp cumin
½ tbsp chili powder
1 cup cheddar, shredded

Place turkey, vegetable stock, black beans, garlic, onion, bell pepper, tomatoes, chiles, cumin, hot sauce, and chili powder in your Instant Pot and stir. Seal the lid, select Manual, and cook for 20 minutes on High pressure. Once done, allow a natural release for 10 minutes, then a quick pressure release, and unlock the lid. Top with cheddar and serve.

## Turkey Stew with Salsa Verde

Serving Size: 4 | Total Time: 52 minutes

1 lb turkey thighs, boneless and diced
2 tbsp olive oil
1 cup pearl onions
1 carrot, julienned
1 cup green peas
1 cup salsa verde
Salt and pepper to taste
¼ tsp turmeric
¼ tsp cumin

Warm olive oil in your IP on Sauté. Add in the turkey pieces and brown for 4-5 minutes, stirring occasionally; set aside. Add pearl onions and carrot to the pot and sauté for 3-4 minutes. Stir in the turmeric, cumin, salt, and pepper and pour in 1 cup of water. Return the turkey. Seal the lid, select Manual, and cook for 20 minutes on High. Once ready, allow a natural pressure release for 10

minutes. Unlock the lid, add in the green peas and salsa verde, and stir. Press Sauté and cook for 3 minutes.

## Potato Skins with Shredded Turkey

Serving Size: 4 | Total Time: 30 minutes

2 cups vegetable broth
1 tsp chili powder
1 tsp ground cumin
½ tsp onion powder
½ tsp garlic powder
1 lb turkey breast
4 potatoes
1 Fresno chili, minced
Salt and pepper to taste

In the pot, combine broth, cumin, garlic powder, onion powder, and chili powder. Toss in turkey to coat. Place a steamer rack over the turkey. On top of the rack, set the steamer basket. Use a fork to pierce the potatoes and transfer to the steamer basket. Seal the lid and cook for 20 minutes on High. Release the pressure quickly.

Remove rack and steamer basket from the cooker. Shred the turkey in a bowl. Place the potatoes on a plate. Cut in half each potato lengthwise and scoop out the insides. Season with salt and pepper. Stuff with shredded turkey. Top with chili pepper.

## Turkey Soup with Noodle

Serving Size: 6 | Total Time: 40 minutes

1 tbsp olive oil
1 onion, minced
3 cloves garlic, minced
1 turnip, chopped
1 cup celery rib, chopped
1 tbsp dry basil
1 bay leaf
6 cups vegetable broth
1 lb turkey breasts, cubed
8 oz dry egg noodles
Salt and pepper to taste

Warm olive oil on Sauté. Stir-fry in garlic and onion for 3 minutes. Mix in celery, bay leaf, basil, and turnip. Pour in 3 cups of broth. Scrape any brown bits from the pan's bottom and add turkey. Seal the lid and cook on High Pressure for 10 minutes. Naturally release the pressure. Transfer turkey breasts to another bowl.

Do away with the skin and bones. Using two forks, shred the meat. Set the cooker on Sauté. Transfer the turkey to the pot; add noodles and the remaining broth. Simmer for 10 minutes until noodles are done. Season and serve.

## Caribbean Turkey Wings

Serving Size: 4 | Total Time: 55 minutes

2 lb turkey wings
2 tbsp vegetable oil
2 tbsp butter
Salt and pepper to taste
1 yellow onion, sliced
½ cup brown sugar
1 tbsp bonnet pepper sauce
¼ cup chives, chopped
1 cup pineapple juice
1 tbsp cornstarch

Warm the vegetable oil and butter in your Instant Pot on Sauté. Sprinkle turkey wings with salt and pepper and place them in the pot. Sear for 5-6 minutes on all sides; set aside. Place onion in the pot and cook for 2 minutes. Stir in pineapple juice, bonnet pepper sauce, brown sugar, and 1/2 cup of water. Put in turkey wings and seal the lid. Select Manual and cook for 20 minutes on High.

When done, allow a natural release for 10 minutes and unlock the lid. Remove wings to a plate. Mix cornstarch and some cooking liquid in a bowl and pour into the pot. Simmer for 5 minutes on Sauté until the sauce thickens. Top with chives and serve with sauce.

## Turkey Meatball Soup with Rice

Serving Size: 4 | Total Time: 30 minutes

1 green bell pepper, chopped
1 habanero pepper, seeded and minced
2 tbsp olive oil
1 onion, chopped
2 garlic cloves, minced
½ lb ground turkey
1 carrot, chopped

1 (14-oz) can diced tomatoes
½ tsp cumin
½ tsp oregano
½ cup white rice, rinsed
Salt and pepper to taste
1 egg, beaten
1 cup yogurt

Mix ground turkey with cumin, oregano, salt, and pepper in a bowl. Shape the mixture into 1-inch balls. Warm olive oil in your Instant Pot on Sauté. Add in onion, bell pepper, habanero pepper, carrot, and garlic. Cook for 3-4 minutes. Add in meatballs, tomatoes, 3 cups water, and rice. Seal the lid, select Manual and cook for 15 minutes.

Once ready, perform a quick pressure release and unlock the lid. Mix the egg and yogurt in a bowl, and temper with one cup of the soup liquid, adding it slowly and whisking constantly to prevent the egg from cooking. Stir this mixture into the pot. Ladle the soup into bowls and serve immediately.

## Hungarian-Style Turkey Stew

Serving Size: 4 | Total Time: 40 minutes

1 lb chopped turkey pieces
2 tbsp butter
1 tsp paprika
1 can (15 oz) diced tomatoes
1 red onion, sliced
2 garlic cloves, chopped
1 red bell pepper, chopped
1 green bell pepper, chopped
1 cup chicken stock
Salt and pepper to taste
6 tbsp sour cream
2 tbsp parsley, chopped

Melt butter in your Instant Pot on Sauté and cook the turkey for 5 minutes, stirring occasionally. Add in onion, garlic, and bell peppers and sauté for another 3 minutes. Stir in paprika, tomatoes, and stock and seal the lid. Select Manual and cook for 20 minutes on High pressure. Once over, perform a quick pressure release and unlock the lid. Adjust the seasoning. Top with sour cream and parsley.

## Buffalo Turkey Chili

Serving Size: 4 | Total Time: 40 minutes

1 lb ground turkey
2 tbsp olive oil
1 onion, diced
½ habanero pepper, diced
½ cup red bell pepper, diced
1 (14 oz) can pinto beans
½ cup hot Buffalo sauce
2 ½ cups chicken stock
1 tsp oregano
1 tbsp chili powder
Salt and pepper to taste
2 tbsp cilantro, chopped

Warm the olive oil in your Instant Pot on Sauté and cook the onion, habanero pepper, and bell pepper until tender, about 3-4 minutes. Stir in ground turkey, beans, chicken stock, buffalo sauce, oregano, chili powder, salt, and pepper. Seal the lid and cook for 15 minutes on Bean/Chili on High pressure. When over, allow a natural release for 10 minutes, then perform a quick pressure release and unlock the lid. Serve topped with cilantro.

## Turkey Sausage with Brussels Sprouts

Serving Size: 4 | Total Time: 40 minutes

1 lb turkey sausage, sliced
2 tbsp olive oil
1 yellow onion, chopped
2 garlic cloves, minced
½ lb Brussels sprouts, sliced
¼ cup chicken broth
1 tsp yellow mustard
1 tsp balsamic vinegar
Salt and pepper to taste

Warm the olive oil in your Instant Pot on Sauté. Place in onion and garlic and cook for 2 minutes. Add in turkey sausage and cook for 5 more minutes. Stir in Brussels sprouts, mustard, vinegar, salt, and pepper for 3 minutes. Pour in chicken broth. Seal the lid, select Manual, and cook for 15 minutes on High pressure. When ready, allow a natural release for 5 minutes, then a quick pressure release, and unlock the lid. Serve right away.

## Potato & Cauliflower Turkey Soup

Serving Size: 4 | Total Time: 35 minutes

1 tbsp olive oil
1 lb ground turkey
2 garlic cloves, minced
1 leek, chopped
1 cup cauliflower florets
1 carrot, chopped
1 celery stalk, chopped
1 cup tomato sauce
½ tsp dried sage
½ tsp dried thyme
4 cups chicken broth
3 potatoes, chopped
Salt and pepper to taste

Warm the olive oil in your Instant Pot on Sauté. Place the ground turkey and garlic and cook for 5-6 minutes. Remove to a bowl. Add the leek, carrot, celery, cauliflower, tomato sauce, chicken broth, potatoes, sage, and thyme to the pot and return the turkey. Seal the lid, select Manual, and cook for 8 minutes on High. When over, allow a natural release for 10 minutes and unlock the lid. Sprinkle with salt and pepper. Serve right away.

## North African Turkey Stew

Serving Size: 4 | Total Time: 60 minutes

1 lb turkey breast, cubed
2 tbsp butter
1 onion, diced
½ tsp garlic powder
2 tsp ras el hanout
1 carrot, sliced
2 celery stalks, chopped
15.5 oz chickpeas, drained
2 oz green olives, pitted
3 ½ cups chicken broth
Salt and pepper to taste
2 tbsp cilantro, chopped

Melt butter in your Instant Pot on Sauté and cook the onion, carrot, and celery for 3-4 minutes. Stir in turkey breast and cook until browned, about 4-5 minutes. Mix in garlic powder, ras el hanout, salt, pepper, chickpeas, and chicken broth. Seal the lid, select Manual, and cook for 25 minutes on High pressure. When done, allow a natural release for 10 minutes and unlock the lid. Serve topped with green olives and cilantro.

## Weekend Turkey with Vegetables

Serving Size: 4 | Total Time: 35 minutes

1 lb turkey breast, chopped
1 tsp red pepper flakes
2 cups canned tomatoes
3 cups chicken broth
1 tsp honey
2 cups zucchini, cubed
3 garlic cloves, chopped
1 onion, finely chopped
2 tbsp tomato paste
1 cup baby carrots, chopped
Salt and pepper to taste
2 tbsp olive oil

Mix turkey, red pepper flakes, tomatoes, broth, honey, zucchini, garlic, onion, tomato paste, carrots, salt, pepper, and olive oil in your Instant Pot. Seal the lid and cook on Meat/Stew for 25 minutes on High Pressure. When ready, do a quick release and open the lid. Serve.

## Turkey with Rice & Peas

Serving Size: 6 | Total Time: 45 minutes

1 ½ lb turkey breasts, sliced
1 tbsp olive oil
1 small onion, sliced
1 cup brown rice
1 cup green peas
2 cups chicken broth
Salt and pepper to taste

Warm the olive oil in your Instant Pot on Sauté. Add in the onion and turkey and cook for 3 minutes, stirring occasionally. Stir in rice for 1 minute and pour in the broth; season with salt and pepper. Seal the lid, select Manual, and cook for 20 minutes on High.

Once ready, allow a natural release for 10 minutes, then perform a quick pressure release and unlock the lid. Mix in green peas and cook for 3-4 minutes on Sauté. Serve.

## Mediterranean Duck with Olives

Serving Size: 4 | Total Time: 20 minutes

½ cup sun-dried tomatoes, chopped
1 lb duck breasts, halved
2 tbsp olive oil
½ tbsp Italian seasoning
Salt and pepper to taste
2 garlic cloves, minced
½ cup chicken stock
¾ cup heavy cream
1 cup kale, chopped
½ cup Parmesan, grated
10 Kalamata olives, pitted

Combine olive oil, Italian seasoning, pepper, salt, and garlic in a bowl. Add in the duck breasts and toss to coat. Set your Instant Pot to Sauté. Place in duck breasts and cook for 5-6 minutes on both sides. Pour in chicken stock and seal the lid. Select Manual and cook for 4 minutes.

When done, perform a quick pressure release and unlock the lid. Mix in heavy cream, tomatoes, Kalamata olives, and kale and cook for 5 minutes on Sauté. Serve topped with Parmesan cheese.

## Honey-Glazed Turkey

Serving Size: 4 | Total Time: 60 minutes

1 large turkey breast
½ cup honey
½ tsp cumin
½ tsp turmeric
Salt and pepper to taste
2 cups chicken stock
1 onion, diced
2 garlic cloves, minced
1 tbsp dry sherry

Combine honey, cumin, turmeric, salt, and pepper in a bowl. Rub the mixture onto the turkey and let sit for 10 minutes. Place onion, garlic, and turkey in your Instant Pot. Add in chicken stock and sherry. Seal the lid and cook for 30 minutes on Manual. When ready, allow a natural release for 10 minutes. Slice turkey before serving.

## Roast Goose with White Wine

Serving Size: 4 | Total Time: 40 minutes
1 lb goose fillets, sliced
1 onion, chopped
4 tbsp butter, softened
2 garlic cloves, crushed
1 cup white wine
2 tbsp fresh celery, chopped
1 tsp dried thyme
Salt and pepper to taste

Season the goose with salt and white pepper. Melt butter on Sauté in your Instant Pot and stir-fry onions, celery, and garlic for 3-4 minutes. Add the goose fillets and brown on both sides for 6-8 minutes. Add in the white wine and thyme. Pour in 1 cup of water, seal the lid, and set to Meat/Stew. Cook for 25 minutes on High Pressure. When ready, do a quick release and set aside Serve.

## Duck Breasts with Honey-Mustard Glaze

Serving Size: 4 | Total Time: 50 minutes
1 lb duck breast
1 tbsp oil
1 tsp onion powder
1 cup honey
¼ cup soy sauce
¼ cup dry sherry
1 tbsp Dijon mustard
3 cups chicken broth
Salt and pepper to taste

Rub the duck with onion powder, salt, and pepper. Place it in the Instant Pot. Pour the broth, seal the lid and cook on Meat/Stew for 35 minutes on High Pressure.

Do a quick release. Remove the duck. Heat oil on Sauté, add soy sauce, honey, sherry, and mustard. Stir well and cook for 3-4 minutes. Add the meat and coat well. Serve the meat topped with the sauce.

# PORK

## Merlot Pork Chops

Serving Size: 4 | Total Time: 50 minutes

4 pork chops
3 carrots, chopped
1 tomato, chopped
1 onion, chopped
2 garlic cloves, minced
¼ cup merlot red wine
½ cup beef broth
1 tsp dried oregano
2 tbsp olive oil
2 tbsp flour
2 tbsp water
2 tbsp tomato paste
1 beef bouillon cube
Salt and pepper to taste

Heat the oil on Sauté. In a bowl, mix in flour, pepper, and salt. Coat the pork chops. Place them in the pressure cooker and cook for a few minutes until browned on all sides. Add the carrots, onion, garlic, and oregano. Cook for 2 more minutes. Stir in tomato, wine, broth, water, tomato paste, and bouillon cube and seal the lid. Cook on Soup/Broth and cook for 25 minutes on High. When ready, do a natural pressure release for 10 minutes, and serve immediately.

## Broccoli & Cauliflower Pork Sausages

Serving Size: 6 | Total Time: 20 minutes

1 lb pork sausage, sliced
½ lb broccoli florets
½ lb cauliflower florets
14 oz can mushroom soup
10 oz evaporated milk
Salt and pepper to taste

Place ¼ of the sausage slices in your pressure cooker. In a bowl, whisk the soup, salt, pepper, and milk. Pour some of the mixtures over the sausages. Top the sausage slices with ¼ of the cauliflower and broccoli florets. Pour some of the soup mixtures again. Repeat the layers until you use up all ingredients. Seal the lid and cook on Pressure Cook for 10 minutes on High. When ready, do a quick release. Serve.

## Friday Night BBQ Pork Butt

Serving Size: 6 | Total Time: 55 minutes

2 lb pork butt
Salt and pepper to taste
1 cup barbecue sauce
¼ tsp cumin powder
½ tsp onion powder
1 ½ cups beef broth

In a bowl, combine the barbecue sauce, cumin, onion powder, salt, and pepper. Brush the pork with the mixture. On Sauté, coat with cooking oil. Add the pork and sear on all sides for 6 minutes. Pour the beef broth around the meat. Seal the lid and cook for 40 minutes on Meat/Stew on High. Do the pressure quickly. Serve.

## Cajun Pork Carnitas

Serving Size: 4 | Total Time: 65 minutes

1 lb pork shoulder, trimmed of excess fat
3 tbsp olive oil
1 onion, chopped
1 cup chicken stock
½ cup sour cream
2 tbsp tomato paste
1 tbsp lemon juice
Salt and pepper to taste
1 tsp cayenne pepper
1 tsp garlic powder
1 tbsp Cajun seasoning
4 tortillas, warm

Warm the olive oil in your Instant Pot on Sauté. Place in the pork and cook for 7-8 minutes on all sides. Stir in onion and cook for 1-2 more minutes. Pour in chicken stock, sour cream, tomato paste, lemon juice, salt, pepper, cayenne pepper, Cajun seasoning, and garlic powder. Seal the lid, select Manual, and cook for 25 minutes on High.

When ready, allow a natural release for 10 minutes and unlock the lid. Remove pork and shred it. Put shredded pork back to the pot and cook for 6-8 minutes on Sauté. Serve with warm tortillas.

## Pork Chops & Mushrooms with Tomato Sauce

Serving Size: 4 | Total Time: 35 minutes

1 cup white button mushrooms, sliced
4 large bone-in pork chops
1 cup tomato sauce
1 onion, chopped
1 tsp garlic, minced
½ cup water
1 tbsp oil

Heat oil on Sauté. Add garlic and onion and cook for 2 minutes until soft. Add pork and cook until browned, 6 minutes. Stir in mushrooms, tomato sauce, and water and seal the lid. Cook for 20 minutes on Meat/Stew. Do a quick pressure release. Carefully unlock the lid. Serve.

## Garlic-Spicy Ground Pork with Peas

Serving Size: 6 | Total Time: 55 minutes

2 lb ground pork
1 onion, diced
1 can diced tomatoes
1 can peas
5 garlic cloves, minced
3 tbsp butter
1 serrano pepper, chopped
1 cup beef broth
1 tsp ground ginger
2 tsp ground coriander
Salt and pepper to taste
¾ tsp cumin
¼ tsp cayenne pepper
½ tsp turmeric

Melt butter on Sauté. Add onion and cook for 3 minutes until soft. Stir in ginger, coriander, salt, pepper, cumin, cayenne pepper, turmeric and garlic and cook for 2 more minutes. Add pork and cook until browned. Pour broth and add serrano pepper, peas, and tomatoes. Seal the lid and cook for 30 minutes on Meat/Stew on High. When ready, release the pressure naturally for 10 minutes. Carefully unlock the lid. Serve immediately.

## Sweet Mustard Pork Chops with Piccalilli

Serving Size: 4 | Total Time: 30 minutes

1 lb pork chops, boneless
2 tbsp olive oil
2 tbsp Dijon mustard
½ tbsp brown sugar
1 tbsp honey
2 garlic cloves, minced
2 tbsp piccalilli
Salt and pepper to taste

Sprinkle pork chops with salt and pepper. Warm the olive oil in your Instant Pot on Sauté. Place the pork chops in the pot and brown for 6-8 minutes on both sides. Mix Dijon mustard, brown sugar, honey, garlic, and 1 cup of water in a bowl. Pour it into the pot and seal the lid. Select Manual and cook for 15 minutes on High pressure. Once done, perform a quick pressure release and unlock the lid. Top with piccalilli and serve.

## Chili-Braised Pork Chops with Tomatoes

Serving Size: 4 | Total Time: 30 minutes

14 oz canned tomatoes with green chilies
4 pork chops
1 onion, chopped
2 tbsp chili powder
1 garlic clove, minced
½ cup beer
½ cup vegetable stock
1 tsp olive oil
Salt and pepper to taste

Heat oil on Sauté. Add onion, garlic, and chili powder and cook for 2 minutes. Add the pork chops and cook until browned on all sides. Stir in the tomatoes, stock, and beer. Season with salt and pepper. Seal the lid and cook for 20 minutes on Meat/Stew on High. When ready, quick Release the pressure and serve hot.

## Chorizo with Macaroni & Cheddar Cheese

Serving Size: 6 | Total Time: 20 minutes

1 lb macaroni
3 oz chorizo, chopped

3 cups water

1 tbsp garlic powder

2 tbsp minced garlic

2 cups milk

2 cups cheddar, shredded

Salt to taste

On Sauté and stir-fry chorizo until crispy for about 6 minutes. Set aside. Wipe the pot with kitchen paper. Add in water, macaroni, garlic, and salt. Seal lid and cook for 5 minutes on High Pressure. Release the pressure quickly. Stir in cheese, garlic powder, and milk until the cheese melts. Top with chorizo and serve.

## Baby Carrot & Onion Pork Chops

Serving Size: 4 | Total Time: 30 minutes

1 ½ lb pork chops

½ lb baby carrots

1 onion, sliced

2 tbsp butter

1 cup vegetable broth

Salt and pepper to taste

Season the pork with salt and pepper. Melt butter on Sauté and brown the pork on all sides. Stir in carrots and onion and cook for 2 more minutes until soft. Pour in the broth. Seal the lid and cook for 20 minutes on Meat/Stew on High. When ready, release the pressure quickly.

## Thai-Style Chili Pork

Serving Size: 4 | Total Time: 29 minutes

2 red Thai chili peppers, chopped

½ lb sugar snap peas, trimmed

1 lb ground pork

2 tbsp olive oil

2 garlic cloves, minced

1-inch piece ginger, grated

2 shallots, thinly sliced

1 ½ cups coconut milk

1 tbsp soy sauce

2 tbsp cilantro, chopped

Warm the olive oil in your Instant Pot on Sauté. Place in ground pork and brown for 5-6 minutes. Add in garlic,

Thai chili, ginger, and shallots and cook for another 2-3 minutes. Stir in coconut milk, sugar snap peas, and soy sauce and seal the lid. Select Manual and cook for 10 minutes on High. When ready, perform a quick pressure release and unlock the lid. Top with cilantro and serve.

## Sweet & Spicy Pork Ribs

Serving Size: 4 | Total Time: 50 minutes

3 lb pork baby back ribs

2 tbsp olive oil

¼ tsp ground coriander

1 tsp garlic powder

2 tsp cayenne pepper

½ cup orange marmalade

2 tbsp ketchup

2 tbsp soy sauce

Salt and pepper to taste

Trim the ribs of excess fat and cut them into individual bones. In a bowl, combine olive oil, ground coriander, garlic powder, cayenne pepper, salt, and pepper and mix well. Add in the ribs and toss to coat. Transfer them to the Instant Pot and pour in 1 cup of water. Seal the lid, select Manual, and cook for 20 minutes on High.

When done, release the pressure naturally for 10 minutes. In a bowl, whisk together the ketchup, orange marmalade, and soy sauce until well combined. Transfer the ribs to a baking tray. Select Sauté and pour the marmalade mixture into the pot. Cook until the sauce has thickened to obtain a glaze texture, about 4-5 minutes. Brush the ribs with some glaze and place under a preheated broiler for 5 minutes or until charred and sticky. Serve the ribs with the remaining glaze.

## BBQ Pork Lettuce Cups

Serving Size: 6 | Total Time: 60 minutes

1-2 little gem lettuces, leaves separated

3 lb pork roast, cut into chunks

2 tbsp olive oil

Salt and pepper to taste

1 cup chicken broth

½ cup BBQ sauce

1 red onion, thinly sliced

2 tbsp cilantro, chopped

Sprinkle pork roast with salt and pepper. Place the roast, olive oil, chicken broth, and BBQ sauce in your Instant Pot and stir. Seal the lid, select Manual, and cook for 40 minutes on High. When ready, allow a natural release for 10 minutes, then perform a quick pressure release, and unlock the lid. Remove roast and shred it using two forks. Divide shredded pork between lettuce leaves. Scatter with onion and cilantro. Serve with the gravy.

## Beer-Braised Pork

Serving Size: 4 | Total Time: 53 minutes

2 lb pork loin roast

2 tbsp butter

1 onion, chopped

2 garlic cloves, minced

1 tsp thyme

1 bay leaf

2 cups beer

Salt and pepper to taste

Melt butter in your Instant Pot on Sauté. Place the pork roast fatty-side down and cook on both sides. Add in onion and garlic and cook for 3 minutes. Put in thyme, salt, pepper, beer, bay leaf, and ½ cup of water and seal the lid. Select Manual and cook for 30 minutes on High. When over, allow a natural release for 10 minutes and unlock the lid. Transfer roast to a bowl and cover it. Press Sauté and cook until the sauce thickens. Cut the roast and top with the sauce.

## Hoisin Spare Pork Ribs

Serving Size: 4 | Total Time: 75 minutes

2 lb pork spare ribs

3 garlic cloves, minced

2 green onions, chopped

3 ginger slices

2 tbsp sesame oil

¼ cup Mirin rice wine

½ cup hoisin sauce

2 red chilies, sliced

1 tbsp honey

2 tbsp cilantro, chopped

Warm sesame oil in your Instant Pot on Sauté. Place in garlic, green onions, chilies, and ginger and cook for 2-3 minutes. Slice spare ribs into individual ribs, place it in the pot, and sauté for 4-5 minutes. Stir in rice wine, honey, 1 cup of water, and hoisin sauce and cook for 3-4 minutes. Seal the lid, select Manual, and cook for 40 minutes.

Once done, allow a natural release for 10 minutes, then perform a quick pressure release, and unlock the lid. Top the ribs with sauce and cilantro and serve.

## Cinnamon BBQ Pork Ribs

Serving Size: 6 | Total Time: 60 minutes

3 lb pork ribs

½ cup apple jelly

1 cup barbecue sauce

1 onion, diced

2 tbsp ground cloves

1 tbsp brown sugar

1 tsp Worcestershire sauce

1 tsp ground cinnamon

Salt and pepper to taste

Whisk together apple jelly, barbecue sauce, onion, cloves, sugar, Worcestershire sauce, cinnamon, salt, and pepper in your pressure cooker. Place the ribs inside and pour in ½ cup water. Seal the lid. Set the cooker to Meat/Stew and cook for 50 minutes. Release the pressure naturally.

## Fruity Pork Steaks

Serving Size: 4 | Total Time: 30 minutes

4 pork steaks

¼ cup milk

8 prunes, pitted

½ cup white wine

2 apples, peeled, sliced

¼ cup heavy cream

1 tbsp fruit jelly

½ tsp ground ginger

Salt and pepper to taste

Place pork, milk, prunes, wine, apples, heavy cream, and ginger in your pressure cooker. Stir and season with salt and pepper. Seal the lid and cook on High Pressure for 15 minutes. Once done, wait 5 minutes and do a quick pressure release. Stir in the jelly and serve.

## Pork Sirloin Chili

Serving Size: 6 | Total Time: 45 minutes

3 lb sirloin pork roast

1 tbsp honey

1 tsp chili powder

1 tbsp rosemary

1 tbsp olive oil

Salt and pepper to taste

Combine chili powder, rosemary, salt, and pepper in a bowl and rub them onto the pork. Heat oil on Sauté and sear the pork on all sides. Stir in honey and seal the lid. Cook for 30 minutes on Meat/Stew. Do a natural pressure release for 10 minutes. Carefully unlock the lid.

## Awesome Herby Pork Butt with Yams

Serving Size: 4 | Total Time: 35 minutes

1 lb pork butt, cut into 4 equal pieces

1 lb yams, diced

2 tsp butter

¼ tsp thyme

¼ tsp oregano

1 ½ tsp sage

1 ½ cups beef broth

Salt and pepper to taste

Season the pork with thyme, sage, oregano, salt, and pepper. Melt butter on Sauté. Add pork and cook until brown, about 5 minutes. Add the yams and pour the broth. Seal the lid and cook for 20 minutes on Meat/Stew. Do a quick release. Serve hot.

## Best Pork Chops with BBQ Sauce & Veggies

Serving Size: 4 | Total Time: 25 minutes

4 pork rib chops

1 cup carrots, thinly sliced

1 cup turnips, thinly sliced

1 cup onions, slice into rings

1 ½ cups BBQ sauce

2 cups water

Add the pork chops to your cooker. Pour in ½ cup of BBQ sauce and 2 cups of water. Select Meat/Stew. Stir in the onions, turnips, and carrots. Lock the lid and cook for 20 minutes on High. Once ready, Release the pressure quickly. Open the lid, drizzle with the remaining BBQ sauce and serve warm.

## Chorizo & Tomato Pork Chops

Serving Size: 4 | Total Time: 40 minutes

4 pork chops, boneless

2 oz chorizo sausage, sliced

1 tsp paprika

2 garlic cloves, minced

2 tbsp olive oil

1 yellow onion, sliced

2 cups chopped tomatoes

Place the pork chops in your Instant Pot and sear for 5 minutes on Sauté. Add in onion and garlic and cook for 3 more minutes. Stir in chorizo, paprika, tomatoes, and ½ cup of water. Seal the lid, select Manual, and cook for 15 minutes on High pressure. When done, allow a natural release for 10 minutes, then perform a quick pressure release, and unlock the lid. Serve right away.

## Tarragon Apple Pork Chops

Serving Size: 4 | Total Time: 25 minutes

2 tbsp olive oil

1 tsp nutmeg

1 tsp Dijon mustard

4 tbsp brown sugar

2 Granny Smith apples, sliced

4 pork chops

Salt and pepper to taste

2 tbsp tarragon, chopped

Combine nutmeg, mustard, and brown sugar in a bowl. Add in apples and toss to coat. Warm oil in your Instant Pot on Sauté. Place the apples in the pot and cook for 2 minutes. Sprinkle pork chops with salt and pepper and put it over the apples. Seal the lid, select Manual, and cook for 15 minutes on High. Once done, perform a quick pressure release. Top with tarragon and serve.

## Paprika Pulled Pork Fajitas

Serving Size: 4 | Total Time: 65 minutes

2 lb pork shoulder, cut into chunks

½ tsp garlic powder

½ tsp dried chili flakes

½ tsp brown sugar

½ tsp cumin

1 yellow onion, sliced

1 ½ cups beef broth

1 tsp smoked paprika

Salt and pepper to taste

4 tortillas

Combine garlic powder, smoked paprika, brown sugar, cumin, salt, and pepper in a bowl. Sprinkle pork shoulder with the spice mixture. Place onion slices in your Instant Pot and top with the pork shoulder. Pour in beef broth and seal the lid. Select Manual and cook for 40 on High. Once done, allow a natural release for 10 minutes, then perform a quick pressure release, and unlock the lid. Remove pork and shred it. Warm each tortilla in a skillet over medium heat for 1 minute. To assemble, divide shredded pork between tortillas and top with chili flakes.

## Mexican Pork Chili Verde

Serving Size: 4 | Total Time: 45 minutes

2 lb pork shoulder, cubed

½ lb tomatillos, quartered

2 serrano peppers, chopped

2 jalapeño peppers, minced

1 onion, chopped

4 garlic cloves, minced

1 tsp cayenne pepper

½ tsp oregano

½ tsp ground coriander

1 tsp cumin

1 cup chicken stock

2 tbsp cilantro, chopped

Salt and pepper to taste

Place pork shoulder, tomatillos, serrano peppers, jalapeño peppers, onion, garlic cloves, cayenne pepper, oregano, ground coriander, cumin, chicken stock, salt, and pepper in your Instant Pot and stir. Seal the lid, select Manual, and cook for 35 minutes on High pressure. Once done, perform a quick pressure release and unlock the lid. Transfer the pork to a plate. Put the cilantro in the pot and blend sauce using an immersion blender. Put the pork back in the pot and toss to coat. Serve immediately.

## Pear & Cider Pork Tenderloin

Serving Size: 4 | Total Time: 55 minutes

1 lb pork loin

1 tbsp garlic powder

2 tbsp olive oil

1 yellow onion, chopped

2 pears, cored and chopped

1 cup apple cider

1 tbsp fennel seeds

Salt and pepper to taste

Sprinkle pork loin with salt, pepper, and garlic powder. Warm the olive oil in your Instant Pot on Sauté. Place the loin and sear for 8 minutes on all sides. Set aside. Add onion to the pot and cook for 3 minutes. Put in pears and apple cider and scrape any brown bits from the bottom. Put loin back to the pot along with fennel seeds.

Seal the lid. Select Manual and cook for 20 minutes on High pressure. When ready, allow a natural release for 10 minutes and unlock the lid. Slice the pork loin before serving and top with sauce.

## Hot Pork Chops with Cheddar Cheese

Serving Size: 4 | Total Time: 30 minutes

4 boneless pork chops

2 tbsp olive oil

1 cup water

4 tbsp habanero pepper sauce

2 tbsp butter

1 cup cheddar, grated

Salt and pepper to taste

2 tbsp parsley, chopped

Warm the olive oil in your Instant Pot on Sauté. Sprinkle pork chops with salt and pepper. Place the chops in the pot and brown for 3 minutes on all sides. Add in 1 cup of water and habanero pepper sauce. Top each pork chop with butter and seal the lid. Select Manual and cook for 15 minutes on High pressure.

When done, perform a quick pressure release and unlock the lid. Scatter pork chops with cheddar cheese and broil in the oven for a few minutes. Top with parsley and serve.

## Juicy Pork Butt Steaks

Serving Size: 4 | Total Time: 57 minutes

2 lb pork butt steaks

2 tbsp olive oil

1 tsp garlic powder

1 onion, chopped

1 cup chicken broth

1 cup tomato sauce

1 tsp ground bay leaf

1 tsp oregano

½ cup red wine

1 tbsp paprika

Salt and pepper to taste

Warm the olive oil in your Instant Pot on Sauté. Place in pork steaks, salt, pepper, and garlic powder and cook for 4-5 minutes. Set aside. Put the onion in the pot and cook for 2 minutes. Pour in red wine and scrape any

brown bits from the bottom. Put pork steaks back to the pot along with chicken stock, tomato sauce, bay leaf, oregano, and paprika.

Seal the lid, select Manual, and cook for 30 minutes on High pressure. When ready, allow a natural release for 10 minutes, then perform a quick pressure release, and unlock the lid. Serve right away.

## Japanese-Style Pork Tenderloin

Serving Size: 4 | Total Time: 30 minutes

2 lb pork tenderloins

2 tbsp peanut butter

1 cup teriyaki sauce

¼ cup coconut milk

1 tbsp sesame seeds

1 tbsp light soy sauce

Salt and pepper to taste

4 green onions, chopped

1 lime, zested

Melt peanut butter in your Instant Pot on Sauté. Sprinkle pork tenderloins with salt and pepper, place it in the pot and brown for a few minutes on all sides. Put in teriyaki sauce, soy sauce, lime zest, coconut milk, and 1/2 cup of water and seal the lid. Select Manual. Cook for 15 minutes on High.

Once done, allow a natural release for 10 minutes, then perform a quick pressure release, and unlock the lid. Slice the tenderloin and garnish with toasted sesame seeds, green onions, and cooking juice. Serve immediately.

## Pork Medallions with Porcini Sauce

Serving Size: 4 | Total Time: 60 minutes

1 oz dried porcini mushrooms

4 boneless pork loin chops

½ cup dry Marsala wine

1 garlic clove, minced

1 tbsp paprika

½ tsp rosemary

1 onion, sliced

2 tbsp butter

Salt and pepper to taste

2 tbsp chopped parsley

Cover the porcini mushrooms with 1 cup of boiling water in a bowl and let soak for 10-15 minutes. Sprinkle pork chops with paprika, salt, and pepper. Melt butter in your Instant Pot on Sauté. Place the pork chops in the pot and sear for 6 minutes on all sides. Set aside.

Add onion and garlic to the pot and cook for 3 minutes. Put pork on top along with Marsala wine, rosemary, and porcini mushrooms with the water. Seal the lid, select Manual, and cook for 15 minutes on High pressure. When over, allow a natural release for 10 minutes and unlock the lid. Garnish with parsley and serve.

## Fennel & Rosemary Pork Belly

Serving Size: 2 | Total Time: 60 minutes

1 lb pork belly
2 tbsp olive oil
¼ tsp ground cinnamon
¼ tsp chili flakes
1 tsp fennel seeds
1 rosemary sprig
1 clove garlic, minced
1 cup red wine
Salt and pepper to taste
2 tbsp chopped chives

Warm the olive oil in your Instant Pot on Sauté. Place the pork belly and cook 4 minutes on both sides. Add in salt, pepper, garlic, fennel seeds, cinnamon, rosemary sprig, chili flakes, red wine, and 1 cup of water. Seal the lid, select Manual, and cook for 35 minutes on High.

Once over, allow a natural release for 10 minutes, then perform a quick pressure release, and unlock the lid. Cut the pork and scatter with chives. Serve warm.

## Spicy Pork Sausage Ragu

Serving Size: 4 | Total Time: 25 minutes

1 lb pork sausage, casings removed
2 tbsp olive oil
2 garlic cloves, minced
1 onion, chopped
1 cup chopped tomatoes
½ tsp oregano
1 tsp red chili flakes

1 cup chicken stock
Salt and pepper to taste
2 tbsp parsley, chopped

Warm the olive oil in your Instant Pot on Sauté. Place in garlic and onion and cook until fragrant. Add and brown the sausage for 8 minutes. Stir constantly, breaking the meat with a wooden spatula. Stir in chicken stock, red chili flakes, oregano, and chopped tomatoes and seal the lid. Select Manual and cook for 10 minutes on High.

When over, perform a quick pressure release and unlock the lid. Adjust seasoning to taste. Cook on Sauté until the sauce thickens. Top with parsley and serve.

## German Pork with Sauerkraut

Serving Size: 4 | Total Time: 40 minutes

2 lb pork belly, cut into 2-inch pieces
3 tbsp lard
2 garlic cloves, minced
1 onion, chopped
1 cup chicken broth
5 cups sauerkraut
1 tsp paprika
1 cup canned diced tomatoes
1 tsp cumin
2 tbsp parsley, chopped
Salt and pepper to taste

Sprinkle the pork with salt and pepper. Melt lard in your Instant Pot on Sauté. Place the pork, onion, and garlic and cook for 5-6 minutes. Stir in paprika and cumin. Put in sauerkraut, chicken broth, tomatoes, and 1/2 cup of water and seal the lid. Select Manual and cook for 30 minutes on High pressure. Once over, perform a quick pressure release and unlock the lid. Serve with parsley.

## Tandoori Pork Butt

Serving Size: 4 | Total Time: 61 minutes

2 lb pork butt, boneless, trimmed of excess fat
1 tsp ground cumin
1 tsp ground coriander
1 tsp paprika
1 green chili, minced
1 tsp garam masala

2 tbsp ghee
1 onion, chopped
2 garlic cloves, minced
1-inch piece ginger, grated
1 can (14 oz) coconut milk
Salt and pepper to taste
Lime wedges for garnish

Mix the salt, pepper, ground coriander, paprika, cumin, and garam masala in a bowl. Sprinkle pork butt with this mixture. Melt ghee in your Instant Pot on Sauté. Place in green chili, ginger, onion, and garlic and cook for 2 minutes. Add in pork butt and cook for 3-4 minutes. Pour in coconut milk and ½ cup of water and seal the lid. Select Manual and cook for 35 minutes on High pressure. Once ready, allow a natural release for 10 minutes, then perform a quick pressure release, and unlock the lid. Cut the butt into slices and serve with lemon wedges.

## Prune & Shallot Pork Tenderloin

Serving Size: 6 | Total Time: 45 minutes

3 lb pork tenderloins, cut into large chunks
2 tbsp olive oil
2 shallots, chopped
Salt and pepper to taste
½ cup vegetable broth
½ cup balsamic vinegar
½ cup dried pitted prunes
1 carrot, sliced diagonally
2 garlic cloves, minced
2 tbsp rosemary, chopped

Warm the olive oil in your Instant Pot on Sauté. Sprinkle pork tenderloins with salt and pepper, place them in the pot, and brown for 2-3 minutes. Add in shallots, garlic, and carrots and cook for 3 minutes. Stir in vegetable broth, balsamic vinegar, prunes, and rosemary. Seal the lid, select Manual, and cook for 20 minutes on High pressure. When done, allow a natural release for 10 minutes, then perform a quick pressure release, and unlock the lid.

## Quick Pork & Vegetable Rice

Serving Size: 4 | Total Time: 40 minutes

4 pork chops
2 tbsp olive oil
1 onion, finely chopped
2 tbsp garlic cloves, minced
1 cup white rice, rinsed
1 ½ cups chicken broth
1 carrot, chopped
1 cup mushrooms, sliced
1 red bell pepper, sliced
Salt and pepper to taste
2 spring onions, sliced

Warm the olive oil in your Instant Pot on Sauté. Place in onion, garlic, carrot, bell pepper, and mushrooms and cook for 5 minutes. Add in rice, salt, and pepper.
Put pork chops over the rice and pour in chicken broth. Seal the lid, select Manual, and cook for 15 minutes on High pressure. Once done, allow a natural release for 10 minutes. Garnish with spring onions and serve.

## Mushroom & Pork Stroganoff

Serving Size: 4 | Total Time: 35 minutes

1 cup button mushrooms, sliced
1 lb pork loin, cut into strips
2 tbsp olive oil
1 leek, chopped
1 celery stalk, chopped
2 cups vegetable broth
2 tsp Dijon mustard
½ cup sour cream
½ cup white wine
Salt and pepper to taste
2 tbsp parsley, chopped

Warm the oil in your Instant Pot on Sauté. Sprinkle pork loin with salt and pepper, place it in the pot and brown on all sides. Set aside. Add leek, mushrooms, and celery to the pot and cook for 3 minutes. Pour in wine and scrape any brown bits from the bottom. Stir in vegetable broth and Dijon mustard. Put pork loin back to the pot.
Seal the lid. Select Manual and cook for 12 minutes on High. Once ready, allow a natural release for 10 minutes and unlock the lid. Mix in sour cream and simmer for 1 minute on Sauté. Top with parsley and serve.

# Cilantro Pork with Avocado

Serving Size: 4 | Total Time: 45 minutes + marinating time

1 lb pork tenderloin, cut into strips
3 garlic cloves, chopped
½ tsp oregano
½ tsp ground cumin
1 tbsp Hungarian paprika
2 tbsp olive oil
2 cups chicken stock
Salt and pepper to taste
1 avocado, sliced
2 tbsp cilantro, chopped

Mix garlic, oregano, cumin, paprika, salt, and pepper in a bowl. Add in pork strips and toss to coat. Let marinate for 30 minutes in the fridge. Warm the olive oil in your Instant Pot on Sauté. Place the strips in the pot and sauté for 10 minutes. Stir in chicken stock and seal the lid. Select Manual and cook for 15 minutes on High pressure.

When done, allow a natural release for 10 minutes, then perform a quick pressure release, and unlock the lid. Scatter with cilantro. Serve topped with avocado slices.

# Parsley Pork with Savoy Cabbage

Serving Size: 6 | Total Time: 35 minutes

2 lb pork roast, cut into chunks
1 head Savoy cabbage, shredded
3 tbsp canola oil
2 garlic cloves, minced
1 onion, chopped
1 tsp cumin
1 tsp mustard powder
1 cup chopped tomatoes
Salt and pepper to taste
2 tbsp parsley, chopped

Warm the canola oil in your Instant Pot on Sauté. Place in garlic and onion and cook for 3 minutes. Add in pork chunks and cook for 5 minutes on all sides. Stir in cumin, mustard powder, salt, pepper, tomatoes, cabbage, and 1 cup of water. Seal the lid, select Manual, and cook for 20 minutes on High pressure. Once ready, perform a quick pressure release. Top with parsley and serve.

# Spiced Pork with Garbanzo Beans

Serving Size: 4 | Total Time: 60 minutes

1 ½ tbsp vegetable oil
1 ½ lb pork shoulder, diced
1 red onion, sliced
1 cup garbanzo beans, soaked
3 cups chicken broth
1 cup tomatoes, chopped
2 garlic cloves, minced
2 tbsp fresh dill, chopped
½ tsp ground mustard
½ tsp paprika
½ tsp dried thyme
½ tsp cayenne pepper
½ tsp garlic powder
Salt and pepper to taste

Mix the paprika, thyme, cayenne pepper, garlic powder, salt, and pepper in a bowl. Sprinkle pork with this mixture. Warm the vegetable oil in your Instant Pot on Sauté. Place in pork and brown for 4-5 minutes.

Remove to a bowl. Add red onion and garlic to the pot and cook for 2 minutes. Pour in chicken broth and scrape any brown bits from the bottom. Add in garbanzo beans, tomatoes, and mustard and seal the lid. Select Manual and cook for 30 minutes on High pressure. When over, allow a natural release for 10 minutes and unlock the lid. Garnish with dill and serve.

# Smoky Shredded Pork with White Beans

Serving Size: 4 | Total Time: 65 minutes

2 lb pork shoulder, halved

2 tbsp vegetable oil

1 onion, chopped

1 cup vegetable broth

2 tbsp liquid smoke

Salt and pepper to taste

1 cup cooked white beans

2 tbsp parsley, chopped

Warm the vegetable oil in your Instant Pot on Sauté. Place in onion and cook for 3 minutes. Sprinkle pork shoulder with salt and pepper, add it to the pot and brown for 5 minutes on all sides. Pour in vegetable broth and liquid smoke and scrape any brown bits from the bottom. Seal the lid, select Manual, and cook for 35 minutes on High.

When ready, allow a natural release for 10 minutes, then perform a quick pressure release, and unlock the lid. Remove pork and shred it. Stir white beans in the pot and put shredded pork back. Top with parsley and serve.

## Pulled Pork Tacos

Serving Size: 6 | Total Time: 55 minutes + marinating time

2 lb pork shoulder, trimmed of excess fat

3 garlic cloves, minced

1 cup onions, sliced

1 tsp ground cinnamon

1 tbsp cumin

1 tsp oregano

¼ tsp red chili flakes

½ cup pineapple juice

1 ½ cups tomatoes, diced

1 Iceberg lettuce, torn

1 red onion, thinly sliced

2 tbsp cilantro, chopped

Salt and pepper to taste

6 tortillas

Slice pork shoulder into 2-inch pieces. Place the garlic, onions, cinnamon, cumin, oregano, chili flakes, salt, and

pepper in a bowl. Add in the pork pieces and toss to coat. Cover with cling film and let marinate for 30 minutes. Transfer to your Instant Pot and pour in pineapple juice and tomatoes. Seal the lid, select Manual and cook for 30 minutes on High pressure. Once done, allow a natural release for 10 minutes and unlock the lid.

Shred the pork and simmer for 5 minutes on Sauté. To assemble, divide shredded pork between tortillas and top with lettuce, red onion, and cilantro. Serve right away.

## Bacon & Potato Brussels Sprouts

Serving Size: 4 | Total Time: 20 minutes

4 bacon slices, chopped

1 lb Brussels sprouts, halved

1 cup potatoes, cubed

½ cup chicken stock

Salt and pepper to taste

Set to Sauté your Instant Pot and add the bacon. Cook for 5-6 minutes until crispy; remove to a paper-lined plate. Add potatoes, Brussels sprouts, chicken stock, salt, and pepper to the pot. Seal the lid, select Manual, and cook for 5 minutes on High. When done, perform a quick pressure release.Top with bacon. Serve warm.

## Spiced Mexican Pork

Serving Size: 4 | Total Time: 55 minutes + marinating time

2 lb pork shoulder, cut into chunks

1 chipotle pepper in adobo sauce, chopped

3 garlic cloves, minced

1 red onion, chopped

½ tsp ground coriander

1 tsp ground cumin

1 tbsp lime juice

¼ cup chile enchilada sauce

1 tsp Mexican oregano

Salt and pepper to taste

Place garlic, onion, ground coriander, cumin, lime juice, Mexican oregano, chipotle pepper, enchilada sauce, salt, pepper, and ½ cup of water in a blender and pulse until smooth. Place the mixture in a large bowl and add in pork chunks; toss to coat. Cover with cling foil and let marinate in the fridge for 30 minutes.

Next, remove from the fridge and transfer to your Instant Pot. Pour in ½ cup of water and seal the lid. Select Manual and cook for 25 minutes on High pressure. When ready, allow a natural release for 15 minutes and unlock the lid. Cook for 5 minutes on Sauté until the sauce thickens. Serve warm.

## Asian Pork & Noodle Soup

Serving Size: 4 | Total Time: 60 minutes
1 lb pork tenderloin, cut into strips
1 (1-inch) piece fresh ginger, halved lengthwise
2 tbsp olive oil
1 yellow onion, halved
2 tsp fennel seeds
1 tsp red pepper flakes
½ tsp coriander seeds
2-star anise
Salt and pepper to taste
8 oz rice noodles
1 lime, cut into wedges
2 tbsp cilantro, chopped

Warm oil on Sauté. Cook ginger and onion for 4 minutes. Add in flakes, fennel seeds, anise, and coriander seeds and cook for 1 minute as you stir. Add in 4 cups of water, salt, pepper, and pork. Seal the lid and cook on High Pressure for 30 minutes.

Soak the rice noodles in hot water for 8 minutes until softened and pliable. Stop the cooking process by draining and rinsing with cold water. Separate the noodles into 4 soup bowls.

Release the pressure naturally for 10 minutes. Remove the pork from the cooker and ladle among the bowls. Strain the broth to get rid of solids. Pour it over the pork and noodles. Season with red pepper flakes. Garnish with lime wedges and cilantro leaves and serve.

## Awesome Pork & Celery Soup

Serving Size: 4 | Total Time: 45 minutes
1 ¼ lb pork ribs
1 leek, chopped

1 onion, chopped
1 cup celery root, diced
½ cup parsley, chopped
4 cups beef broth
1 tsp salt
1 tsp red chili flakes
2 bay leaves
A handful of basil, torn
2 tbsp olive oil

Heat oil on Sauté. Add the ribs in batches and brown on all sides for 5-6 minutes. Add leek, onion, celery, parsley, broth, salt, red chili flakes, bay leaves, and basil.

Seal the lid and cook on Meat/Stew on High for 30 minutes. Do a quick release. Serve.

## Delicious Pork & Vegetables Soup

Serving Size: 4 | Total Time: 50 minutes
2 (8-oz) pork chops
1 tbsp cayenne pepper
1 tsp chili powder
½ tsp garlic powder
4 cups beef broth
2 tbsp olive oil
2 large carrots, chopped
2 celery stalks, diced
1 onion, diced
2 tbsp soy sauce

Warm the olive oil in your Instant Pot on Sauté and stir-fry the onion until translucent, 3 minutes. Add celery stalks, carrots, cayenne, and chili pepper. Give it a good stir and continue to cook for 6-7 minutes. Add in pork chops, garlic, and soy sauce.

Pour in the broth and seal the lid. Cook on Manual for 25 minutes on High. Do a quick release. Let chill for 5 minutes. Serve.

# Cajun Orange Pork Shoulder

Serving Size: 6 | Total Time: 60 minutes + marinating time

3 lb pork shoulder, trimmed of excess fat

2 garlic cloves, sliced

1 tsp cumin

1 tsp Cajun seasoning

1 large onion, sliced

¼ cup lime juice

¼ cup orange juice

Salt and pepper to taste

2 tbsp olive oil

2 tbsp cilantro, chopped

Mix the cumin, Cajun seasoning, garlic, onion, lime juice, orange juice, salt, and pepper in a bowl. Place in the pork shoulder and toss to coat. Let sit covered in the fridge for 30 minutes. Warm the olive oil in your Instant Pot on Sauté. Place in pork shoulder and cook for 10 minutes on all sides. Set aside.

Pour the remaining marinade into the pot and scrape any brown bits from the bottom. Pour in 1 cup of water and fit in a trivet. Place the pork inside the trivet and seal the lid. Select Manual and cook for 30 minutes on High.

When over, allow a natural release for 10 minutes, then perform a quick pressure release, and unlock the lid. Remove and slice the pork. Top with cilantro. Serve.

# Garlic & Thyme Pork

Serving Size: 4 | Total Time: 58 minutes

1 lb pork brisket

2 garlic cloves, minced

2 tsp paprika

1 tsp ground cumin

1 tsp onion powder

2 tbsp flour

2 tbsp olive oil

1 ½ cups chicken broth

½ cup red wine

6 garlic cloves, minced

1 tbsp thyme, chopped

1 tbsp butter

1 cup mushrooms, sliced

Salt and pepper to taste

Mix the onion powder, paprika, cumin, salt, pepper, and garlic in a bowl. Sprinkle pork brisket with this mixture. Cover all brisket with flour. Warm the oil in your Instant Pot on Sauté. Place in brisket and cook for 8 minutes on all sides. Pour in red wine and scrape any brown bits from the bottom. Add in garlic, thyme, and broth and seal the lid. Select Manual and cook for 30 minutes.

When ready, allow a natural release for 10 minutes, then perform a quick pressure release, and unlock the lid. Remove brisket to a plate and cooking liquid in a bowl. Melt butter in your Instant Pot on Sauté. Place in mushrooms and cook until they are soft. Pour in reserved liquid and cook for another minute. Cut brisket in slices and top with mushroom sauce. Serve warm.

# German-Style Red Cabbage with Apples

Serving Size: 4 | Total Time: 20 minutes

1 cup Granny Smith apples, cubed

1 head red cabbage, shredded

2 tbsp olive oil

4 oz bacon, chopped

1 sweet onion, chopped

2 garlic cloves, chopped

1 tbsp red wine vinegar

1 tsp ground cumin

Salt and pepper to taste

Warm olive oil in your Instant Pot on Sauté. Place the bacon, onion, and garlic and cook for 5 minutes.

Put in cabbage, vinegar, apples, cumin, salt, pepper, and 1 cup of water and seal the lid. Select Manual and cook for 10 minutes on High pressure. When done, perform a quick pressure release. Carefully unlock the lid. Adjust the taste with salt and pepper and serve.

## Gruyere Mushroom & Mortadella Cups

Serving Size: 4 | Total Time: 20 minutes

4 eggs, beaten
1 tsp olive oil
½ tsp paprika
½ cup mushrooms, chopped
1 cup mortadella, chopped
1 tbsp parsley, minced
Salt and pepper to taste
2 tbsp Gruyere, grated

Mix the eggs, olive oil, 1 tbsp of water, and paprika in a bowl. Add in mushrooms, parsley, salt, pepper, and mortadella. Divide the mixture between ramekins and top with Gruyere cheese.

Pour 1 cup of water into your Instant Pot and fit in a trivet. Place the ramekins on the trivet and seal the lid. Select Manual and cook for 12 minutes on High pressure. Once ready, perform a quick pressure release. Carefully unlock the lid. Serve warm.

## Asparagus Wrapped in Parma Ham

Serving Size: 4 | Total Time: 15 minutes

1 lb asparagus, trimmed
½ lb Parma ham, sliced
2 tbsp Parmesan, grated

Pour 1 cup of water into your Instant Pot and fit in a trivet. Wrap each asparagus spear with a ham slice and place on the trivet. Seal the lid, select Manual, and cook for 3 minutes on High pressure.

When over, allow a natural release for 5 minutes, then perform a quick pressure release, and unlock the lid. Transfer the wraps to a greased baking dish and sprinkle with the Parmesan cheese. Place under preheated broiler for about 4 minutes until the cheese is melted. Serve.

## Ranch Potatoes with Ham

Serving Size: 4 | Total Time: 20 minutes

1 lb Yukon gold potatoes, quartered
4 oz cooked ham, chopped
1 tsp garlic powder
2 tsp chives, chopped
Salt to taste
1/3 cup Ranch dressing

Cover potatoes with salted water in your Instant Pot and seal the lid. Select Manual and cook for 7 minutes on High pressure.

When done, perform a quick pressure release and unlock the lid. Drain the potatoes and transfer to a bowl. Stir in ranch dressing, garlic powder, and ham. Sprinkle with chives and serve.

# BEEF & LAMB

## Gingered Beef Pot Roast

Serving Size: 6 | Total Time: 45 minutes

2 lb beef chuck roast, cubed

2 tbsp olive oil

Salt and pepper to taste

1 cup beef broth

½ cup soy sauce

3 minced garlic cloves

1 tbsp grated ginger

2-star anise

1 jalapeño pepper, minced

Warm the olive oil in your Instant Pot on Sauté. Sprinkle beef with salt and pepper and place it in the pot and garlic, ginger, and jalapeño pepper and cook until browned. Remove to a plate.

Pour beef broth in the pot and scrape any brown bits from the bottom. Stir in soy sauce and star anise. Put the beef back in the pot and seal the lid. Select Manual and cook for 35 minutes on High pressure. Once ready, perform a quick pressure release and unlock the lid.

## Beef Lasagna with Eggplant & Almonds

Serving Size: 4 | Total Time: 25 minutes

2 lb stewed beef, boneless, sliced

3 oz toasted almonds, chopped

3 eggplants, halved

2 tomatoes, chopped

2 red bell peppers, sliced

¼ tbsp tomato paste

2 tbsp parsley, chopped

2 tbsp capers

¼ cup olive oil

Grease the Instant Pot with 2 tbsp of olive oil. Make the first layer with halved eggplants tucking the ends gently to fit in. Make the second layer with beef slices, tomatoes, and red bell peppers. Spread the tomato paste evenly over, sprinkle with almonds and capers. Add in the remaining olive oil. Pour 1 ½ cups of water and seal the lid. Cook on High Pressure for 13 minutes. Do a quick release. Serve with fresh parsley.

## T-Bone Steaks with Basil & Mustard

Serving Size: 4 | Total Time: 40 minutes + marinating time

1 lb T-bone steak

Salt and pepper to taste

2 tbsp Dijon mustard

¼ cup oil

½ tsp dried basil, crushed

Whisk together oil, mustard, salt, pepper, and basil. Brush each steak and Refrigerate for 1 hour. Then, insert a steamer tray in the Instant Pot. Pour in 1 cup of water and arrange the steaks on the tray. Seal the lid and cook on Manual for 25 minutes on High. Do a quick release. Discard the liquid, remove the tray, and hit Sauté. Brown the steaks for 5 minutes, turning once.

## Stewed Beef with Potatoes

Serving Size: 4 | Total Time: 60 minutes

1 lb russet potatoes, cut into chunks

1 lb beef shoulder

2 carrots, chopped

1 onion, finely chopped

4 tbsp olive oil

2 tbsp tomato paste

1 tbsp flour

4 cups beef broth

1 celery stalk, chopped

1 tbsp parsley, chopped

1 cayenne pepper, chopped

Salt and pepper to taste

Warm oil on Sauté. Stir-fry onion, carrots, and potatoes for 7-8 minutes. Stir in flour and press Cancel. Add beef, tomato paste, broth, celery, parsley, cayenne pepper, salt, and pepper Seal the lid and cook on High Pressure for 40 minutes. Do a quick release.

## Carrot Casserole with Beef & Potato

Serving Size: 3 | Total Time: 20 minutes

1 lb lean beef, with bones

2 carrots

1 potato, sliced

3 tbsp olive oil

½ tsp salt

Mix beef, carrots, potato, olive oil, and salt in the Instant Pot. Pour enough water to cover and seal the lid. Cook on High Pressure for 15 minutes. Do a quick release and serve hot.

## Beef Goulash with Cabbage & Potatoes

Serving Size: 6 | Total Time: 45 minutes

1 cup sun-dried tomatoes, diced

2 lb beef stew meat

3 potatoes, cut into chunks

1 onion, chopped

1 carrot, chopped

1 cabbage head, shredded

4 cups beef broth

3 tbsp tomato paste

1 tsp tabasco sauce

Salt and pepper to taste

3 tbsp butter

Melt the butter oil in your Instant Pot on Sauté and cook the onion until translucent for 2 minutes. Add the tomato paste and stir. Add the beef, tomatoes, potatoes, carrot, cabbage, broth, tabasco sauce, salt, and pepper and seal the lid. Cook on High Pressure for 35 minutes. Do a quick release.

## Beef Arancini with Potatoes

Serving Size: 4 | Total Time: 40 minutes

1 lb lean ground beef

6 oz rice

2 onions, peeled, chopped

2 garlic cloves, crushed

1 egg, beaten

1 potato peeled, chopped

3 tbsp olive oil

1 tsp salt

In a bowl, combine beef, rice, onions, garlic, egg, and salt. Shape the mixture into 15-16 meatballs. Grease the inner pot with 1 tbsp of olive oil. Press Sauté and cook the meatballs for 3-4 minutes, or until slightly brown.

Remove the meatballs. Add the remaining oil and make a layer of potato. Top with meatballs, cover with water and seal the lid. Adjust the release steam handle. Cook on Meat/Stew for 15 minutes on High. Do a quick release.

## Green Pea & Beef Ragout

Serving Size: 4 | Total Time: 25 minutes

2 lb beef, tender cuts, cut into bits

2 cups green peas

1 onion, diced

1 tomato, diced

3 cups beef broth

½ cup tomato paste

1 tsp cayenne pepper

1 tbsp flour

1 tsp salt

½ tsp dried thyme

½ tsp red pepper flakes

Add beef, green peas, onion, tomato, broth, tomato paste, cayenne pepper, flour, salt, thyme, and red pepper flakes to the Instant Pot. Seal the lid, press Manual/Pressure Cook and cook for 10 minutes on High Pressure. When done, release the steam naturally for 10 minutes. Serve.

## Classic Mushroom Beef Stroganoff

Serving Size: 6 | Total Time: 45 minutes

1 lb beef steak, cut into bite-sized pieces

1 cup button mushrooms, chopped

1 cup sour cream

2 cups beef broth

3 tbsp Worcestershire sauce

3 tbsp olive oil

1 tbsp flour

1 onion, chopped

Salt and pepper to taste

In a bowl, mix flour, salt, and pepper. Coat steaks with the mixture. Place the meat and broth in the inner pot. Seal the lid and cook for 10 minutes on High Pressure. Do a quick release. Add mushrooms, onion, and Worcestershire sauce. Seal the lid and cook on High

Pressure for 15 minutes. Do a quick release. Stir in sour cream. Let simmer for 10 minutes and serve.

## Eggplant & Beef Stew with Parmesan

Serving Size: 6 | Total Time: 70 minutes

9 oz beef neck, cut into bite-sized pieces

2 cups fire-roasted tomatoes

1 eggplant, chopped

½ tbsp fresh green peas

1 tbsp cayenne pepper

1 tbsp beef broth

4 tbsp olive oil

2 tbsp tomato paste

1 tbsp ground chili pepper

½ tsp salt

Parmesan, for garnish

Rub the meat with salt, cayenne, and chili pepper. Grease the Instant Pot with oil and brown the meat for 5-7 minutes or until golden on Sauté. Add tomatoes, eggplant, green peas, broth, and tomato paste and seal the lid. Cook on Meat/Stew for 40 minutes on High. Do a natural release for 10 minutes. Carefully unlock the lid. Serve warm sprinkled with grated Parmesan cheese.

## Tasty Spicy Beef

Serving Size: 6 | Total Time: 33 minutes

2 lb lean beef, cut into bite-sized pieces

5 onions, chopped

5 garlic cloves, minced

1 jalapeño pepper, chopped

Salt and pepper to taste

1 tsp cayenne pepper

2 tbsp tomato sauce

2 tbsp vegetable oil

Heat oil on Sauté. Stir-fry onions and garlic for 3 minutes. Add in the meat, salt, pepper, cayenne pepper, jalapeño pepper, and tomato sauce. Mix and cover with water. Seal the lid. Cook for 20 minutes on High Pressure. Do a quick pressure release. Carefully unlock the lid. Serve.

## Red Wine Beef & Vegetable Hotpot

Serving Size: 6 | Total Time: 40 minutes

2 sweet potatoes, cut into chunks

2 lb stewing beef meat

¾ cup red wine

1 tbsp ghee

6 oz tomato paste

6 oz baby carrots, chopped

1 onion, finely chopped

½ tsp salt

4 cups beef broth

½ cup green peas

1 tsp dried thyme

3 garlic cloves, crushed

Heat ghee on Sauté. Add beef and brown for 5-6 minutes. Add onion and garlic, and keep stirring for 3 more minutes. Add the sweet potatoes, wine, tomato paste, carrots, salt, broth, green peas, and thyme and seal the lid. Cook on Meat/Stew for 20 minutes on High Pressure. Do a quick release. Serve.

## Beef Bones with Beans & Chili Pepper

Serving Size: 4 | Total Time: 30 minutes

14.5 oz canned beans

12 oz beef bones

1 onion, chopped

3 garlic cloves

1 carrot, chopped

1 tbsp parsley, chopped

1 bay leaf

Salt and pepper to taste

1 chili pepper, minced

3 tbsp vegetable oil

Place beans, beef bones, onion, garlic, carrot, parsley, bay leaf, salt, pepper, chili pepper, and oil in the Instant Pot. Pour water enough to cover. Seal the lid. Cook on High Pressure for 15 minutes. Release the steam naturally for 10 minutes. Let it chill for a while before serving.

## Beef & Potatoes Moussaka

Serving Size: 4 | Total Time: 35 minutes

2 lb potatoes, chopped

1 lb lean ground beef

1 onion, chopped

Salt and pepper to taste

½ cup milk

2 eggs, beaten

1 tbsp vegetable oil

Sour cream for serving

Grease the pot with vegetable oil. Make 1 layer of potatoes and brush with milk. Spread the beef on top and make another layer of potatoes. Brush with the remaining milk. Seal the lid and cook for 15 minutes on High Pressure. Do a quick release. Sprinkle with salt and pepper and top with the eggs and onion. Seal the lid and let it stand for about 10 minutes. Top with sour cream.

## Beef with Potatoes & Mushrooms

Serving Size: 6 | Total Time: 40 minutes

2 lb round roast

2 tbsp olive oil

2 cups vegetable broth

2 garlic cloves, minced

1 celery stalk, chopped

Salt and pepper to taste

1 tsp oregano

2 cups sliced mushrooms

1 large white onion, diced

1 lb potatoes, quartered

Place the olive oil, vegetable broth, garlic, salt, pepper, and oregano in your Instant Pot and stir. Mix in the round roast, mushrooms, potatoes, celery, and onion. Seal the lid, select Manual, and cook for 25 minutes on High pressure. When done, perform a quick pressure release and unlock the lid. Serve immediately.

## Chinese Beef with Bok Choy

Serving Size: 4 | Total Time: 45 minutes

1 lb stew beef meat, cubed

1 onion, quartered

1 garlic clove, minced

2 tbsp sesame oil

1 carrot, thinly chopped

1 tbsp rice wine

1 (12 oz) bok choy, sliced

12 oz broccoli florets

1 red chili, sliced

1 tsp ground ginger

1 cup beef broth

¼ cup soy sauce

2 tbsp fish sauce

Warm the sesame oil in your Instant Pot on Sauté. Add in beef meat, onion, garlic, carrot, ginger, and red chili and cook for 5-6 minutes. Stir in beef broth, rice wine, soy sauce, and fish sauce and seal the lid. Select Manual and cook for 30 minutes on High pressure. When done, perform a quick pressure release. Put in broccoli and bok choy and cook for 4-5 minutes on Sauté. Serve.

## Simple Beef with Rice & Cheese

Serving Size: 4 | Total Time: 65 minutes

2 lb beef shoulder

1 cup rice

2 cups beef broth

3 tbsp butter

¼ cup Parmesan, grated

Salt and pepper to taste

Rub the beef with salt and pepper. Place it in the pot and pour in broth. Seal the lid and cook on Meat/Stew for 25 minutes on High. Do a quick release. Unlock the lid and remove the meat but keep the broth. Add rice and stir in 1 tbsp butter. Season with pepper and salt. Seal the lid. Cook on Manual for 20 minutes on High. Do a quick release. Remove the rice and wipe the pot clean. Melt 2 tbsp of butter on Sauté. Add meat and lightly brown for 10 minutes. Serve with rice topped with Parmesan.

# Fall Beef Steak with Vegetables

Serving Size: 4 | Total Time: 51 minutes

1 lb beef chuck roast, cut into chunks
2 tbsp olive oil
1 leek, sliced
2 garlic cloves, minced
1 tsp thyme
1 tsp steak seasoning
2 green bell peppers, sliced
1 cup mushrooms, sliced
1 carrot, chopped
1 celery stalk, chopped
1 cup beef stock
Salt and pepper to taste

Warm the olive oil in your Instant Pot on Sauté. Place in garlic and leek and cook for 3-4 minutes. Stir in beef chunks and brown for 6-7 minutes, stirring occasionally. Mix in steak seasoning, bell peppers, celery, carrot, mushrooms, beef stock, thyme, salt, and pepper. Seal the lid, select Manual, and cook for 30 minutes on High pressure. When done, perform a quick pressure release and unlock the lid. Serve right away.

# Calf's Liver Venetian-Style

Serving Size: 2 | Total Time: 55 minutes

1 lb calf's liver, rinsed
3 tbsp olive oil
2 garlic cloves, crushed
1 tbsp mint, chopped
½ tsp cayenne pepper
½ tsp Italian seasoning

In a bowl, mix oil, garlic, mint, cayenne, and Italian seasoning. Brush the liver and chill for 30 minutes. Remove from the fridge and pat dry with paper. Place the liver into the inner pot. Seal the lid and cook on High Pressure for 5 minutes. When ready, release the steam naturally for about 10 minutes.

# Thyme Ground Beef Roll

Serving Size: 6 | Total Time: 50 minutes

2 lb ground beef

2 large eggs
½ tsp minced garlic
1 cup all-purpose flour
1 tsp dried thyme
3 tbsp olive oil
½ tsp salt

In a bowl, combine the meat, garlic, flour, and eggs. Sprinkle with thyme and salt. Mix with hands and set aside. Grease a baking dish with olive oil. Form the meatloaf at the bottom. Add 1 cup water and place a trivet in your cooker. Lay the baking dish on the trivet. Seal the lid, press Meat/Stew, and cook for 40 minutes on High. Do a quick release. Carefully transfer the meatloaf to a serving dish. Garnish with salad and serve.

# Pino Noir Beef Pot Roast

Serving Size: 6 | Total Time: 61 minutes

3 lb beef chuck roast
2 tbsp olive oil
1 cup beef broth
4 carrots, julienned
1 lb potatoes, chopped
2 celery stalks, chopped
3 garlic cloves, peeled
1 cup Pino Noir red wine
1 onion, sliced
2 sprigs rosemary
2 tbsp tomato puree
Salt and pepper to taste

Warm the olive oil in your Instant Pot on Sauté. Add in the beef roast and brown for 5-6 minutes on all sides. Remove to a plate. Pour in the red wine and scrape any brown bits from the bottom. Stir in onion, garlic, carrots, potatoes, celery, tomato puree, rosemary sprigs, salt, and pepper. Put the beef back on the vegetables and add in the beef broth.

Seal the lid. Select Manual and cook for 35 minutes on High. When over, allow a natural release for 10 minutes and unlock the lid. Discard rosemary sprigs and remove beef to a plate. Serve with gravy and vegetables.

## Beer-Braised Beef Short Ribs

Serving Size: 6 | Total Time: 70 minutes

3 lb beef short ribs
Salt and pepper to taste
2 tbsp olive oil
3 garlic cloves, minced
4 carrots, chopped
1 onion, diced
1 tsp dried thyme
1 ½ cups beef broth
1 cup pilsner beer

Sprinkle beef ribs with salt and pepper. Warm the olive oil in your Instant Pot on Sauté. Add in the ribs and cook for 10 minutes on all sides until browned; set aside. Add carrot, onion, garlic, and thyme to the pot and cook for 5 more minutes. Pour in beef broth and scrape any brown bits from the bottom. Mix in beer and return the ribs.

## Maple Beef Teriyaki

Serving Size: 4 | Total Time: 50 minutes

2 lb flank steak, cut into strips
2 garlic cloves, minced
¼ cup soy sauce
¼ cup maple syrup
¼ cup tamari sauce
1-inch piece grated ginger

Place the soy sauce, garlic, maple syrup, tamari sauce, ginger, and ½ cup of water in your Instant Pot and cook for 5 minutes on Sauté. Stir in steak strips.

Seal the lid. Select Manual and cook for 25 minutes on High pressure. Once over, allow a natural release for 10 minutes, then perform a quick pressure release. Carefully unlock the lid. Serve immediately.

## Beef with Snow Peas

Serving Size: 4 | Total Time: 46 minutes

1 lb beef brisket, cubed
Salt and pepper to taste
2 tbsp olive oil
1 onion, chopped
2 garlic cloves, minced

2 bay leaves
8 oz bag snow peas, trimmed
1 carrot, chopped
1 turnip, chopped
1 lb potatoes, cut into quarters
Bearnaise sauce for serving

Warm the olive oil in your Instant Pot on Sauté. Place in beef brisket, onion, garlic, carrot, and turnip and cook for 5 minutes. Add in 2 cups of water, potatoes, bay leaves, salt, and pepper and seal the lid. Select Manual and cook for 25 minutes on High pressure. When ready, perform a quick pressure release and unlock the lid. Discard bay leaves and put in snow peas, and cook for 6 minutes on Sauté. Serve with bearnaise sauce.

## Italian Roast Beef

Serving Size: 4 | Total Time: 75 minutes

1 lb boneless beef chuck roast
2 oz dried porcini mushrooms
4 oz pancetta, diced
1 onion, chopped
2 garlic cloves, minced
1 cup chicken broth
1 tsp tomato paste
14 oz can crushed tomatoes
½ cup Chianti red wine
1 tsp dried oregano
2 bay leaves
½ tsp Italian seasonings
Salt and pepper to taste
2 tbsp parsley, chopped

In a bowl, place porcini mushrooms and pour in ½ cup of boiling water to cover. Let sit for 10 minutes. Set your Instant Pot to Sauté. Place in pancetta and cook for 5 minutes until crispy; set aside. Add in onion and garlic and cook for 3 minutes until fragrant. Stir in the beef roast, pancetta, soaked mushrooms with their water, chicken broth, tomato paste, tomatoes, red wine, oregano, bay leaves, Italian seasonings, salt, and pepper.

Seal the lid, select Meat/Stew, and cook for 35 minutes on High pressure. Once over, allow a natural release for 10 minutes, then perform a quick pressure release, and unlock the lid. Serve topped with parsley.

# Classic Beef Stroganoff

Serving Size: 6 | Total Time: 45 minutes

2 lb chuck roast, thin slices

2 tbsp butter

1 tbsp olive oil

1 onion, sliced

Salt and pepper to taste

1 cup mushrooms, sliced

2 garlic cloves, minced

1 ¼ cups beef broth

½ cup crème fraiche

2 cup cooked rice

Warm the olive oil and butter in your Instant Pot on Sauté. Place in onion and cook for 3 minutes. Sprinkle chuck roast with salt and pepper and place it in the pot and brown for 2 minutes on all sides. Add in mushrooms and garlic and cook for another 3 minutes. Stir in beef broth and seal the lid.

Select Manual and cook for 20 minutes on High pressure. Once ready, perform a quick pressure release and unlock the lid. Mix in créme fraiche and lock the lid. Let sit for 5 minutes. Serve with rice.

# Sambal Beef Noodles

Serving Size: 4 | Total Time: 65 minutes

1 lb beef chuck roast, cubed

2 tbsp sesame oil

Salt and pepper to taste

1 chopped onion

2 minced garlic cloves

3 tbsp sambal oelek chili paste

2 cups water

8 oz egg noodles

Warm the sesame oil in your Instant Pot on Sauté. Place in the beef roast and cook for 6-7 minutes, stirring often. Add in salt, pepper, onion, sambal oelek chili paste, garlic, and 1 cup of water. Seal the lid, select Manual, and cook for 30 minutes on High pressure.

Once done, allow a natural release for 10 minutes, then perform a quick pressure release. Transfer beef roast to a plate. Pour in 1 cup of water in the pot and bring to a boil on Sauté. Add in noodles and cook for 4-5 minutes. Put the beef back to the pot and stir. Serve warm.

# Beef Tikka Masala

Serving Size: 4 | Total Time: 50 minutes

2 tbsp tikka masala powder

1 lb beef chuck steak, cubed

2 tbsp olive oil

1 green chili, chopped

2 tsp ginger purée

2 tsp garlic purée

1 onion, chopped

1 cup beef broth

1 (14 oz) diced tomatoes

½ cup coconut cream

Salt and pepper to taste

3 tbsp chopped cilantro

Warm the olive oil in your Instant Pot on Sauté. Sprinkle beef steak with salt and pepper. Place it in the pot and sauté for 4-5 minutes, stirring periodically; set aside. Add onion, ginger puree, garlic puree, green chili, tikka masala powder, salt, and pepper in the pot.

Cook for 3 minutes. Pour in beef broth and scrape any brown bits from the bottom. Put back beef to the pot and diced tomatoes and seal the lid. Select Manual and cook for 25 minutes on High pressure.

Once done, perform a quick pressure release and unlock the lid. Mix in coconut cream for 4-5 minutes. Scatter cilantro on top and serve.

# Traditional American Beef Meatloaf

Serving Size: 6 | Total Time: 45 minutes

2 lb ground beef

½ cup milk

½ cup breadcrumbs

1 onion, grated

1 egg, beaten

1 tsp allspice

Salt and pepper to taste

¼ cup ketchup

½ garlic powder

½ tsp brown sugar

2 tbsp tomato paste

I a bowl, add ground beef, beaten egg, onion, milk, breadcrumbs, allspice, salt, and pepper and stir with your hands. Pour 1 cup of water into your Instant Pot and fit in a trivet. Place the meatloaf on an aluminum sheet and shape a loaf. Combine ketchup, garlic powder, brown sugar, and tomato paste in a bowl.

Spread the ketchup mixture on top of the meatloaf and place it on the trivet. Seal the lid, select Manual, and cook for 25 minutes on High pressure. Once over, allow a natural release for 10 minutes and unlock the lid. Cut into slices and serve with rice or cooked potatoes.

## Savory Herb Meatloaf

Serving Size: 4 | Total Time: 45 minutes

1 lb ground beef

1 egg, beaten

1 tsp garlic powder

1 tsp onion powder

1 shredded potato

½ tsp rosemary

½ tsp thyme

1 ½ tsp parsley

Salt and pepper to taste

Dill pickles, to serve

Add the ground beef, egg, onion powder, garlic powder, shredded potato, rosemary, thyme, parsley, salt, and pepper to a bowl and combine them until everything is well mixed. Press the meatloaf mixture to a greased cooking pan. Pour 1 cup of water into your Instant Pot and fit in a trivet. Place the pan on the trivet and seal the lid. Select Manual and cook for 25 minutes on High.

When ready, allow a natural release for 10 minutes, then perform a quick pressure release, and unlock the lid. Remove the meatloaf to a plate and let cool before slicing. Serve with dill pickles.

## Beef Steak with Mustard Sauce

Serving Size: 4 | Total Time: 55 minutes

1 lb flank steak, sliced

2 tbsp olive oil

Salt and pepper to taste

½ cup beef broth

¼ cup apple cider vinegar

1 tbsp onion powder

1 tbsp Worcestershire sauce

1 cup heavy cream

1 tbsp yellow mustard

Warm 1 tbsp of olive oil in your Instant Pot on Sauté. Season the flank steak with onion powder, salt, and pepper and place in the pot; brown for 4-5 minutes on both sides. Stir in beef broth, vinegar, and Worcestershire sauce and seal the lid. Cook on Meat/Stew for 30 minutes.

Once ready, allow a natural release for 10 minutes, then perform a quick pressure release, and unlock the lid. Mix in heavy cream and mustard. Serve immediately.

Seal the lid, select Manual, and cook for 35 minutes on High pressure. Once done, allow a natural release for 10 minutes, then perform a quick pressure release, and unlock the lid. Serve with vegetables or potatoes.

## Thai Beef Short Ribs

Serving Size: 6 | Total Time: 55 minutes

3 tbsp Thai yellow curry paste

12 beef short ribs

2 tbsp olive oil

Salt to taste

½ cup soy sauce

2 tbsp tomato paste

2 tbsp apple cider vinegar

4 garlic cloves, minced

1 tbsp ginger root, grated

2 tbsp sriracha sauce

¼ cup raw honey

Warm the olive oil in your Instant Pot on Sauté. Sprinkle beef ribs with salt and place them in the pot. Sear until browned on all sides; set aside. Place the soy sauce, curry paste, tomato paste, vinegar, garlic, ginger, sriracha, and honey in the pot. Stir well and scrape any bits from the bottom. Put ribs back to the pot. Pour in 1 cup of water.

Seal the lid, select Manual, and cook for 35 minutes on High pressure. When over, allow a natural release for 10 minutes and unlock the lid. Serve with gravy.

## Mediterranean Beef Stew with Olives

Serving Size: 6 | Total Time: 50 minutes

2 cups canned spicy diced tomatoes with juice

2 lb beef stew meat, cubed

3 tbsp olive oil

1 onion, sliced

2 garlic cloves, minced

½ cup dry white wine

1 red pepper, sliced

20 kalamata olives, pitted

Salt and pepper to taste

Warm the oil in your Instant Pot on Sauté. Place in the beef cubes and cook for 4-5 minutes or until no longer pink, stirring often. Add in onion, garlic, red pepper, salt, and pepper and cook for another 3 minutes. Pour in white wine and scrape any brown bits from the bottom. Stir in tomatoes, kalamata olives, and 1 cup of water.

Seal the lid. Select Manual and cook for 30 minutes on High pressure. Once done, perform a quick pressure release and unlock the lid. Adjust the seasoning with salt and pepper. Serve with potatoes or cooked rice.

## Smoky Chipotle Beef Brisket

Serving Size: 4 | Total Time: 60 minutes + marinating time

1 tsp seasoned meat tenderizer

2 lb beef brisket, flat cut

¼ tsp garlic salt

1 tbsp smoked paprika

1 tbsp Worcestershire sauce

1 cup smoky chipotle sauce

Combine garlic salt, smoked paprika, Worcestershire sauce, and seasoned meat tenderizer in a bowl. Rub the brisket with the mixture. Cover with cling film and allow to marinate for 30 minutes in the fridge.

Place 1 cup of water, smoky chipotle, and brisket with its marinate in your Instant Pot and seal the lid. Select Manual and cook for 40 minutes on High pressure.

Once done, allow a natural release for 10 minutes, then perform a quick pressure release, and unlock the lid. Remove brisket to a plate. Slice before serving with sauce.

## Beef Ragù Bolognese

Serving Size: 4 | Total Time: 40 minutes

½ cup Pecorino Romano cheese, shredded

1 lb ground beef

2 tbsp butter

1 onion, chopped

1 carrot, chopped

1 celery stalk, chopped

Salt and pepper to taste

2 tbsp basil, chopped

1 tbsp red wine

16 oz tomato sauce

2 tbsp passata

16 oz fettuccine pasta

In the Instant Pot, add the pasta and cover with salted water. Seal the lid, press Manual, and cook for 4 minutes on High. Once ready, do a quick pressure release. Drain the pasta and remove to a bowl; cover with foil to keep warm.

Melt the butter on Sauté. Add in onion, carrot, and celery. Cook for 3-4 minutes. Mix in the ground beef and brown for 8-10 minutes, stirring occasionally. Pour in red wine, tomato sauce, and passata, and season with salt and black pepper. Seal the lid and select Manual.

Cook for 10 minutes on High. When ready, do a quick pressure release. Carefully unlock the lid. Pour the Bolognese sauce over the pasta, sprinkle with Pecorino Romano cheese, and top with basil to serve.

## Leftover Beef Sandwiches

Serving Size: 4 | Total Time: 30 minutes

1 lb leftover roast beef

4 ciabatta rolls

Salt and pepper to taste

1 tsp brown sugar

½ tsp garlic powder

1 tsp mustard powder

1 tsp paprika

2 tsp onion flakes

2 cups beef stock

2 tbsp Worcestershire sauce

1 tbsp balsamic vinegar

4 tsp butter, softened

4 cheddar cheese slices

In a bowl, mix salt, pepper, sugar, garlic powder, mustard powder, paprika, and onion flakes and rub the beef roast with the mixture. Transfer to your Instant Pot and add beef stock, Worcestershire sauce, and balsamic vinegar.

Seal the lid, select Manual, and cook for 10 minutes on High pressure. When over, allow a natural release for 10 minutes, then perform a quick pressure release, and unlock the lid. Remove beef roast and shred it.

Discard sauce and reserve 1 cup for serving. Brush ciabatta rolls with butter and top with cheddar cheese. Stuff the rolls with some shredded beef. Serve sandwiches with sauce.

## Rich Beef & Vegetable Casserole

Serving Size: 4 | Total Time: 40 minutes

1 cup mixed mushrooms, sliced

1 lb stewing steak, cubed

2 tbsp olive oil

1 onion, chopped

2 garlic cloves, minced

1 celery stalk, chopped

Salt and pepper to taste

1 red bell pepper, chopped

2 tbsp tomato paste

1 lb tomatoes, chopped

½ cup red wine

½ cup green olives

2 tbsp oregano, chopped

Warm the olive oil in your Instant Pot on Sauté. Add in the steak and cook for 5 minutes until browned, stirring often. Add in onion, bell pepper, garlic, celery, mushrooms, salt, and pepper and sauté for 3-4 minutes. Stir in tomato paste, tomatoes, red wine, 1 cup of water, and green olives and seal the lid. Select Manual and cook for 20 minutes on High pressure. Once ready, perform a quick pressure release and unlock the lid. Serve topped with fresh oregano.

## Rosemary Braised Beef in Red Wine

Serving Size: 6 | Total Time: 75 minutes

3 lb diced braising steak

3 tbsp olive oil

Salt and pepper to taste

10 pearl onions, peeled

1 tsp Worcestershire sauce

4 baby carrot, chopped

1 celery stalk, diced

1 tbsp tomato paste

2 garlic cloves, minced

1 cup beef broth

1 cup red wine

2 sprigs fresh rosemary

1 bay leaf

1 tbsp cornstarch

Warm the olive oil in your Instant Pot on Sauté. Sprinkle beef with salt and pepper and place it in the pot. Cook for 8-10 minutes on all sides; reserve. Add pearl onions, garlic, baby carrot, celery, and tomato paste to the pot and cook for 4-5 minutes. Pour in red wine and scrape any brown bits from the bottom. Put meat back to the pot and thyme, Worcestershire sauce, beef broth, rosemary sprigs, and bay leaf.

Seal the lid, select Manual, and cook for 40 minutes on High pressure. When over, allow a natural release for 10 minutes, then perform a quick pressure release, and unlock the lid. Remove meat to a plate and let cool before slicing. Discard the rosemary and bay leaf. Combine cornstarch with 1 cup of cooking liquid and pour in the pot, and simmer on Sauté until the sauce thickens. Serve brisket with the sauce.

## Beef & Bean Chili

Serving Size: 4 | Total Time: 70 minutes

1 lb ground beef

2 tbsp olive oil

½ lb white beans, soaked

14 oz can diced tomatoes

1 tbsp tomato paste

1 white onion, diced

2 garlic cloves, chopped

1 green bell pepper, diced

1 cup beef broth

Salt and pepper to taste

½ tsp oregano

1 jalapeño pepper, minced

1 tsp ground cumin

Heat olive oil on Sauté. Add onion, garlic, green pepper, and jalapeño pepper, and sauté for 3-5 minutes until tender. Stir in beef and cook for another 6 minutes. Season with oregano, cumin, salt, and pepper, and pour in tomato paste, tomatoes, beef broth, and white beans. Seal the lid, select the Bean/Chili and cook for 25 minutes on High. When the timer is over, let the pressure release naturally for 10 minutes. Unlock the lid. Select Sauté to cook for another 8-10 minutes until the desired texture and thickness is reached. Ladle into bowls and serve.

## Garlicky Herb-Rubbed Beef Brisket

Serving Size: 4 | Total Time: 60 minutes + marinating time

2 lb beef brisket, flat cut

2 garlic cloves, minced

Salt and pepper to taste

½ tsp oregano

½ tsp marjoram

½ tsp ground cumin

½ tsp dried rosemary

1 ½ cups beef stock

Combine garlic, salt, pepper, marjoram, oregano, cumin, and rosemary in a bowl. Add in the brisket, toss to coat, and marinate for 30 minutes in the fridge. Place the brisket and beef stock in your Instant Pot and seal the lid. Select Manual and cook for 40 minutes on High pressure. When done, allow a natural release for 10 minutes, then perform a quick pressure release, and unlock the lid. Slice before serving.

## Beef & Lentil Stew

Serving Size: 4 | Total Time: 45 minutes

2 lb beef shoulder, cut into chunks

2 tbsp olive oil

Salt and pepper to taste

1 cup lentils

1 cup beef broth

½ cup sun-dried tomatoes

1 onion, sliced

2 garlic cloves, minced

½ tsp oregano

½ tsp marjoram

Combine the beef shoulder, olive oil, salt, pepper, lentils, beef broth, sun-dried tomatoes, onion, garlic cloves, oregano, and marjoram in your Instant Pot and stir. Seal the lid, select Manual, and cook for 25 minutes on High pressure. Once ready, allow a natural release for 10 minute and unlock the lid. Serve.

## Beef & Vegetable Stew

Serving Size: 6 | Total Time: 55 minutes

2 lb beef stew meat, cubed

Salt and pepper to taste

½ tsp onion powder

1/3 cup flour

1 tsp Italian seasoning

2 tbsp olive oil

1 onion, chopped

3 garlic cloves, minced

1 tbsp red wine

1 tbsp tomato paste

4 potatoes, peeled, chopped

1 cup green beans, trimmed

1 tsp paprika

1 cup tomatoes, chopped

1 celery rib, chopped

2 carrots, sliced

3 cups beef broth

1 bay leaf

2 tbsp parsley, chopped

Combine salt, pepper, onion powder, flour, and Italian seasoning in a bowl. Add in beef meat and toss to coat. Warm the olive oil in your Instant Pot on Sauté. Place the meat in the pot and cook for 5-6 minutes, stirring occasionally; set aside. Place the onion, garlic, celery, carrot, and paprika in the pot and cook for 3-4 minutes.

Pour in wine and scrape any brown bits from the bottom. Put the meat back to the pot and tomato paste, tomatoes, potatoes, green beans, broth, bay leaf, salt, and pepper and stir. Seal the lid, select Manual, and cook for 25 minutes on High. When ready, allow a natural release for 10 minutes. Serve topped with parsley.

## Beef & Root Vegetable Pot

Serving Size: 4 | Total Time: 65 minutes

1 lb beef stew meat, cubed

2 tbsp olive oil

Salt and pepper to taste

1 leek, chopped

2 garlic cloves, minced

1 tsp dried thyme

2 tbsp flour

1 cup dry red wine

2 cups chopped tomatoes

1 turnip, chopped

1 lb sweet potatoes, sliced

2 carrots, chopped

2 cups beef broth

¼ cup parsley, chopped

Warm the olive oil in your Instant Pot on Sauté. Sprinkle beef meat with salt and pepper and place it in the pot. Sauté for 6-7 minutes on all sides until browned; set aside. Add leek and garlic to the pot and cook for 3 minutes. Stir in thyme and flour and cook for 1 minute. Pour in red wine and scrape any brown bits from the bottom.

Add in turnip, carrots, sweet potatoes, tomatoes, and beef broth. Put the meat back to the pot and seal the lid. Select Manual and cook for 30 minutes on High pressure. Once over, allow a natural release for 10 minutes and unlock the lid. Serve topped with parsley.

## Beef & Butternut Squash Chili

Serving Size: 4 | Total Time: 65 minutes

2 tbsp olive oil

1 lb stewed beef meat, cubed

1 lb butternut squash, cubed

1 cup canned tomatoes, diced

1 onion, diced

2 garlic cloves

2 cups beef broth

Salt and pepper to taste

2 tbsp tomato paste

1 tsp chili powder

1 tsp ground cumin

1 tsp oregano

1 tsp cayenne pepper

Warm the olive oil in your Instant Pot on Sauté. Place in beef meat and cook for 7-8 minutes on all sides; reserve. Add onion, garlic, chili powder, cumin, oregano, cayenne pepper, salt, and pepper to the pot and cook for 5 minutes. Put in butternut squash, tomato paste, tomatoes, and beef broth and return the beef.

Seal the lid, select Manual, and cook for 30 minutes on High pressure. When ready, allow a natural release for 10 minutes, then perform a quick pressure release, and unlock the lid. Serve warm.

## Beef Neapolitan Ragù

Serving Size: 4 | Total Time: 53 minutes

1 ½ lb beef steak, cut into strips

2 tbsp lard

1 onion, chopped

2 cups crushed tomatoes

1 carrot, chopped

1 celery stalk, chopped

1 cup beef broth

½ cup red wine

1 tbsp passata

Salt and pepper to taste

Melt lard in your Instant Pot on Sauté. Place in onion, carrot, and celery and sauté until fragrant. Add in beef steak and cook for 3 minutes, stirring often. Pour in tomatoes, beef broth, red wine, passata, salt, and pepper and seal the lid. Select Meat/Stew.

Cook for 30 minutes on High pressure. When over, allow a natural release for 10 minutes, then perform a quick pressure release, and unlock the lid. Serve immediately.

## Boeuf Bourguignon

Serving Size: 4 | Total Time: 63 minutes

1 lb flank steak
2 tbsp olive oil
1 cup pearl onions
2 garlic cloves, minced
1 cups crimini mushrooms
1 carrot, sliced
4 oz bacon, chopped
1 cup beef broth
1 cup Burgundy red wine
Salt and pepper to taste
1 bay leaf
2 tbsp thyme, chopped

Warm the oil in your Instant Pot on Sauté. Place in the steak and cook for 6-8 minutes in total. Set aside. Add onions, garlic, mushrooms, carrots, and bacon to the pot and cook for 4-5 minutes. Stir in beef broth and wine. Put the meat back to the pot and salt, pepper, and bay leaf and seal the lid. Select Manual and cook for 30 minutes on High. When over, allow a natural release for 10 minutes, then perform a quick pressure release, and unlock the lid. Discard bay leaf. Top with thyme.

## Pulled BBQ Beef

Serving Size: 6 | Total Time: 65 minutes

3 lb beef chuck roast
2 tbsp olive oil
1 cup BBQ sauce
1 tbsp Dijon mustard
1 tsp smoked paprika
Salt and pepper to taste
2 cups beef broth
3 tbsp cilantro, chopped

Warm the olive oil in your Instant Pot on Sauté. Sprinkle beef with salt and pepper and place it in the pot and cook for 8-10 minutes on all sides. Add in BBQ sauce, Dijon mustard, smoked paprika, salt, pepper, and beef broth and seal the lid. Select Manual and cook for 35 minutes on High pressure.

Once ready, allow a natural release for 10 minutes, then perform a quick pressure release, and unlock the lid.

Remove beef and shred it using 2 forks. Put it back to the pot and mix with the remaining liquid. Top with cilantro and serve.

## Beef Meatballs with Tomato-Basil Sauce

Serving Size: 4 | Total Time: 30 minutes

2 cups tomato and basil pasta sauce
1 ¼ lb ground beef
1 tsp garlic powder
1 tsp onion powder
1 tsp oregano
2 tbsp breadcrumbs
Salt and pepper to taste
2 tbsp olive oil

Combine ground beef, garlic powder, onion powder, oregano, breadcrumbs, salt, and pepper in a bowl. Make 2-inch meatballs of the mixture. Warm the olive oil in your Instant Pot on Sauté. Add in the meatballs and cook for 4-5 minutes on all sides until browned. Stir in tomato and basil pasta sauce and ¼ cup of water.

Seal the lid, select Manual, and cook for 10 minutes on High pressure. When done, allow a natural release for 10 minutes, then perform a quick pressure release, and unlock the lid. Serve immediately.

## Vietnamese Beef

Serving Size: 6 | Total Time: 60 minutes

2 lb beef steak, sliced
3 tbsp olive oil
Salt and pepper to taste
4 garlic cloves, minced
1 tsp minced ginger
3 white onions, chopped
3 tbsp fish sauce
1 tbsp brown sugar
2 tbsp cornflour
2 tbsp mint leaves, chopped
1 red chili pepper, minced

Sprinkle beef steak with salt and pepper. Warm the olive oil in your Instant Pot on Sauté. Place in the steak and sauté for 10-12 minutes on all sides. Set aside.

Add garlic, ginger, red chili pepper, and onions to the pot and cook for 2-3 minutes. Stir in fish sauce, brown sugar, and 1 ¼ cups of water. Put the steak back to the pot.

Seal the lid. Select Manual and cook for 25 minutes on High pressure. When done, allow a natural release for 10 minutes, then perform a quick pressure release, and unlock the lid. Combine ½ cup of water and cornflour in a bowl and pour it into the pot. Simmer on Sauté until the liquid thickens. Serve topped with mint leaves.

## Greek-Style Stuffed Peppers

Serving Size: 4 | Total Time: 39 minutes

¼ cup Halloumi cheese, grated

2 tbsp olive oil

1 lb ground beef

2 onions, chopped

Salt and pepper to taste

4 bell peppers, tops removed

1 tsp oregano

1 tsp paprika

½ tsp ground cinnamon

1 cup canned tomato sauce

1 tbsp flour

Mix the cheese, ground beef, onions, paprika, cinnamon, salt, and pepper in a bowl. Stuff each bell pepper with the mixture. Pour the tomato sauce and ½ of water in your Instant Pot and fit in a trivet. Place the peppers on the trivet and seal the lid. Select Manual and cook for 15 minutes on High pressure.

When over, allow a natural release for 10 minutes and unlock the lid. Remove peppers to a plate. Whisk the flour and oregano with some cooking sauce in a bowl. Pour it in the pot and select Sauté; cook until the sauce thickens, about 3-4 minutes. Adjust the seasoning before pouring it over the peppers.

## Chipotle Shredded Beef

Serving Size: 4 | Total Time: 45 minutes

2 lb beef shoulder roast

2 tbsp vegetable oil

1 onion, chopped

3 garlic cloves, minced

3 cups beef broth

2 tbsp tomato salsa

1 tsp chipotle chili pepper

Salt and pepper to taste

4 tbsp sour cream

2 tbsp cilantro, chopped

Rub the beef roast with chipotle chili pepper, salt, and pepper on all sides. Warm the vegetable oil in your Instant Pot on Sauté. Place the onion and garlic and cook for 2-3 minutes. Add in the beef roast and beef broth and seal the lid.

Select Manual and cook for 30 minutes on High pressure. Once ready, perform a quick pressure release and unlock the lid. Remove meat and shred it. Pour tomato salsa in the pot and cook until the sauce thickens on Sauté. Stir in shredded beef. Top with cilantro and serve with a dollop of sour cream on the side.

## Veal Chops with Greek Yogurt

Serving Size: 4 | Total Time: 60 minutes

2 lb boneless veal shoulder, cubed

3 tomatoes, chopped

2 tbsp flour

3 tbsp butter

1 tbsp cayenne pepper

1 tsp salt

1 tbsp parsley, chopped

1 cup Greek yogurt

1 pide bread

Grease the bottom of the inner pot with 1 tbsp of butter. Make a layer with veal pieces and Pour water to cover. Season with salt and seal the lid. Cook on High Pressure for 45 minutes. Do a quick release.

Melt the remaining butter in a skillet. Add the cayenne pepper and flour and briefly stir-fry, about 2 minutes. Slice pide bread and arrange on a serving plate. Place the meat and tomatoes on top. Drizzle with cayenne pepper, Top with yogurt and sprinkle with parsley to serve.

## Lamb Shanks with Garlic & Thyme

Serving Size: 4 | Total Time: 65 minutes

2 ½ lb lamb shanks, trimmed of excess fat

Salt and pepper to taste

10 whole garlic cloves, peeled

1 cup vegetable broth

1 (14-oz) can diced tomatoes

1 onion, sliced

2 tbsp tomato paste

½ cup red wine

2 tbsp fresh thyme, chopped

2 tbsp butter

2 tsp balsamic vinegar

Sprinkle lamb shanks with salt and pepper. Warm the butter in your Instant Pot on Sauté. Place in lamb shanks and cook for 4-5 minutes on all sides until browned. Add in onion and garlic and sauté for 2 more minutes. Stir in vegetable broth, tomato paste, red wine, tomatoes, and thyme and seal the lid. Select Manual and cook for 35 minutes on High.

Once done, allow a natural release for 10 minutes and unlock the lid. Remove lamb to a plate. Stir the butter and balsamic vinegar in the pot and select Sauté; cook until the sauce thickens. Serve the lamb with sauce.

## Lamb with Tomato & Green Peas

Serving Size: 4 | Total Time: 65 minutes

1 cup green peas

1 lb lamb, cubed

1 tomato, roughly chopped

1 onion, peeled, chopped

2 carrots, peeled, chopped

1 celery stalk, chopped

2 tbsp parsley, chopped

2 garlic cloves, crushed

4 tbsp tomato sauce

2 tbsp olive oil

4 cups vegetable stock

Salt and pepper to taste

Warm the olive oil in your Instant Pot on Sauté. Cook the onion, carrots, celery, and garlic for 8 minutes until tender. Add in the lamb and sauté for another 5-6 minutes. Season with salt and black pepper. Add in green peas, tomato, tomato sauce, and stock and seal the lid. Cook on High Pressure for 30 minutes. Do a natural pressure release for about 10 minutes. Carefully fully unlock the lid. Top with parsley to serve.

## Minty Lamb

Serving Size: 6 | Total Time: 55 minutes

3 lb lamb, boneless and cubed

2 tbsp butter

4 garlic cloves, minced

4 green onions, chopped

1 tsp cumin seeds

1 tsp coriander seeds

3 tbsp flour

1 ½ cups vegetable stock

1 cup carrots, sliced

4 mint sprigs

Salt and pepper to taste

Sprinkle the lamb with salt and pepper and coat in flour. Melt butter in your Instant Pot on Sauté. Add in onion and garlic and cook for 3 minutes. Put in lamb and cook for 5-6 minutes until browned. Stir in stock, carrots, cumin and coriander seeds, and mint sprigs and seal the lid. Select Manual and cook for 25 minutes on High.

When ready, allow a natural release for 10 minutes. Carefully unlock the lid. Discard the mint sprigs. Top the lamb with sauce and serve warm.

## Hot Paprika & Oregano Lamb

Serving Size: 4 | Total Time: 70 minutes + marinating time

1 lb lamb shoulder

1 tsp hot paprika

1 tsp oregano

1 tsp cumin

¼ tsp ground cinnamon

2 tbsp tomato puree

¼ cup red wine

¼ cup chicken stock

1 tbsp olive oil

½ cup water

2 tbsp butter

Salt and pepper to taste

Mix the oregano, hot paprika, salt, black pepper, cumin, and cinnamon in a bowl. Add in lamb and toss to coat. Cover and let marinate for 20-30 minutes. Warm the olive oil in your Instant Pot on Sauté. Place in lamb shoulder and brown for 5 minutes on all sides. Pour in red wine, chicken stock, tomato puree, butter, and ½ cup of water.

Seal the lid, select Manual, and cook for 45 minutes on High pressure. Once over, allow a natural release for 10 minutes, then perform a quick pressure release, and unlock the lid. Remove the lamb to a cutting board shred it. Return to the pot and stir. Serve warm.

## Mediterranean Lamb

Serving Size: 4 | Total Time: 55 minutes

1 lb lamb meat, cut into strips

1 tsp vegetable oil

4 tomatoes, chopped

2 tbsp tomato paste

1 red bell pepper, sliced

2 garlic cloves, minced

1 yellow onion, chopped

1 carrot, sliced

2 thyme sprigs

½ cup dry white wine

10 black olives, sliced

Salt and pepper to taste

2 tbsp parsley, chopped

Warm oil in your Instant Pot on Sauté. Add in lamb and cook for 8 minutes on all sides. Stir in tomatoes, tomato paste, bell pepper, garlic, onion, carrots, salt, pepper and sauté for 5 more minutes. Pour in wine and enough water to cover everything. Add in thyme sprigs and olives. Seal the lid, select Manual, and cook for 30 minutes on High.

Once done, perform a quick pressure release and unlock the lid. Remove the lamb to a plate, discard bones and shred it. Put the shredded lamb back to the pot and stir parsley. Serve immediately.

## Quick French-Style Lamb with Sesame

Serving Size: 4 | Total Time: 45 minutes

12 oz lamb, tender cuts, ½-inch thick

1 cup rice

1 cup green peas

3 tbsp sesame seeds

4 cups beef broth

1 tsp salt

½ tsp dried thyme

3 tbsp butter

Mix the meat in the pot with broth. Seal the lid and cook on High Pressure for 15 minutes. Do a quick release. Remove the meat but keep the liquid. Add rice and green peas. Season with salt and thyme. Stir well and top with the meat. Seal the lid and cook on Manual for 18 minutes on High. Do a quick release. Carefully unlock the lid. Stir in butter and sesame seeds. Serve immediately.

## Lamb Stew with Lemon & Parsley

Serving Size: 4 | Total Time: 60 minutes

2 potatoes, cut into bite-sized pieces

1 lb lamb neck, boneless

2 large carrots, chopped

1 tomato, diced

1 red bell pepper, chopped

1 garlic head, whole

2 tbsp parsley, chopped

¼ cup lemon juice

Salt and pepper to taste

Add the meat and season with salt. Add in potatoes, carrots, tomato, bell pepper, lemon juice, and pepper, tuck in one garlic head in the middle of the pot and add 2 cups water. Add parsley and seal the lid. Cook on High Pressure for 45 minutes. When ready, do a quick release. Carefully unlock the lid. Serve.

## Simple Roast Lamb

Serving Size: 4 | Total Time: 40 minutes

2 lb lamb leg

1 tbsp garlic powder

3 tbsp extra virgin olive oil

Salt and pepper to taste

4 rosemary sprigs, chopped

Grease the inner pot with oil. Rub the meat with salt, pepper, and garlic powder, and place in the Instant Pot. Pour enough water to cover and seal the lid. Cook on Meat/Stew for 30 minutes on High. Do a quick release. Make sure the meat is tender and falls off the bones. Top with cooking juices and rosemary. Serve.

## Traditional Lamb with Vegetables

Serving Size: 6 | Total Time: 30 minutes

1 lb lamb chops, 1-inch thick

1 cup green peas, rinsed

3 carrots, chopped

3 onions, chopped

1 potato, chopped

1 tomato, chopped

3 tbsp olive oil

1 tbsp paprika

Salt and pepper to taste

Grease the Instant Pot with olive oil. Rub salt onto the lamb and make a bottom layer. Add peas, carrots, onions, potato, and tomato. Season with paprika. Add olive oil, 1 cup of water, salt, and pepper. Give it a good stir and seal the lid. Cook on Meat/Stew for 20 minutes on High Pressure. When ready, do a natural pressure release. Carefully unlock the lid. Serve hot.

## Garlic Lamb with Thyme

Serving Size: 4 | Total Time: 60 minutes

2 lb lamb, cubed

2 garlic cloves, minced

1 cup onions, chopped

1 cup red wine

2 cups beef stock

2 tbsp butter, softened

2 celery stalks, chopped

1 tbsp fresh thyme

2 tbsp flour

Salt and pepper to taste

Rub the lamb with salt and pepper. Melt butter on Sauté and cook onions, celery, and garlic for 5 minutes. Add lamb and fry until browned for about 5-6 minutes. Dust the flour and stir. Pour in the stock and red wine. Seal the lid, and cook on High Pressure for 30 minutes. Do a natural release for 10 minutes. Serve with thyme.

## Leg of Lamb with Garlic and Pancetta

Serving Size: 6 | Total Time: 40 minutes

2 lb lamb leg

6 garlic cloves

1 large onion, chopped

6 pancetta slices

1 tsp rosemary

Salt and pepper to taste

2 tbsp oil

3 cups beef broth

Heat the oil in your Instant Pot on Sauté. Add the pancetta and onion, making two layers. Season with salt and pepper and cook for 3 minutes until lightly browned. Place the lamb on a separate dish. Using a sharp knife, make 6 incisions into the meat and place a garlic clove in each. Rub the meat with rosemary and transfer to the pot. Press Cancel and pour in the beef broth. Seal the lid and cook on High Pressure for 25 minutes. When done, do a natural pressure release. Serve.

## Savory Irish Lamb Stew

Serving Size: 4 | Total Time: 36 minutes

1 lb lamb, cut into pieces

1 ½ tbsp canola oil

1 onion, sliced

2 tbsp cornstarch

2 potatoes, cubed

2 carrots, chopped

2 ½ cups beef broth

½ tsp dried oregano

Salt and pepper to taste

Season the lamb with salt and pepper. Heat the canola oil in your Instant Pot on Sauté. Sear the lamb until browned on all sides, about 4-5 minutes. Add onion, potatoes, carrots, broth, and oregano, and stir. Seal the lid and cook on High Pressure for 18 minutes. When ready, do a quick pressure release. Whisk the cornstarch with a little bit of water and stir it into the stew. Cook on Sauté for 3 more minutes. Serve hot.

## Asian-Style Lamb Curry

Serving Size: 4 | Total Time: 55 minutes + marinating time

1 ½ lb lamb stew meat, cubed
½ cup coconut milk
4 garlic cloves, minced
Juice of ½ lime
1-inch piece ginger, grated
Salt and pepper to taste
2 tbsp yellow curry paste
½ tsp turmeric
2 tbsp butter
1 tbsp soy sauce
14 oz canned tomatoes, diced
3 carrots, sliced
1 onion, diced
1 eggplant, diced
2 tbsp cilantro, chopped
2 cups basmati rice, cooked

Mix coconut milk, garlic, lime juice, ginger, salt, and pepper in a bowl. Add in lamb cubes and toss to coat. Let marinate for 30 minutes. Set your Instant Pot to Sauté. Melt butter and add onion, curry paste, turmeric, eggplant, and carrots and cook for 3-4 minutes. Stir in tomatoes, soy sauce, and 1 cup water.

Add in the marinated lamb with their juice and seal the lid. Select Manual and cook for 30 minutes on High pressure. Once ready, allow a natural release for 10 minutes, then perform a quick pressure release, and unlock the lid. Serve with the rice topped with cilantro.

## Spicy Lamb & Bean Chili

Serving Size: 4 | Total Time: 53 minutes

1 cup chopped green chilies
1 cup cannellini beans, soaked
1 lb ground lamb
2 tbsp olive oil
1 onion, chopped
½ tbsp chili powder
½ tsp cayenne pepper
1 tsp cumin
1 tsp fennel seeds
1 (14-oz) can diced tomatoes
1 tbsp tomato paste
3 cups chicken broth
Salt and pepper to taste

Warm the olive oil in your Instant Pot on Sauté. Add in ground lamb and cook for 5 minutes until mostly brown. Stir in onion, chili powder, cayenne pepper, cumin, fennel seeds, salt, and pepper and sauté for 3 minutes. Pour in tomatoes, tomato paste, green chilies, cannellini beans, and chicken broth and seal the lid. Select Manual and cook for 25 minutes on High.

When ready, allow a natural release for 10 minutes and unlock the lid. Serve with sour cream.

## Fennel Lamb Ribs

Serving Size: 4 | Total Time: 47 minutes

3 lb lamb ribs
2 tbsp olive oil
4 garlic cloves, chopped
3 tbsp all-purpose flour
1 ½ cups vegetable stock
½ tsp cumin
½ fennel bulb, sliced
2 carrots, chopped
4 rosemary sprigs
Salt and pepper to taste

Warm olive oil in your Instant Pot on Sauté. Sprinkle lamb ribs with salt and pepper and add them to the pot. Cook for 6-7 minutes on all sides. Add in garlic, cumin and fennel and cook for 3 more minutes. Stir in flour, stock, rosemary, and carrots and seal the lid. Select Manual and cook for 22 minutes on High. When ready, allow a natural release for 5 minutes and unlock the lid. Remove rosemary sprigs. Serve the ribs with sauce.

# Lamb Chops with Mashed Potatoes

Serving Size: 6 | Total Time: 20 minutes

8 lamb chops

Salt to taste

3 sprigs rosemary, chopped

3 tbsp butter, softened

2 tbsp olive oil

1 tbsp tomato puree

1 green onion, chopped

1 cup beef stock

5 potatoes, peeled, chopped

1/3 cup milk

2 tbsp cilantro, chopped

Rub rosemary leaves and salt to the lamb chops. Warm oil and 2 tbsp of butter on Sauté. Brown lamb chops for 1 minute per each side; set aside. In the pot, mix tomato puree and green onion and cook for 2-3 minutes. Add the stock into the pot to deglaze and scrape the bottom to get rid of any browned food bits. Return the lamb chops to the pot. Set a steamer rack on lamb chops. Place the steamer basket on the rack. Pour in the potatoes.

Seal the lid and cook on High Pressure for 4 minutes. Release the pressure quickly. Remove trivet and steamer basket.

In a blender, add potatoes, milk, salt, and remaining butter. Blend well until you obtain a smooth consistency. Place the potato mash on a serving dish. Lay lamb chops on the mash. Drizzle with cooking liquid and top with cilantro.

## Vegetable & Lamb Casserole

Serving Size: 4 | Total Time: 50 minutes

1 lb lamb stew meat, cubed

2 tbsp olive oil

1 onion, chopped

3 garlic cloves, minced

2 tomatoes, chopped

½ lb baby potatoes

½ lb green beans, chopped

1 carrot, chopped

1 onion, chopped

1 celery stalk, chopped

2 tbsp white wine

2 cups lamb stock

1 tsp Hungarian paprika

1 tsp cumin, ground

¼ tsp oregano, dried

¼ tsp rosemary, dried

Salt and pepper to taste

Warm the olive oil in your Instant Pot on Sauté. Add in lamb cubes and cook for 5-6 minutes until no longer pink. Stir in onion and garlic and sauté for another 3 minutes. Pour in tomatoes, potatoes, green beans, carrot, onion, celery, white wine, lamb stock, paprika, cumin, oregano, rosemary, salt, and pepper and seal the lid. Select Manual and cook for 20 minutes on High pressure. When over, allow a natural release for 10 minutes and unlock the lid.

## Balsamic Lamb

Serving Size: 4 | Total Time: 45 minutes

2 lb lamb shanks

2 tbsp sesame oil

2 garlic cloves, peeled

1 onion, chopped

1 cup vegetable broth

1 tbsp tomato paste

½ tsp thyme

¼ tsp dried dill weed

1 tbsp balsamic vinegar

1 tbsp butter

Warm sesame oil in your Instant Pot on Sauté. Place in onion and garlic and sauté for 3 minutes. Stir in broth, tomato paste, dill, and thyme. Add in the lamb and seal the lid. Select Manual and cook for 25 minutes on High. When ready, allow a natural release for 5 minutes and unlock the lid. Remove the lamb to a bowl. Stir the balsamic vinegar and butter in the pot for 1-2 minutes until the butter melts. Serve the lamb with sauce.

# Lamb Chorba

Serving Size: 4 | Total Time: 35 minutes

2 lb lamb shanks
2 tbsp olive oil
2 garlic cloves, peeled
1 onion, chopped
1 celery stalk, chopped
1 tomato, chopped
1 carrot, chopped
2 tbsp oregano, chopped
Salt and pepper to taste
4 cups vegetable broth
1 tbsp white wine vinegar

Warm the olive oil in your Instant Pot on Sauté. Place in the lamb, celery, onion, carrot, and garlic and sauté for 6 minutes. Stir in vegetable broth, tomato, salt, and pepper Seal the lid. Select Manual and cook for 20 minutes. Release the pressure quickly. Drizzle with vinegar and sprinkle with oregano to serve.

# FISH & SEAFOOD

## Haddock with Edamame Soybeans

Serving Size: 4 | Total Time: 25 minutes

1 pack (12-oz) edamame soybeans
1 lb haddock fillets
1 clove garlic, minced
2 tsp grated ginger
¼ red chili, sliced
1 tbsp honey
2 tbsp soy sauce
Salt and pepper to taste

Pour 1 cup of water into your Instant Pot and fit in a trivet. Mix garlic, ginger, red chili, honey, soy sauce, salt, and pepper in a bowl. Add in the haddock fillets and toss to coat. Spread the fillets on a greased baking pan; scatter edamame soybeans around. Place the pan on the trivet.

Seal the lid. Cook on Steam for 6 minutes on High pressure. When done, allow a natural release for 10 minutes, then perform a quick pressure release. Serve.

## Italian Steamed Sea Bream with Lemon

Serving Size: 4 | Total Time: 50 minutes

2 pieces sea bream (2 lb), cleaned
¼ cup olive oil
¼ cup lemon juice
1 tbsp fresh thyme sprigs
1 tbsp Italian seasoning
½ tsp sea salt
1 tsp garlic powder
4 cups fish stock

In a bowl, mix oil, lemon juice, thyme, Italian seasoning, sea salt, and garlic powder. Brush onto fish and wrap tightly with a plastic foil. Refrigerate for 30 minutes. Pour fish stock into the pot. Set the steamer rack and place the fish on top. Seal the lid. Cook on Steam for 8 minutes on High. Do a quick release. Unwrap the fish. Serve immediately with steam vegetables.

## Tilapia with Basil Pesto & Rice

Serving Size: 2 | Total Time: 15 minutes

2 tilapia fillets
2 tbsp basil pesto
½ cup basmati rice
Salt and pepper to taste

Place the rice and 1 cup of water in your Instant Pot and season with salt and pepper; fit in a trivet. Place tilapia fillets in the middle of a parchment paper sheet. Top each fillet with pesto and roll all the edges to form a packet. Place it on the trivet and seal the lid.

Select Manual and cook for 6 minutes on Low pressure. Once ready, perform a quick pressure release. Carefully unlock the lid. Fluff the rice with a fork and transfer to a plate. Top with tilapia and serve.

## Tilapia Fillets with Hazelnut Crust

Serving Size: 4 | Total Time: 15 minutes

4 tilapia fillets
2 tsp olive oil
¼ tsp lemon pepper
2 tbsp Dijon mustard
½ cup chopped hazelnuts
2 tbsp parsley, chopped
Salt and pepper to taste

Pour 1 cup of water into your Instant Pot and fit in a trivet. Mix the olive oil, lemon pepper, and Dijon mustard in a bowl. Rub each fillet with mustard mixture, then roll them in the hazelnuts to coat.

Place the fillets on the trivet, sprinkle with salt and pepper, and seal the lid. Select Manual, and cook for 5 minutes on High. When done, perform a quick pressure release. Unlock the lid. Serve scattered with parsley.

## Lemon & Leek Tilapia

Serving Size: 2 | Total Time: 15 minutes

2 tilapia fillets

¼ tsp garlic powder

2 sprigs fresh dill

4 slices lemon

1 leek, white part, sliced

1 tbsp cold butter, sliced

Salt and pepper to taste

Pour 1 cup of water into your Instant Pot and fit in a trivet. Season the tilapia fillets with salt, pepper, and garlic and place on the trivet. Top each fillet with 1 sprig of dill, 2 lemon slices, leek slices, and butter and seal the lid. Select Manual and cook for 5 minutes on High pressure. When done, perform a quick pressure release.

## Thyme Sea Bass with Turnips

Serving Size: 4 | Total Time: 15 minutes

1 white onion, chopped into thin rings

1 lemon, chopped

4 sea bass fillets

4 sprigs thyme

2 turnips, sliced

Salt and pepper to taste

2 tsp olive oil

Add 1 cup water and set a rack into the pot. Line a parchment paper to the bottom of the steamer basket.

Place lemon slices in a single layer on the basket. Arrange fillets on the top of the lemons, cover with onion and thyme sprigs. Top with turnips. Sprinkle pepper, salt, and oil over the mixture. Put a steamer basket onto the rack.

Seal lid and cook on High Pressure for 8 minutes. Release the pressure quickly. Carefully unlock the lid. Serve over the delicate onion rings and thinly turnips.

## Stuffed Tench with Herbs & Lemon

Serving Size: 2 | Total Time: 20 minutes

1 tench, cleaned, gutted

1 lemon, quartered

2 tbsp olive oil

1 tsp rosemary, chopped

¼ tsp dried thyme

2 garlic cloves, crushed

In a bowl, mix olive oil, garlic, rosemary, and thyme. Stir to combine. Brush the fish with the previously prepared mixture and stuff with lemon. Pour 4 cups of water into the Instant Pot, set the steamer tray, and place the fish on top. Seal the lid and cook on Steam for 15 minutes on High Pressure. Do a quick release. Unlock the lid. For a crispier taste, briefly brown the fish in a grill pan.

## Pollock & Tomato Stew

Serving Size: 4 | Total Time: 30 minutes

1 lb pollock fillets

4 cloves, crushed

1 lb tomatoes, chopped

2 bay leaves, whole

2 cups fish stock

Salt and pepper to taste

1 onion, finely chopped

½ cup olive oil

Heat 2 tbsp olive oil on Sauté. Add onion and sauté for 3 minutes. Add tomatoes and cook until soft. Press Cancel. Add pollock fillets, cloves, bay leaves, stock, salt, and pepper and seal the lid. Cook on High pressure for 15 minutes. When ready, do a quick release. Serve warm.

## Dijon Catfish Fillets with White Wine

Serving Size: 3 | Total Time: 15 minutes + cooling time

1 lb catfish fillets

1 lemon, juiced

½ cup parsley, chopped

2 garlic cloves, crushed

1 onion, finely chopped

1 tbsp dill, chopped

1 tbsp rosemary, chopped

2 cups white wine

2 tbsp Dijon mustard

1 cup extra virgin olive oil

In a bowl, mix lemon juice, parsley, garlic, onion, dill, rosemary, wine, mustard, and oil. Stir well. Submerge the fillets and cover with a tight lid. Refrigerate for 1 hour. Insert a trivet in the Instant Pot. Remove the fish from the fridge and place it on the rack. Pour in 1 cup of water and marinade. Seal the lid. Cook on Steam for 8 minutes on High. Release the pressure quickly. Serve immediately.

## Chili Steamed Catfish

Serving Size: 4 | Total Time: 70 minutes

1 lb flathead catfish

1 cup orange juice

¼ cup lemon juice

½ cup olive oil

1 tbsp dried thyme

1 tbsp dried rosemary

1 tsp chili flakes

1 tsp sea salt

In a bowl, mix orange juice, lemon juice, olive oil, thyme, rosemary, chili flakes, and salt. Brush the fish with the mixture and refrigerate for 30 minutes. Remove from the fridge, drain, and reserve the marinade. Insert a trivet in the pot. Pour in 1 cup of water and marinade. Place the fish onto the top. Seal the lid and cook on High Pressure for 10 minutes. Do a quick release. Serve immediately.

## Mackerel with Potatoes & Spinach

Serving Size: 4 | Total Time: 20 minutes

4 mackerels, skin on

1 lb spinach, torn

5 potatoes, peeled, chopped

3 tbsp olive oil

2 garlic cloves, crushed

2 tbsp mint leaves, chopped

1 lemon, juiced

Sea salt to taste

Heat 2 tbsp of the olive oil on Sauté. Stir-fry garlic for 1 minute. Stir in spinach and salt and cook for 4-5 minutes until wilted; set aside. Make a layer of potatoes in the pot. Top with fish and drizzle with lemon juice, remaining olive oil, and salt. Pour in 1 cup of water, seal the lid, and cook on Steam for 7 minutes on High. When ready, do a quick release. Carefully unlock the lid. Plate the fish and potatoes with spinach and serve topped with mint leaves.

## Corn & Mackerel Chowder

Serving Size: 4 | Total Time: 45 minutes

6 oz mackerel fillets

½ cup wheat groats, soaked

½ cup kidney beans, soaked

¼ cup sweet corn

1 lb tomatoes, chopped

4 cups fish stock

4 tbsp olive oil

2 garlic cloves, crushed

Heat olive oil on Sauté. Stir-fry tomatoes and garlic for 5 minutes. Add in stock, corn, kidney beans, and wheat groats. Seal the lid and cook on High Pressure for 25 minutes. Do a quick release. Add mackerel fillets. Seal the lid and cook on Steam for 8 minutes on High. Do a quick release. Serve.

## Steamed Halibut Packets

Serving Size: 4 | Total Time: 20 minutes

4 halibut fillets

1 lb cherry tomatoes, halved

1 cup olives, chopped

2 tbsp olive oil

1 garlic clove, minced

½ tsp thyme

Salt and pepper to taste

Arugula for garnish

Pour 1 cup of water into your Instant Pot and insert a trivet. Divide the halibut fillets, cherry tomatoes, and olives between 4 sheets of aluminum foil. Drizzle with olive oil and season with salt, pepper, garlic, and thyme. Close the packets and seal the edges. Place them on the trivet. Secure the lid, select Steam, and cook for 4 minutes on Low. When done, allow a natural release for 10 minutes. Serve scattered with arugula.

## Seafood & Fish Stew

Serving Size: 6 | Total Time: 25 minutes

2 lb different fish and seafood

3 tbsp olive oil

2 onions, peeled, chopped

2 carrots, grated

2 tbsp parsley, chopped

2 garlic cloves, crushed

3 cups water

1 tsp sea salt

Heat olive oil on Sauté. Stir-fry onions and garlic for 3-4 minutes, or until translucent. Add carrots, fish and seafood, parsley, water, and salt. Seal the lid, and cook on High Pressure for 10 minutes. Do a quick release. Serve.

## Vietnamese Fish & Noodle Soup

Serving Size: 6 | Total Time: 32 minutes
2 tbsp sesame oil
1 lb snapper fillets, chopped
12 oz squid
5 oz rice noodles
¼ cup soy sauce
¼ tsp thyme
½ tbsp cilantro, chopped
1 tsp chili flakes
1 garlic clove, sliced
1 onion, thinly sliced
Salt and pepper to taste

Heat the sesame oil in your Instant Pot on Sauté. Add in onion, garlic, salt, and pepper and cook for 2 minutes. Stir in fish, squid, chili flakes, and thyme and sauté for 5-6 minutes. Pour in soy sauce and 5 cups of water and seal the lid. Select Manual and cook for 10 minutes.

Once ready, perform a quick pressure release. Press Sauté and add in the rice noodles. Cook for 3-4 minutes until just tender. Ladle into bowls and serve scattered cilantro.

## Seafood Medley with Rosemary Rice

Serving Size: 4 | Total Time: 45 minutes
1 lb frozen seafood mix
1 cup brown rice
1 tbsp calamari ink
2 tbsp extra virgin olive oil
2 garlic cloves, crushed
1 tbsp chopped rosemary
½ tsp salt
3 cups fish stock
½ lemon

Add in seafood mix, rice, calamari ink, olive oil, garlic, rosemary, salt, stock, and lemon, seal the lid and cook on

Manual for 25 minutes on High. Release the pressure naturally for 10 minutes. Squeeze lemon juice and serve.

## Seafood Chowder with Oyster Crackers

Serving Size: 4 | Total Time: 40 minutes
20 oz canned mussels, drained, liquid reserved
¼ cup grated Pecorino Romano cheese
1 lb potatoes, peeled and cut chunks
2 cups oyster crackers
2 tbsp olive oil
½ tsp garlic powder
Salt and pepper to taste
2 pancetta slices, chopped
2 celery stalks, chopped
1 medium onion, chopped
1 tbsp flour
¼ cup white wine
1 tsp dried rosemary
1 bay leaf
1 ½ cups heavy cream
2 tbsp chopped fresh chervil

Fry pancetta on Sauté for 5 minutes until crispy. Remove to a paper towel-lined plate and set aside. Sauté the celery and onion in the same fat for 1 minute, stirring until the vegetables soften. Mix in the flour to coat the vegetables. Pour in the wine simmer. Cook for about 1 minute or until reduced by about one-third.

Pour in 1 cup water, the reserved mussel liquid, potatoes, salt, rosemary, and bay leaf. Seal the lid and cook on High Pressure for 4 minutes. Do a natural pressure release for 10 minutes. Stir in mussels and heavy cream.

Press Sauté and bring the soup to a simmer to heat the mussels through. Discard the bay leaf. Top with pancetta chervil, cheese, and crackers and serve.

## Seafood Traditional Spanish Paella

Serving Size: 4 | Total Time: 30 minutes
2 tbsp olive oil
1 onion, chopped
4 garlic cloves, minced
½ cup dry white wine
1 cup rice

1 ½ cups chicken stock
1 ½ tsp sweet paprika
1 tsp turmeric powder
1 lb small clams, scrubbed
1 lb prawns, deveined
1 red bell pepper, diced
1 lemon, cut into wedges

Cook onion and garlic in 1 tbsp of oil on Sauté for 3 minutes. Pour in wine to deglaze, scraping the bottom of the pot of any brown. Cook for 2 minutes until the wine is reduced by half. Add in rice and broth. Stir in paprika, turmeric, and bell pepper. Seal the lid and cook on High Pressure for 10 minutes. Do a quick release. Remove to a plate and wipe the pot clean. Heat the remaining oil on Sauté. Cook clams and prawns for 6 minutes until the shrimp are pink. Discard unopened clams. Arrange seafood and lemon wedges over paella to serve.

## Easy Seafood Paella

Serving Size: 4 | Total Time: 20 minutes
1 cup tiger prawns, peeled and deveined
1 lb mussels, cleaned and debearded
½ tsp guindilla (cayenne pepper)
½ lb clams
2 tbsp olive oil
1 onion, chopped
2 garlic cloves, minced
1 red bell pepper, chopped
1 cup rice
2 cups clam juice
¾ cup green peas, frozen
1 tbsp parsley, chopped
1 tbsp turmeric
1 whole lemon, quartered

Warm the olive oil in your Instant Pot on Sauté. Add in prawns, red pepper, onion, and garlic and cook for 3 minutes. Stir in rice for 1 minute and pour in clam juice, turmeric, mussels, and clams. Seal the lid, select Manual, and cook for 5 minutes on High pressure. When ready, perform a quick pressure release and unlock the lid. Stir in green peas and guindilla for 3-4 minutes. Top with lemon quarters and parsley. Serve immediately.

## Seafood Pilaf

Serving Size: 6 | Total Time: 35 minutes
1 lb chopped catfish fillets
2 cups mussels and shrimp
4 tbsp olive oil
1 onion, diced
2 garlic cloves, minced
½ tsp cayenne pepper
½ tsp basil
½ tsp oregano
1 red bell pepper, diced
1 green bell pepper, diced
2 cups Jasmine rice
A few saffron threads
3 cups fish stock
Salt and pepper to taste

Warm the olive oil in your Instant Pot on Sauté. Add in onion, garlic, and bell peppers and cook for 4 minutes. Add in catfish, rice, and saffron and cook for another 2 minutes. Add mussels, shrimps, cayenne pepper, basil, oregano, stock, salt, and pepper, stir, and seal the lid. Select Manual and cook for 6 minutes. When done, allow a natural release for 10 minutes. Serve.

## Seafood Hot Pot with Rice

Serving Size: 4 | Total Time: 20 minutes
½ lb shrimp, deveined
½ lb scallops
2 tbsp butter
1 onion, chopped
1 bell pepper, sliced
1 carrot, shredded
1 cup basmati rice
Salt and pepper to taste
2 cups fish broth
1 lemon, sliced

Melt the butter in your Instant Pot on Sauté. Add in onion, bell pepper, and carrot and cook for 3-4 minutes. Stir in rice, shrimp, scallops, salt, pepper, and fish broth and seal the lid. Press Manual and cook for 6 minutes on High pressure. Once done, use a quick pressure release and unlock the lid. Top with lemon slices and serve.

## Spicy Pasta with Seafood

Serving Size: 4 | Total Time: 20 minutes

2 tbsp olive oil

1 onion, diced

16 oz penne

24 oz arrabbiata sauce

3 cups chicken broth

Salt and pepper to taste

16 oz scallops

¼ cup Parmesan, grated

Basil leaves for garnish

Heat oil on Sauté. Stir-fry onion for 3 minutes. Stir in penne, arrabbiata sauce, salt, pepper, and 2 cups of broth. Seal the lid and cook for 6 minutes on High Pressure. Do a quick release. Remove to a plate. Pour the remaining broth and add scallops. Press Sauté and cook for 4 minutes. Mix in the pasta and serve topped with Parmesan cheese and basil leaves.

## Creole Seafood Gumbo

Serving Size: 4 | Total Time: 20 minutes

12 oz pollock filets, cut into chunks

1 lb medium raw shrimp, deveined

Salt and pepper to taste

1 tbsp creole seasoning

1 olive oil

1 yellow onion, diced

2 celery ribs, diced

1 cup chicken broth

14 oz diced tomatoes

¼ cup tomato paste

2 bay leaves

6 oz okra, trimmed

Sprinkle the pollock with salt, pepper, and creole seasoning. Warm the olive oil in your Instant Pot on Sauté. Add in the fish and cook for 4 minutes. Set aside. Add onions and celery to the pot and cook for 2 minutes. Put in chicken broth, tomatoes, tomato paste, bay leaves, okra, shrimp, and cooked fish and seal the lid. Select Manual and cook for 5 minutes on High pressure. When ready, perform a quick pressure release. Serve.

## Shrimp with Chickpeas & Olives

Serving Size: 6 | Total Time: 25 minutes

2 lb shrimp, deveined

2 garlic cloves, minced

1 carrot, chopped

1 cup chickpeas, soaked

3 cups fish broth

½ cup olives, pitted

Salt and pepper to taste

1 cup tomatoes, chopped

2 tbsp olive oil

1 onion, chopped

Warm the olive oil in your Instant Pot on Sauté. Add in onion, garlic, carrot, salt, and pepper and cook for 4 minutes until soft. Add tomatoes, chickpeas, olives and broth. Simmer for 5 minutes. Add the shrimp and toss to coat in the sauce. Seal the lid and cook on High Pressure for 4 minutes. Release the pressure naturally. Serve warm.

## Shrimp Boil with Chorizo Sausages

Serving Size: 4 | Total Time: 15 minutes

3 red potatoes

3 ears corn, cut into rounds

1 cup white wine

4 chorizo sausages, chopped

1 lb shrimp, deveined

2 tbsp of seafood seasoning

Salt to taste

1 lemon, cut into wedges

¼ cup butter, melted

Add potatoes, corn, wine, chorizo, shrimp, seafood seasoning, and salt. Do not stir. Add in 2 cups of water. Seal the lid and cook for 2 minutes on High Pressure. Release the pressure quickly. Drain the mixture through a colander. Transfer to a plate. Serve with melted butter and lemon wedges.

## Party Shrimp with & Rice Veggies

Serving Size: 4 | Total Time: 36 minutes

¼ cup olive oil

1 onion, chopped

1 red bell pepper, diced

2 garlic cloves, minced

1 tsp turmeric

Salt and pepper to taste

1 cup rice

¼ cup green peas

2 cups fish broth

1 lb shrimp, deveined

Chopped fresh parsley

1 lemon, cut into wedges

Warm oil on Sauté. Add in bell pepper and onion and garlic and cook for 5 minutes until fragrant. Season with pepper, salt, and turmeric and cook for 1 minute. Stir in fish broth and rice. Seal the lid and cook on High Pressure for 15 minutes. Release the pressure quickly. Stir in green peas and shrimp and cook for 5 minutes on Sauté. Serve with parsley and lemon.

## Quick Shrimp Gumbo with Sausage

Serving Size: 4 | Total Time: 30 minutes

1 lb jumbo shrimp

2 tbsp olive oil

1/3 cup flour

1 ½ tsp Cajun seasoning

1 onion, chopped

1 red bell pepper, chopped

2 celery stalks, chopped

2 garlic cloves, minced

1 serrano pepper, minced

2 ½ cups chicken broth

6 oz andouille sausage, sliced

2 green onions, finely sliced

Salt and pepper to taste

Heat olive oil on Sauté. Whisk in the flour with a wooden spoon and cook 3 minutes, stirring constantly. Stir in Cajun seasoning, onion, bell pepper, celery, garlic, and serrano pepper for about 5 minutes. Pour in the chicken broth, ¾ cup water, and andouille sausage. Seal and cook for 6 minutes on High Pressure. Do a natural pressure for 5 minutes. Stir the shrimp into the gumbo to eat it up for 3 minutes. Adjust the seasoning. Ladle the gumbo into bowls and garnish with the green onions.

## Hot Shrimp & Potato Chowder

Serving Size: 4 | Total Time: 35 minutes

4 slices pancetta, chopped

4 tbsp minced garlic

1 onion, chopped

2 potatoes, chopped

16 oz canned corn kernels

4 cups vegetable stock

1 tsp dried rosemary

Salt and pepper to taste

1 lb jumbo shrimp, deveined

1 tbsp olive oil

½ tsp red chili flakes

¾ cup heavy cream

Fry pancetta for 5 minutes until crispy on Sauté and set aside. Add in onion and stir-fry for 3 minutes. Pour in the potatoes, corn, stock, rosemary, salt, and pepper. Seal the lid and cook on High Pressure for 10 minutes. Do a quick pressure release. Carefully unlock the lid.

In a bowl, toss the shrimp in the garlic, salt, olive oil, and flakes. Remove the chowder from the pot to a serving bowl. Wipe the pot clean and fry shrimp for 3-4 minutes until pink. Mix in the heavy cream and cook for 2 minutes. Add shrimp to chowder and garnish with the reserved pancetta. Ladle into bowls and serve.

## Shrimp with Okra & Brussels Sprouts

Serving Size: 4 | Total Time: 40 minutes

1 lb large shrimp, cleaned, rinsed

6 oz Brussels sprouts

4 oz okra, whole

2 carrots, chopped

2 cups vegetable broth

2 tomatoes, diced

2 tbsp tomato paste

½ tsp cayenne pepper

Salt and pepper to taste
2 tbsp olive oil
¼ cup balsamic vinegar
1 tbsp rosemary, chopped
2 tbsp sour cream

Mix olive oil, vinegar, rosemary, salt, and pepper in a large bowl. Stir the shrimp into the mixture. Toss well to coat. Mix tomatoes, tomato paste, and cayenne pepper in the pressure cooker. Cook on Sauté for 5 minutes, stirring constantly. Set aside. Pour broth, Brussels sprouts, carrots, and okra into the pot. Cook on High pressure for 15 minutes. Do a quick release.

Remove the vegetables and add the shrimp to the remaining broth in the pot. Press Sauté and cook for 5 minutes. Add in the cooked vegetables. Cook for 2-3 minutes, stirring constantly. Stir in sour cream and serve.

## Spinach & Shrimp Fusilli

Serving Size: 4 | Total Time: 15 minutes
1 ¼ lb shrimp, deveined
2 tbsp melted butter
2 garlic cloves, minced
¼ cup white wine
10 oz fusilli pasta
1/3 cup tomato puree
½ tsp red chili flakes
1 tsp lemon zest
1 tbsp lemon juice
6 cups spinach

On Sauté, pour the white wine and bring to simmer for 2 minutes to reduce the liquid by half. Stir in the fusilli pasta, 2 ½ cups water, garlic, puréed tomato, shrimp, melted butter, and chili flakes. Seal the lid. Cook for 5 minutes on High pressure. Do a quick release. Stir in lemon zest, juice, and spinach until wilted and soft. Serve.

## Jalapeño Shrimp with Herbs & Lemon

Serving Size: 4 | Total Time: 25 minutes
1 lb shrimp, deveined
½ cup olive oil
1 tsp garlic powder
1 tsp rosemary, chopped
1 tsp thyme, chopped
½ tsp basil, chopped
½ tsp sage, chopped
½ tsp salt
1 tsp jalapeño pepper

Pour 1 cup of water into the inner pot. In a bowl, mix oil, garlic, rosemary, thyme, basil, sage, salt, and jalapeño pepper. Brush the marinade over the shrimp. Insert a steamer rack in the pot and arrange the shrimp on top. Seal the lid and cook on Steam for 3 minutes on High. Release the steam naturally for 10 minutes. Press Sauté and stir-fry for 2 more minutes or until golden brown.

## Creole Shrimp with Okra

Serving Size: 2 | Total Time: 10 minutes
1 lb shrimp, deveined
6 oz okra, trimmed
2 tbsp olive oil
1 tsp garlic powder
½ tsp cayenne pepper
½ tbsp Creole seasoning
Salt and pepper to taste

Pour 1 cup water into your Instant Pot and fit in a trivet. In a baking dish, combine shrimp, okra, olive oil, garlic powder, cayenne pepper, Creole seasoning, salt, and pepper and mix to combine. Place the dish on the trivet. Seal the lid and cook for 2 minutes on Steam on High. When ready, perform a quick pressure release. Serve.

## Rich Shrimp Risotto

Serving Size: 4 | Total Time: 30 minutes
¾ cup Pecorino Romano cheese, grated
1 lb shrimp, deveined
4 tbsp butter
2 garlic cloves, minced
1 yellow onion, chopped
1 ½ cups Arborio rice
2 tbsp dry white wine
4 cups fish broth
½ tsp Italian seasoning
2 tbsp heavy cream
Salt and pepper to taste

Melt half of the butter in your Instant Pot. Add in garlic and onion and cook for 4 minutes. Stir in rice and cook for another minute. Mix in white wine and cook for 3 minutes until the wine evaporates. Pour in 3 cups of fish broth and Italian seasoning and seal the lid. Select Manual and cook for 10 minutes on High pressure.

When ready, perform a quick pressure release and unlock the lid. Add in shrimp and the remaining broth and cook for 4-5 minutes on Sauté. Stir in Pecorino Romano cheese, heavy cream, and the remaining butter.

## Tangy Shrimp Curry

Serving Size: 4 | Total Time: 15 minutes

1 lb shrimp, deveined
2 tbsp sesame oil
1 onion, chopped
½ tsp fresh ginger, grated
1 garlic clove, minced
1 tsp cayenne pepper
1 tbsp lime juice
1 cup coconut milk
1 tbsp curry powder
Salt and pepper to taste

Heat the sesame oil in your Instant Pot on Sauté and cook the onion, garlic, and ginger for 3-4 minutes. Stir in curry powder, cayenne pepper, salt, and pepper and cook for 3 minutes. Pour in coconut milk, shrimp, and 1 cup of water and seal the lid. Select Manual and cook for 4 minutes on Low pressure. Once done, perform a quick pressure release. Drizzle with lime juice and serve.

## Chinese Shrimp with Green Beans

Serving Size: 2 | Total Time: 20 minutes

1 tbsp sesame oil
1 lb shrimp, deveined
½ cup diced onion
2 cloves garlic, minced
1 carrot, cut into strips
½ lb green beans, chopped
2 cups vegetable stock
3 tbsp soy sauce
2 tbsp rice wine vinegar

10 oz lo mein egg noodles
½ tsp toasted sesame seeds
Sea Salt and pepper to taste

Warm oil on Sauté. Stir-fry the shrimp for 5 minutes; set aside. Add in garlic and onion and cook for 3 minutes until fragrant. Mix in soy sauce, carrot, stock, beans, and rice wine vinegar. Add in noodles and ensure they are covered. Season with pepper and salt. Seal the lid and cook on High Pressure for 5 minutes. Release the pressure quickly. Place the main in 2 plates. Add the reserved shrimp, sprinkle with sesame seeds, and serve.

## Cheesy Shrimp Scampi

Serving Size: 4 | Total Time: 10 minutes

1 lb shrimp, deveined
2 tbsp olive oil
1 clove garlic, minced
1 tbsp tomato paste
10 oz canned tomatoes, diced
½ cup dry white wine
1 tsp red chili pepper
1 tbsp parsley, chopped
Salt and pepper to taste
1 cup Grana Padano, grated

Warm the olive oil in your Instant Pot on Sauté. Add in garlic and cook for 1 minute. Stir in shrimp, tomato paste, tomatoes, white wine, chili pepper, parsley, salt, pepper, and ¼ cup of water and seal the lid. Select Manual and cook for 3 minutes on High pressure. Once done, perform a quick pressure release and unlock the lid. Serve garnished with Grana Padano cheese.

## Indian Prawn Curry

Serving Size: 4 | Total Time: 30 minutes

1 ½ lb prawns, deveined
2 tbsp ghee
2 garlic cloves, minced
1 onion, chopped
1 tsp ginger, grated
½ tsp ground turmeric
1 tsp red chili powder
2 tsp ground cumin

2 tsp ground coriander

2 tbsp curry paste

2 cups coconut milk

1 cup tomatoes, chopped

2 habanero peppers, minced

Salt and pepper to taste

1 tbsp fresh lemon juice

Melt the ghee in your Instant Pot on Sauté. Add in garlic, onion, and ginger and cook for 4 minutes. Stir in the turmeric, chili powder, cumin, coriander, and curry paste and cook for 1 more minute. Stir in coconut milk, prawns, tomatoes, habanero peppers, salt, and pepper. Seal the lid. Select Manual and cook for 5 minutes on Low. Once ready, allow a natural release for 10 minutes, then perform a quick pressure release, and unlock the lid. Top with lemon juice and serve.

## Butter & Wine Lobster Tails

Serving Size: 4 | Total Time: 10 minutes

1 lb lobster tails, cut in half

½ cup white wine

½ cup butter, melted

1 tsp red pepper flakes

Pour ½ cup of water and white wine in your Instant Pot and fit in a trivet. Place lobster tails on the trivet and seal the lid. Select Steam and cook for 5 minutes on Low. When ready, perform a quick pressure release. Drizzle with butter and top with red pepper flakes to serve.

## Ginger & Garlic Crab

Serving Size: 4 | Total Time: 15 minutes

1 lb crabs, halved

2 tbsp butter

1 shallot, chopped

1 garlic cloves, minced

1 cup coconut milk

1-inch ginger, sliced

1 lemongrass stalk

Salt and pepper to taste

1 lemon, sliced

Melt the butter in your Instant Pot on Sauté. Place in shallot, garlic, and ginger and cook for 3 minutes. Pour

in coconut milk, crabs, lemongrass, salt, and pepper and seal the lid. Select Manual and cook for 6 minutes on High pressure. Once ready, perform a quick pressure release and unlock the lid. Serve with lemon slices.

## Herby Crab Legs with Lemon

Serving Size: 4 | Total Time: 10 minutes

3 lb king crab legs, broken in half

1 tsp rosemary

1 tsp thyme

1 tsp dill

¼ cup butter, melted

Salt and pepper to taste

1 lemon, cut into wedges

Pour 1 cup of water into your Instant Pot and fit in a trivet. Season the crab legs with rosemary, thyme, dill, salt, and pepper; place on the trivet. Seal the lid, select Manual, and cook for 3 minutes. When ready, perform a quick pressure release. Remove crab legs to a bowl and drizzle with melted butter. Serve with lemon wedges.

## Black Squid Ink Tagliatelle

Serving Size: 4 | Total Time: 25 minutes

18 oz squid ink tagliatelle, cooked

1 lb fresh seafood mix

¼ cup olive oil

4 garlic cloves, crushed

1 tbsp parsley, chopped

1 tsp rosemary, chopped

½ tbsp white wine

Heat 3 tbsp olive oil on Sauté and stir-fry the garlic for 1-2 minutes until fragrant. Add seafood, parsley, and rosemary and stir. Add the remaining oil, wine, and ½ cup of water. Seal the lid and cook on High Pressure for 4 minutes. Do a quick release and set aside. Open the lid, add the pasta, and stir. Serve hot.

## Crab Pilaf with Broccoli & Asparagus

Serving Size: 4 | Total Time: 30 minutes

½ lb asparagus, trimmed and cut into 1-inch pieces
½ lb broccoli florets
Salt to taste
2 tbsp olive oil
1 small onion, chopped
1 cup rice
1/3 cup white wine
2 cups vegetable stock
8 oz lump crabmeat

Heat oil on Sauté and cook the onion for 3 minutes until soft. Stir in rice and cook for 1 minute. Pour in the wine. Cook for 2 to 3 minutes, stirring until the liquid has almost evaporated. Add vegetable stock and salt; stir. Place a trivet on top. Arrange the broccoli and asparagus on the trivet. Seal the lid and cook on High Pressure for 8 minutes. Do a quick release. Remove the vegetables to a bowl. Fluff the rice with a fork and add in the crabmeat, heat for a minute. Taste and adjust the seasoning. Serve immediately topped with broccoli and asparagus.

## Red Wine Squid

Serving Size: 4 | Total Time: 25 minutes

2 lb squid, chopped
2 tbsp olive oil
Salt and pepper to taste
½ cup red wine
½ fennel bulb, sliced
28 oz can crushed tomatoes
1 red onion, sliced
2 garlic cloves, minced
1 tsp Italian seasoning
½ cup parsley, chopped

Mix the olive oil, squid, salt, and pepper in a bowl. Pour the red wine, tomatoes, onion, garlic, Italian seasoning, and fennel in your Instant Pot and fit in a steamer basket. Put in the squid and seal the lid. Select Manual and cook for 4 minutes on High pressure. When ready, allow a natural release for 10 minutes, then perform a quick pressure release. Serve scattered with parsley.

## White Wine Marinated Squid Rings

Serving Size: 3 | Total Time: 25 minutes + cooling time

1 lb fresh squid rings
1 cup dry white wine
1 cup olive oil
2 garlic cloves, crushed
1 lemon, juiced
2 cups fish stock
¼ tsp red pepper flakes
¼ tsp dried oregano
1 tbsp rosemary, chopped
1 tsp sea salt

In a bowl, mix wine, olive oil, lemon juice, garlic, flakes, oregano, rosemary, and salt. Submerge squid rings in this mixture and cover with a lid. Refrigerate for 1 hour. Remove the squid from the fridge and place it in the pot along with stock and half of the marinade. Seal the lid. Cook on High Pressure for 6 minutes. Release the pressure naturally for 10 minutes. Transfer the rings to a plate and drizzle with some marinade to serve.

## Mussels With Lemon & White Wine

Serving Size: 5 | Total Time: 10 minutes

2 lb mussels, cleaned and debearded
1 cup white wine
½ cup water
1 tsp garlic powder
Juice from 1 lemon

In the pot, mix garlic powder, water, and wine. Put the mussels into the steamer basket; rounded-side should be placed facing upwards to fit as many as possible.
Insert a rack into the cooker and lower the steamer basket onto the rack. Seal the lid and cook on Low Pressure for 1 minute. Release the pressure quickly. Remove unopened mussels. Coat the mussels with the wine mixture and lemon juice and serve.

# Chili Squid

Serving Size: 4 | Total Time: 35 minutes

1 lb squid, sliced into rings
1 tsp onion powder
2 tbsp flour
1 garlic clove, minced
1 tbsp chives
¼ tsp chili pepper, chopped
¼ tsp smoked paprika
1 tbsp lemon juice
1 cup vegetable broth
2 tbsp butter
Salt and pepper to taste
2 tbsp parsley, chopped

Mix the onion powder, smoked paprika, flour, garlic, chives, chili pepper, salt, and pepper in a bowl. Add in the squid slices and toss to coat. Let sit for 10 minutes.

Melt the butter in your Instant Pot on Sauté. Place in the squid mixture and cook for 3-4 minutes. Pour in the vegetable broth and seal the lid. Cook on Manual for 12 minutes on High. Once done, perform a quick pressure release and unlock the lid. Serve sprinkled with parsley.

# Spicy Mussels & Anchovies with Rice

Serving Size: 4 | Total Time: 40 minutes

1 cup rice
6 oz mussels
1 onion, finely chopped
1 garlic clove, crushed
1 tbsp dried rosemary
¼ cup capers
Salt and chili pepper to taste
3 tbsp olive oil
4 salted anchovies

Add rice to the pot and pour 2 cups of water. Seal the lid and cook on Manual for 18 minutes on High. Do a quick release. Remove the rice and set aside. Grease the pot with oil, and stir-fry garlic and onion for 2 minutes on Sauté. Add mussels and rosemary. Cook for 10 more minutes. Stir in rice and season with salt and chili pepper. Serve with anchovies and capers.

# Beer-Steamed Mussels

Serving Size: 4 | Total Time: 15 minutes

3 lb mussels, debearded
4 tbsp butter
1 shallot, chopped
2 garlic cloves, minced
2 tbsp parsley, chopped
1 cup beer
1 cup chicken stock

Melt butter in your Instant Pot on Sauté. Add in shallot and garlic and cook for 2 minutes. Stir in beer and cook for 1 minute. Mix in stock and mussels and seal the lid. Select Manual and cook for 3 minutes on High pressure. Once ready, perform a quick pressure release. Discard unopened mussels. Serve sprinkled with parsley.

# Basil Clams with Garlic & White Wine

Serving Size: 4 | Total Time: 15 minutes

1 lb clams, scrubbed
2 tbsp butter
4 green garlic, chopped
1 tbsp lemon juice
½ cup white wine
½ cup chicken stock
Salt and pepper to taste
2 tbsp basil, chopped

Melt the butter in your Instant Pot on Sauté. Add in the garlic and clams and cook for 3-4 minutes. Stir in lemon juice and chicken stock, white wine, salt, and pepper and seal the lid. Select Manual and cook for 3 minutes on High pressure. Once done, perform a quick pressure release and unlock the lid. Discard unopened clams. Serve topped with basil.

# Saucy Clams with Herbs

Serving Size: 4 | Total Time: 15 minutes

1 lb clams, scrubbed
2 tsp olive oil
2 garlic cloves, minced
1 onion, chopped
2 celery stalks, diced
1 bell pepper, diced

1 tbsp tomato paste
28 oz can crushed tomatoes
1/2 tsp basil
1 tsp rosemary
1/2 tsp oregano
Salt and pepper to taste
1/4 tsp chili pepper

Warm the olive oil in your Instant Pot on Sauté. Place in garlic, onion, celery, and bell pepper and cook for 3-4 minutes. Add in tomato paste and cook for another 1 minute. Stir in clams, tomatoes, basil, rosemary, oregano, salt, pepper, and chili pepper and seal the lid. Select Manual and cook for 2 minutes on High pressure. Once done, perform a quick pressure release and unlock the lid. Discard unopened clams. Serve with cooked rice.

## Sicilian Seafood Linguine

Serving Size: 4 | Total Time: 25 minutes

2 tbsp olive oil

1 onion, chopped

2 garlic cloves, minced

2 tomatoes, chopped

1 red bell pepper, chopped

½ cup dried white wine

3 cups vegetable stock

16 oz linguine

½ lb prawns, peeled

4 sardines, chopped

2 tbsp parsley, chopped

1 tbsp tomato purée

Salt and pepper to taste

½ cup Parmesan, grated

Warm the olive oil in your Instant Pot on Sauté. Add in the onion and garlic and cook for 3 minutes. Pour in tomatoes and bell pepper and cook for another 3-4 minutes. Stir in white wine and simmer for 3 minutes. Mix in vegetable stock, linguine, prawns, tomato puree, salt, and pepper and seal the lid. Select Manual on High. Cook for 4 minutes on High. When ready, perform a quick pressure release and unlock the lid. Stir in sardines and parsley. Scatter with Parmesan cheese and serve.

## Spicy Rice Noodles with Tofu & Chives

Serving Size: 6 | Total Time: 15 minutes

½ cup soy sauce

2 tbsp brown sugar

2 tbsp rice vinegar

1 tbsp sweet chili sauce

1 tbsp sesame oil

1 tsp fresh minced garlic

20 oz tofu, cubed

8 oz rice noodles

¼ cup chopped chives

Heat the oil on Sauté. Fry the tofu for 5 minutes until golden brown; reserve. To the pot, add 2 cups water, garlic, vinegar, sugar, soy sauce, and chili sauce and mix until smooth. Stir in rice noodles. Seal the lid and cook on High Pressure for 3 minutes. Divide noodles between bowls. Top with tofu and sprinkle with chives and serve.

## Beef Garam Masala with Rice

Serving Size: 4 | Total Time: 30 minutes

¼ cup yogurt

2 cloves garlic, smashed

1 tbsp olive oil

1 lime, juiced

Salt and pepper to taste

2 lb beef stew meat, cubed

1 tbsp garam masala

1 tbsp fresh ginger, grated

1 ½ tbsp smoked paprika

1 tsp ground cumin

¼ tbsp cayenne pepper

3 tbsp butter

1 onion, chopped

14-oz can puréed tomatoes

1 cup beef broth

1 cup basmati rice, rinsed

½ cup heavy cream

2 tbsp cilantro, chopped

In a bowl, mix garlic, lime juice, olive oil, pepper, salt, and yogurt. Add in the beef and toss to coat. In another bowl, mix paprika, garam masala, cumin, ginger, and cayenne pepper. Melt butter on Sauté and stir-fry the onion for 3 minutes. Sprinkle spice mixture over onion and cook for about 30 seconds. Add in the beef-yogurt mixture. Sauté for 3 to 4 minutes until the meat is slightly cooked. Mix in broth and puréed tomatoes.

Set trivet over beef in the Pressure cooker's inner pot. In an oven-proof bowl, mix 2 cups of water and rice. Set the bowl onto the trivet. Seal the lid and cook on High Pressure for 10 minutes. Release pressure quickly. Remove the bowl with rice and trivet. Add pepper, salt, and heavy cream into beef and stir. Use a fork to fluff rice and divide into serving plates; apply a topping of beef. Garnish with cilantro and serve.

# Spinach, Garlic & Mushroom Pilaf

Serving Size: 6 | Total Time: 45 minutes

2 cups button mushrooms, sliced

1 tbsp olive oil

2 cloves garlic, minced

1 onion, chopped

1 cup spinach, chopped

4 cups vegetable stock

2 cups white rice

1 tsp salt

2 sprigs parsley, chopped

Select Sauté and heat oil. Add mushrooms, onion, and garlic, and stir-fry for 5 minutes until tender. Mix in rice, stock, spinach, and salt. Seal the lid and cook on High Pressure for 20 minutes. Release pressure naturally for 10 minutes. Fluff the rice and top with parsley. Serve.

# Salmon & Tomato Farfalle

Serving Size: 4 | Total Time: 15 minutes

16 oz farfalle pasta

2 tbsp olive oil

2 garlic cloves, sliced

2 cups tomatoes, diced

¼ tsp chili pepper

¼ tsp oregano

¾ cup red wine

4 oz smoked salmon, flaked

10 green olives, sliced

½ cup Parmesan, grated

Warm olive oil in your Instant Pot on Sauté. Add in garlic and cook for 1 minute. Stir in tomatoes, farfalle, chili pepper, 4 cups water, red wine, and oregano. Seal the lid.

Select Manual, and cook for 5 minutes on High. Once ready, perform a quick pressure release. Mix in salmon and green olives. Serve sprinkled with Parmesan cheese.

# Vegetarian Wild Rice with Carrots

Serving Size: 6 | Total Time: 32 minutes

4 cups vegetable broth

2 carrots, chopped

2 cups wild rice

3 tbsp butter

Zest and juice from 1 lemon

Salt and pepper to taste

Add rice, carrots, lemon zest, butter, and broth. Stir, seal the lid, and cook on High Pressure for 12 minutes. Release pressure naturally for 10 minutes. Carefully unlock the lid. Sprinkle salt, lemon juice, and pepper over the rice and use a fork to gently fluff. Serve warm.

# Risotto with Spring Vegetables & Shrimp

Serving Size: 4 | Total Time: 40 minutes

1 tbsp avocado oil

1 lb asparagus, chopped

1 cup spinach, chopped

1 cup mushrooms, sliced

1 cup rice

1 ¼ cups chicken broth

¾ cup coconut milk

1 tbsp coconut oil

1 lb shrimp, deveined

Salt and pepper to taste

¾ cup Parmesan, shredded

Warm the avocado oil on Sauté. Add spinach, mushrooms, and asparagus and sauté for 5 minutes until cooked through. Add in rice, coconut milk, and chicken broth as you stir. Seal the lid, press Manual, and cook for 20 minutes on High Pressure.

Do a quick release. Place the rice on a serving plate. Press Sauté. Heat the coconut oil. Add shrimp and cook for 6 minutes until it turns pink. Set the shrimp over rice and season with pepper and salt. Serve topped with Parmesan cheese.

# Stuffed Mushrooms with Rice & Cheese

Serving Size: 4 | Total Time: 25 minutes

4 portobello mushrooms, stems and gills removed

2 tbsp melted butter

½ cup brown rice, cooked

1 tomato, chopped

¼ cup black olives, chopped

1 green bell pepper, diced

½ cup feta, crumbled

Salt and pepper to taste

2 tbsp cilantro, chopped

1 cup vegetable broth

Brush the mushrooms with butter. Arrange them in a single layer on a greased baking pan. In a bowl, mix the rice, tomato, olives, bell pepper, feta cheese, salt, and black pepper. Spoon the rice mixture into the mushrooms. Pour in the broth.

Pour 1 cup of water into the Instant Pot and insert a trivet. Place the baking dish on the trivet. Seal the lid and cook on High Pressure for 10 minutes. Do a quick release. Garnish with fresh cilantro and serve immediately.

### Risotto with Broccoli & Grana Padano

Serving Size: 6 | Total Time: 35 minutes

2 tbsp Grana Padano cheese flakes

10 oz broccoli florets

1 onion, chopped

3 tbsp butter

2 cups carnaroli rice, rinsed

¼ cup dry white wine

4 cups chicken stock

Salt and pepper to taste

2 tbsp Grana Padano, grated

Warm butter on Sauté. Stir-fry onion for 3 minutes until translucent. Add in broccoli and rice and cook for 5 minutes, stirring occasionally. Pour wine into the pot and scrape away any browned bits of food from the pan. Stir in stock, pepper, and salt. Seal the lid, press Manual and cook on High for 15 minutes. Release the pressure quickly. Sprinkle with grated Grana Padano cheese and stir well. Top with flaked Grana Padano cheese to serve.

### Arugula & Wild Mushroom Risotto

Serving Size: 4 | Total Time: 30 minutes

½ cup wild mushrooms, chopped

4 tbsp pumpkin seeds, toasted

1/3 cup grated Pecorino Romano cheese

2 tbsp olive oil

1 onion, chopped

2 cups arugula, chopped

1 cup arborio rice

1/3 cup white wine

3 cups vegetable stock

Heat oil on Sauté and cook onion and mushrooms for 5 minutes until tender. Add the rice and cook for a minute. Stir in white wine and cook for 2-3 minutes until almost evaporated. Pour in the stock. Seal the lid and cook on High Pressure for 10 minutes. Do a quick release. Stir in arugula and Pecorino Romano cheese to melt and serve scattered with pumpkin seeds.

### Yummy Mexican-Style Rice & Pinto Beans

Serving Size: 4 | Total Time: 30 minutes

3 tbsp olive oil

1 small onion, chopped

2 garlic cloves, minced

1 serrano pepper, chopped

1 cup rice

1/3 cup red salsa

¼ cup tomato sauce

½ cup vegetable broth

1 tsp Mexican seasoning

16 oz canned pinto beans

1 tsp salt

1 tbsp chopped parsley

Warm oil on Sauté and cook onion, garlic, and serrano pepper for 2 minutes, stirring occasionally until fragrant. Stir in rice, salsa, tomato sauce, vegetable broth, Mexican seasoning, beans, and salt. Seal the lid and cook on High Pressure for 10 minutes. Do a natural pressure release for 10 minutes. Sprinkle with fresh parsley and serve.

### Butternut Squash with Rice & Feta

Serving Size: 4 | Total Time: 30 minutes

2 cups vegetable broth

1 lb butternut squash, sliced

2 tbsp melted butter

Salt and pepper to taste

1 cup feta cheese, cubed

1 tbsp coconut aminos

2 tsp arrowroot starch

1 cup jasmine rice, cooked

Pour the rice and broth into the pot and stir to combine. In a bowl, toss butternut squash with 1 tbsp of melted butter and season with salt and black pepper. Mix in the pot with the rice. In another bowl, mix the remaining butter, water, and coconut aminos. Toss feta in the mixture, add the arrowroot starch, and toss again to combine well. Transfer to a greased baking dish.

Lay a trivet over the rice butternut squash and place the baking dish on the trivet. Seal the lid and cook on High for 15 minutes. Do a quick pressure release. Fluff the rice with a fork and serve with feta cheese.

## Avocado & Cherry Tomato Jasmine Rice

Serving Size: 6 | Total Time: 25 minutes

2 avocados, chopped

½ lb cherry tomatoes, halved

2 cups jasmine rice

2 tsp olive oil

½ tsp salt

2 tbsp cilantro, chopped

Place the rice, 2 cups water, olive oil, and salt in your Instant Pot and stir. Seal the lid, select Manual, and cook for 4 minutes on High pressure. Once done, allow a natural release for 10 minutes and unlock the lid. Using a fork, fluff the rice and add in avocados and cherry tomatoes. Top with cilantro and serve.

## Date & Apple Risotto

Serving Size: 4 | Total Time: 30 minutes

1 tbsp butter

1 ½ cups Arborio rice

1/3 cup brown sugar

2 apples, cored and sliced

1 cup apple juice

2 cups milk

1 ½ tsp cinnamon powder

½ cup dates, pitted

Melt butter in your Instant Pot on Sauté and place in rice; cook for 1-2 minutes. Stir in brown sugar, apples, apple juice, milk, and cinnamon. Seal the lid, select

Manual, and cook for 6 minutes on High pressure. Once done, allow a natural release for 6 minutes and unlock the lid. Mix in dates and cover with the lid. Let sit for 5 minutes.

## Butternut Squash & Cheese Risotto

Serving Size: 4 | Total Time: 45 minutes

½ lb butternut squash, cubed

3 tbsp olive oil

2 cloves garlic, minced

1 yellow onion, chopped

2 cups arborio rice

4 cups chicken stock

½ cup pumpkin puree

1 tsp thyme, chopped

½ tsp nutmeg

½ tsp ginger, grated

½ tsp cinnamon

½ cup heavy cream

Salt and pepper to taste

¼ cup shaved Parmesan

Preheat the oven to 360°F. Spread the squash cubes on a baking tray and drizzle with olive oil. Roast for 20 minutes until tender. Warm oil in your Instant Pot on Sauté and add garlic and onion; cook for 3 minutes.

Stir in rice, stock, pumpkin puree, thyme, nutmeg, ginger, and cinnamon. Seal the lid, select Manual, and cook for 10 minutes on High. When done, perform a quick pressure release. Mix in heavy cream, salt, and pepper. Top with pumpkin cubes and Parmesan shaves and serve.

## Spring Risotto

Serving Size: 6 | Total Time: 40 minutes

3 tbsp Pecorino Romano cheese, shredded

½ cup green peas

1 cup baby spinach

2 tbsp olive oil

2 spring onions, chopped

1 ½ cups arborio rice

3 ½ cups chicken stock

Salt and pepper to taste

Warm olive oil in your Instant Pot on Sauté. Add spring onions and cook for 3 minutes. Pour in rice and stock. Seal the lid and cook for 15 minutes on Manual.

Once done, allow a natural release for 10 minutes and unlock the lid. Adjust the seasoning with salt and pepper. Mix in green peas and spinach and cover with the lid. Let sit for 5 minutes until everything is heated through. Top with Pecorino Romano cheese and serve.

## Arroz con Pollo

Serving Size: 4 | Total Time: 40 minutes
2 tbsp olive oil
1 sweet onion, diced
2 garlic cloves, minced
1 lb boneless chicken thighs
Salt and pepper to taste
½ tsp chili powder
2 carrots, diced
1 cup white jasmine rice
1 ½ cups chicken stock
½ tsp Mexican oregano

Warm olive oil in your Instant Pot on Sauté. Add in onion and garlic and cook until fragrant, about 3 minutes. Stir in chicken, salt, and pepper and cook for 5 minutes more. Mix in carrots, rice, chili powder, chicken stock, and oregano. Seal the lid, select Manual, and cook for 10 minutes on High pressure. Once done, allow a natural release for 10 minutes and unlock the lid. Fluff the rice.

## Chicken & Broccoli Rice

Serving Size: 4 | Total Time: 40 minutes
1 red chili, finely chopped

2 tbsp butter
1 lb chicken breasts, sliced
1 onion, chopped
2 cloves garlic, minced
Salt and pepper to taste
1 cup long-grain rice
2 cups chicken broth
10 oz broccoli florets
2 tbsp cilantro, chopped

Melt butter in your Instant Pot on Sauté and add chicken, onion, red chili, garlic, salt, and pepper; cook for 5 minutes, stirring often. Stir in rice, chicken broth, milk, and broccoli. Seal the lid, select Manual, and cook for 15 minutes on High. When ready, allow a natural release for 10 minutes. Sprinkle with cilantro and serve.

## Hawaiian Rice

Serving Size: 4 | Total Time: 30 minutes
2 tsp olive oil
1 ½ cups coconut water
1 cup jasmine rice
2 green onions, sliced
½ pineapple, and chopped
Salt to taste
¼ tsp red pepper flakes

Stir olive oil, water, rice, pineapple, and salt in your Instant Pot. Seal the lid, select Manual, and cook for 10 minutes on low pressure. Once over, allow a natural release for 10 minutes, then a quick pressure release. Carefully unlock the lid. Using a fork, fluff the rice. Scatter with green onions and red pepper flakes and serve.

# BEANS & GRAINS

## Barley & Smoked Salmon Salad

Serving Size: 4 | Total Time: 30 minutes

4 smoked salmon fillets, flaked

1 cup pearl barley

Salt and pepper to taste

1 cup arugula

1 green apple, chopped

Place the barley, 2 cups of water, salt, and pepper in your Instant Pot. Seal the lid, select Manual, and cook for 20 minutes on High pressure.

Once ready, perform a quick pressure release and unlock the lid. Remove barley to a serving bowl. Mix in apple and salmon. Top with arugula.

## Tomato & Feta Pearl Barley

Serving Size: 4 | Total Time: 30 minutes

½ cup sundried tomatoes in oil, chopped

½ cup feta, crumbled

1 cup pearl barley

2 cups chicken broth

Salt to taste

2 tbsp butter, melted

Place barley, chicken broth, and salt in your Instant Pot. Seal the lid, select Manual, and cook for 25 minutes on High pressure. When done, allow a natural release for 15 minutes and unlock the lid. Mix in tomatoes and top with feta and butter to serve.

## Cranberry Millet Pilaf

Serving Size: 4 | Total Time: 20 minutes

½ cup dried cranberries. chopped

2 tbsp olive oil

1 garlic clove, minced

1 shallot, chopped

1 cup long-grain white rice

1 cup millet

Salt and pepper to taste

Warm olive oil in your Instant Pot on Sauté. Add in shallot and garlic and cook for 3 minutes. Stir in rice, millet, 3 cups water, cranberries, salt, and pepper.

Seal the lid and for 10 minutes on Rice. When ready, perform a quick pressure release and unlock the lid. Using a fork, fluff the pilaf. Serve immediately.

## Rich Millet with Herbs & Cherry Tomatoes

Serving Size: 4 | Total Time: 20 minutes

1 cup millet

2 cups vegetable stock

1 sweet onion, chopped

1 cup cherry tomatoes, halved

1 tbsp fresh sage, chopped

1 tsp fresh thyme, chopped

1 tsp parsley, chopped

Salt and pepper to taste

Add millet, onion, and vegetable stock. Seal the lid and cook for 10 minutes on High Pressure. Release pressure quickly. Fluff the millet with a fork, add in sage, thyme, parsley, and tomatoes, and season with pepper and salt.

## Feta & Vegetable Faro

Serving Size: 4 | Total Time: 30 minutes

1 cup faro, rinsed

2 cups chicken broth

1 celery stalk, chopped

4 cups spinach

1 bell pepper, chopped

½ cup feta, crumbled

Place faro, broth, celery, spinach, and bell pepper in your Instant Pot. Seal the lid, select Manual, and cook for 10 minutes on High. When ready, allow a natural release for 10 minutes. Top with feta cheese and serve.

## Harissa Chicken with Fruity Farro

Serving Size: 4 | Total Time: 45 minutes

2 tbsp dried cherries, chopped

1 lb chicken breasts, sliced

1 tbsp harissa paste

1 cup whole-grain farro

Salt to taste

3 tbsp olive oil

1 tbsp apple cider vinegar

4 green onions, chopped

10 mint leaves, chopped

In a bowl, place chicken, apple cider vinegar, 1 tbsp of olive oil, and harissa paste and combine everything thoroughly. Allow marinating covered for 15 minutes.

Heat the remaining olive oil on Sauté and cook green onion for 3 minutes. Stir in farro and salt and pour 2 cups of water. Insert a trivet over the farro and place the chicken on the trivet. Seal the lid, select Manual, and cook for 20 minutes on High. When ready, do a quick pressure release. Open the lid, remove the chicken and the trivet. Add dried cherries and mint to the farro. Stir and transfer to a plate. Top with chicken and serve.

## Gluten-Free Porridge

Serving Size: 4 | Total Time: 25 minutes

1 cup buckwheat groats

2 cups rice milk

1 banana, sliced

¼ cup raisins

1 tsp ground cardamom

½ tsp vanilla

2 tbsp pistachios, chopped

Place buckwheat, milk, raisins, cardamom, and vanilla in your Instant Pot. Seal the lid, select Manual, and cook for 6 minutes on High pressure. When done, allow a natural release for 10 minutes and unlock the lid. Serve topped with banana and pistachios.

# APPETIZERS & SIDE DISHES

## Old-Fashioned Apple Pie

Serving Size: 6 | Total Time: 30 minutes

2 lb apples, cubed

¼ cup sugar

¼ cup breadcrumbs

2 tsp cinnamon

¼ tbsp oil

1 egg, beaten

¼ cup flour

Pie dough

Combine breadcrumbs, sugar, apples, and cinnamon in a bowl. On a lightly floured surface, roll out the pie dough, making 2 circle-shaped crusts. Place one pie crust on a greased baking dish. Spoon the apple mixture on top, and cover with the remaining crust. Seal by crimping edges and brush with beaten egg. Pour 1 cup of water into the Instant Pot and lay a trivet. Lower the baking sheet onto the trivet. Seal the lid and cook on High Pressure for 20 minutes. When ready, do a quick release. Carefully unlock the lid. Serve chilled.

## Easy Camembert Cakes

Serving Size: 4 | Total Time: 45 minutes

1 cup Camembert cheese, cubed

2 tbsp butter

1 white onion, sliced

2 cups spinach, chopped

Salt and pepper to taste

¼ cup dry white wine

1 pie pastry, thawed

3 thinly sliced green onions

Melt 1 tbsp of butter on Sauté and cook onion and spinach for 5 minutes until tender. Season with salt and pepper, then pour in white wine and cook until evaporated, about 2 minutes. Set aside. Unwrap the pie pastry and cut it into 4 squares. Prink the dough with a fork and brush both sides with the remaining butter. Share half of the cheese over the pie pastry squares. Cover with spinach and remaining cheese. Arrange the tarts in a buttered baking dish. Pour 1 cup of water into

the pot. Insert a trivet and lower the baking dish on top. Seal the lid and cook on High Pressure for 30 minutes. Do a quick release. Serve topped with green onions.

## Chili Deviled Eggs

Serving Size: 6 | Total Time: 15 minutes

1 cup water

10 large eggs

¼ cup cream cheese

¼ cup mayonnaise

Salt and pepper to taste

¼ tsp chili powder

Add 1 cup of water and a steamer basket in the Instant Pot. Add in the eggs. Seal the lid. Cook on Pressure cook for 5 minutes. Release the pressure quickly. Drop eggs into an ice bath to cool. Peel eggs and halve them. Transfer yolks to a bowl and use a fork to mash; Stir in cream cheese, chili powder, mayonnaise, salt, and pepper. Spoon into egg white halves.

## Hard-Boiled Eggs with Paprika

Serving Size: 4 | Total Time: 20 minutes

4 large eggs

Salt and pepper to taste

A pinch of paprika

In the pot, add 1 cup water and place a trivet. Lay your eggs on top. Seal the lid and cook for 5 minutes on High Pressure. Do a natural release for 10 minutes. Transfer the eggs to ice-cold water to cool completely. Peel and season with paprika, salt, and pepper before serving.

## Traditional Italian Rice & Cheese Balls

Serving Size: 6 | Total Time: 35 minutes

1 cup canned Kernel sweet corn, drained

½ cup + 1 tbsp olive oil

1 white onion, diced

2 garlic cloves, minced

5 cups chicken stock

½ cup apple cider vinegar

2 cups short-grain rice

1 ½ cups grated cheddar

¼ cup grated Parmesan

Salt and pepper to taste

2 cups fresh bread crumbs

2 eggs

On Sauté, heat 1 tbsp of oil and cook onion and garlic for 3 minutes until translucent. Stir in the stock, vinegar, and rice. Seal the lid and cook on High Pressure for 7 minutes. Do a natural pressure release for 10 minutes. Stir in cheddar cheese, corn, salt, and pepper. Spoon into a bowl and let cool completely. Wipe clean the pot. In a bowl, pour the breadcrumbs.

In a separate bowl, beat the eggs. Form balls out of the rice mixture, dip each into the beaten eggs, and coat in the breadcrumb mixture. Heat the remaining oil on Sauté and fry balls until crispy. Sprinkle with Parmesan cheese and serve.

## Egg Bites with Mushrooms & Arugula

Serving Size: 4 | Total Time: 15 minutes

12 oz button mushrooms, sliced

4 oz asiago cheese, shredded

8 oz arugula

4 eggs

2 tbsp butter, melted

½ red chili flakes

Place a trivet in the Instant Pot and pour in 1 cup water. Grease 4 heatproof cups with the butter. In a bowl, whisk the eggs and stir in the mushrooms and arugula. Pour the mixture into the cups. Top with the cheese and chili flakes. Arrange the cups on the trivet. Seal the lid and cook on Manual for 7 minutes. Do a quick release. Serve chilled.

## Kale & Artichoke Cheese Bites

Serving Size: 4 | Total Time: 30 minutes

¼ cup chopped artichoke hearts

¼ cup chopped kale

¼ cup ricotta cheese

2 tbsp grated Parmesan

¼ cup goat cheese

1 large egg white

1 tsp dried basil

1 lemon, zested

Salt and pepper to taste

4 frozen filo dough, thawed

1 tbsp extra-virgin olive oil

In a bowl, combine kale, artichoke, ricotta, parmesan, goat cheese, egg white, basil, lemon zest, salt, and pepper. Place a filo dough on a clean flat surface. Brush with olive oil. Place a second filo sheet on the first and brush with more oil. Continue layering to form a pile of four oiled sheets. Working from the short side, cut the phyllo sheets into 8 strips and half them.

Spoon 1 tbsp of filling onto one short end of every strip. Fold a corner to cover the filling and a triangle; continue folding over and over to the end of the strip, creating a triangle-shaped filo packet. Repeat the process with the other filo bites. Place a trivet and 1 cup water into the pot. Put the bites on the trivet. Seal the lid. Cook on Manual for 15 minutes. Do a quick release.

## Juicy Hot Chicken Wings

Serving Size: 4 | Total Time: 15 minutes

¼ cup ranch salad dressing mix

½ cup sriracha sauce

2 tbsp butter, melted

Juice from ½ lemon

2 lb chicken vignettes

½ tsp paprika

Mix chicken, 1 cup water, sriracha, butter, and lemon in the inner pot. Seal the lid and cook on High Pressure for 5 min minutes. Do a quick pressure release. Serve with the paprika and ranch dressing.

## Picante Chicken Wings

Serving Size: 4 | Total Time: 25 minutes

2 lb chicken wings

¼ cup hot pepper sauce

2 tbsp oil

4 tbsp butter

2 tbsp Worcestershire sauce

1 tsp tabasco

4 cups chicken broth

Grease the pot with oil and place the chicken wings. Pour in broth and hot pepper sauce. Seal the lid and cook on Manual for 15 minutes on High. When ready, do a quick release. Unlock the lid Remove the wings and discard the broth. In the pot, melt the butter on Sauté. Brown the wings for 3 minutes, turning once. Add the Worcestershire sauce and tabasco and stir. Serve hot.

## Paprika Chicken Wings

Serving Size: 4 | Total Time: 25 minutes

2 lb chicken wings

¼ cup olive oil

2 garlic cloves, crushed

1 tbsp rosemary, chopped

Salt and pepper to taste

1 tsp paprika

1 tbsp grated ginger

¼ cup lime juice

½ cup apple cider vinegar

In a bowl, mix oil, garlic, rosemary, white pepper, salt, paprika, ginger, lime juice, and apple cider vinegar. Submerge wings into the mixture and cover. Refrigerate for one hour. Remove the wings from the marinade and pat dry.

Insert the steaming rack, 1 cup of water, and place the chicken on the rack. Seal the lid and cook on High Pressure for 8 minutes. Release the steam naturally for about 10 minutes. Serve with fresh vegetable salad.

# BROTHS & SAUCES

## Tasty Beef Neck Bone Stock

Serving Size: 6 | Total Time: 2 hours 10 minutes

1 carrot, chopped

2 onions, chopped

2 cups celery, chopped

2 lb beef neck bones

12 cups water, or more

1 tsp cider vinegar

2 bay leaves

10 peppercorns

Salt to taste

Add carrot, peppercorns, salt, bay leaves, celery, vinegar, onions, and beef bones. Add enough water to cover the ingredients. Seal the lid and cook on High Pressure for 120 minutes. Release pressure naturally.

Remove the bones and bay leaves, and discard. Use a fine-mesh strainer to strain the liquid. Allow the broth to cool. From the surface, skim fat and throw away. Refrigerate for a maximum of 7 days.

## Herby Chicken Stock

Serving Size: 6 | Total Time: 60 minutes

2 lb chicken wings

4 spring onions, diced

2 large carrots, diced

4 cloves garlic

1 small handful of parsley

1 bay leaf

Add chicken, carrots, parsley, onions, garlic, and bay leaf in your Instant Pot. Pour in 6 cups of water. Seal the lid and cook on High Pressure for 45 minutes. Release Pressure naturally for about 10 minutes. Carefully unlock the lid. Use a fine-mesh strainer to strain the broth and allow it to cool. Transfer the broth to containers and seal. Refrigerate for up to a week.

## Best Vegetable Broth Ever

Serving Size: 6 | Total Time: 35 minutes

2 onions, chopped

2 cups celery, chopped

2 carrots, chopped

4 garlic cloves

1 cup kale

1 cup bell pepper, chopped

A handful of rosemary

A handful of parsley

10 peppercorns

2 bay leaves

Salt to taste

Add onions, carrots, parsley, bay leaves, garlic, kale, celery, bell pepper, salt, rosemary, and peppercorns in your Instant Pot. Cover with cold water. Seal the lid and cook on High Pressure for 15 minutes. Do a natural release for 15 minutes. Use a wide and shallow bowl to hold the stock you strain through a fine-mesh strainer. Let cool. Seal into jars and refrigerate for up to 14 days.

## Ginger & Vegetable Beef Broth

Serving Size: 6 | Total Time: 1 hour

2 lb beef stew meat

2 onions, chopped

2 cups celery, chopped

2 red chilies, chopped

2 carrots, chopped

1 tsp fresh ginger, grated

4 garlic cloves

Salt to taste

In the pot, mix meat, celery, garlic, carrots, onions, red chilies, and ginger. Pour in 6 cups of water. Seal the lid and cook on High Pressure for 45 minutes. Release pressure naturally for 10 minutes. Carefully unlock the lid. Use a fine-mesh strainer to strain the broth into a bowl. Season with salt. Store in sealable containers.

# Homemade Chicken Stock

Serving Size: 6 | Total Time: 40 minutes

2 lb chicken carcasses

4 carrots, cut into chunks

1 cup leeks, chopped

1 onion, quartered

1 cup celery, chopped

2 large garlic cloves

1 sprig fresh thyme

1 bunch fresh parsley

Salt to taste

10 peppercorns

2 bay leaves

Add chicken, onion, peppercorns, thyme, celery, carrots, garlic, parsley, leeks, bay leaves, and salt. Cover with water. Seal the lid and cook for 30 minutes on High Pressure. Release the pressure quickly. Unlock the lid. Use a colander to drain the broth and do away with solids. Allow cooling for about an hour before storing it.

# Simple Beef Bolognese Sauce

Serving Size: 6 | Total Time: 55 minutes

4 slices bacon, chopped

1 tbsp olive oil

1 onion, minced

2 celery stalks, minced

1 carrot, chopped

1 ½ lb ground beef

3 tbsp red wine

28 oz can tomatoes, diced

2 bay leaves

Salt and pepper to taste

½ cup yogurt

¼ cup chopped basil

Set to Sauté the Instant Pot. Cook bacon until crispy, 4-5 minutes. Add in olive oil, celery, carrot, and onion and continue cooking for about 5 minutes until vegetables are softened. Add in the beef and cook for 4 minutes until golden brown. Season with salt and pepper. Stir in the wine and allow to sit for 4 more minutes. Add in bay leaves and tomatoes. Seal the lid and cook for 15 minutes on High Pressure. Release pressure naturally for 10 minutes. Carefully unlock the lid. Add yogurt and stir. Serve alongside noodles and use basil to garnish.

# Authentic Neapolitan Sauce

Serving Size: 4 | Total Time: 50 minutes

1 lb mushrooms, sliced

14 oz can tomatoes, diced

1 carrot, chopped

1 onion, chopped

1 celery stick, chopped

1 tbsp olive oil

2 garlic cloves

½ tsp paprika

1 tsp fish sauce

Heat olive oil on Sauté. Stir-fry carrot, onion, celery, and paprika for 5 minutes. Add mushrooms, garlic, and fish sauce, and pour in 1 cup water. Cook for 5-6 more minutes until the meat is slightly browned. Seal the lid. Cook on High Pressure for 10 minutes. Release the steam naturally for 10 minutes. Hit Sauté, add in tomatoes and cook for 7-8 minutes to thicken the sauce.

# Cranberry Orange Sauce

Serving Size: 4 | Total Time: 20 minutes

2 cups cranberries

1 tsp orange zest

½ cup orange juice

¼ cup brown sugar

1 cup water

2 tbsp maple syrup

Combine maple syrup, water, cranberries, and orange juice in the Instant Pot. Sprinkle with orange zest. Seal the lid, and cook on High Pressure for 5 minutes. When done, release the pressure naturally for about 10 minutes. Press Sauté, add brown sugar, and stir until a thick sauce mixture is formed. Turn off the heat and transfer the sauce to the serving dish.

## Mushroom-Spinach Cream Soup

Serving Size: 4 | Total Time: 30 minutes

2 sweet potatoes, peeled and chopped

1 tbsp dry porcini mushrooms, soaked

8 button mushrooms, sliced

2 tbsp olive oil

2 garlic cloves, minced

1 cup spinach, chopped

1 red onion, chopped

4 cups vegetable stock

Salt and pepper to taste

1 cup creme fraiche

Set your Instant Pot to Sauté and warm the olive oil. Sauté the sliced mushrooms for 5 minutes until tender. Remove 2 tbsp of them and set aside on a plate. Add onion and garlic to the pot and cook for 3 minutes until the onion becomes translucent. Mix in the potatoes, soaked mushrooms, vegetable stock, spinach, and salt.

Seal the lid and cook on High Pressure for 5 minutes. Quick-release the pressure. Add in creme fraiche and mix. Season with salt and pepper. Using an immersion blender, whizz the mixture until smooth. Garnish with the reserved mushrooms and a drizzle of olive oil. Serve.

## Red Soup with Cheesy Croutons

Serving Size: 4 | Total Time: 1 hour

2 tbsp olive oil

1 onion, chopped

2 garlic cloves, minced

1 carrot, chopped

Salt and pepper to taste

1 cup vegetable stock

28 oz canned tomatoes

1 cup heavy cream

2 Monterey Jack slices

4 bread slices

2 gouda cheese slices

2 tbsp butter, softened

Warm oil on Sauté. Stir-fry onion, garlic, carrot, pepper, and salt for 6 minutes until soft. Add in vegetable stock to deglaze. Scrape any brown bits from the pot. Mix the stock with tomatoes. Seal the lid and cook on High Pressure for 30 minutes. Allow for a natural release for 10 minutes. Transfer soup to a blender and process until smooth. Add in heavy cream and stir.

Place 1 slice Monterey Jack cheese on 1 bread slice and cover with 1 Gouda cheese slice and the second slice of bread. Brush the bread with butter. Do the same with the rest of the ingredients. Heat a skillet over medium heat. Place the sandwiches on the skillet. Cook each side for 3 to 5 minutes until browned and all cheese melts. Transfer sandwiches to a cutting board and chop them into bite-sized pieces. Divide the soup into serving plates and top with cheese croutons before serving.

## Homemade Vichyssoise Soup with Chives

Serving Size: 4 | Total Time: 30 minutes

2 tbsp butter

3 leeks, chopped

2 cloves garlic, minced

4 cups vegetable broth

3 potatoes, peeled, cubed

½ cup sour cream

2 tbsp rosemary

Salt and pepper to taste

2 tbsp chives, chopped

Melt butter on Sauté. Stir in garlic and leeks and cook for 3-4 minutes until soft. Stir in potatoes, rosemary, and broth. Seal the lid and cook on High Pressure for 15 minutes. Release pressure quickly. Transfer soup to a food processor and puree to obtain a smooth consistency. Season with salt and pepper. Top with fresh chives and sour cream. Serve

## Celery-Cauliflower Soup with Blue Cheese

Serving Size: 5 | Total Time: 20 minutes

2 tbsp butter

½ tbsp olive oil

1 onion, chopped

2 stalks celery, chopped

10 oz cauliflower florets

1 potato, finely diced

3 cups vegetable broth

Salt and pepper to taste

2 cups milk

1 bay leaf

4 oz blue cheese, crumbled

Warm oil and butter on Sauté. Add celery and onion and sauté for 3-5 minutes until fragrant. Stir in half the cauliflower and cook for 5 minutes until golden brown. Add in broth, bay leaf, potato, and the remaining cauliflower. Seal the lid. Cook on High Pressure for 5 minutes. Release the pressure quickly.

Remove the bay leaf. Puree the soup with an immersion blender until smooth. Stir in the milk. Adjust the seasoning. Top with blue cheese before serving.

## Simple Chicken Soup with Fennel

Serving Size: 4 | Total Time: 55 minutes

1 lb chicken drumsticks, boneless

4 celery stalks

1 fennel bulb, chopped

1 onion, diced

1 carrot, diced

2 garlic cloves, minced

2 bay leaves

Salt and pepper to taste

½ cup matzo meal

1 egg, beaten

2 tbsp canola oil

In the pot, add chicken, bay leaves, onion, carrot, celery, pepper, garlic, salt, and fennel. Add enough water such that ingredients are covered by 2 inches. Seal the lid and cook for 30 minutes on High Pressure. Release pressure quickly. In a bowl, mix egg, canola oil, pepper, salt, and matzo meal. Use a plastic wrap to close the bowl and refrigerate for 10 minutes.

Get rid of celery stalks from the pot. Transfer chicken to a cutting board, strip, and shred it from the bones. Take back to the pot. Select Sauté and boil the soup. Roll matzo mixture into 1-inch balls and place in the boiling soup. Cook for 3 mins to heat through as you gently stir.

## Broccoli, Potatoes & Cheese Cream Soup

Serving Size: 4 | Total Time: 30 minutes

1/3 cup butter

1 lb broccoli florets

2 cloves garlic, minced

1 onion, chopped

2 lb potatoes, chopped

4 cups vegetable broth

½ cup heavy cream

Cheddar cheese, grated

½ cup chopped scallions

Melt butter on Sauté. Add onion and garlic and Sauté for 5 minutes. Add in broth, potatoes, and broccoli, and mix well. Seal the lid and cook for 5 minutes on High Pressure. Release pressure naturally for 10 minutes. Transfer the potato mixture to a blender and pulse until smooth. Stir in heavy cream. Divide between bowls and top with cheese and scallions. Serve.

## Homemade Chicken & Quinoa Soup

Serving Size: 6 | Total Time: 25 minutes

2 tbsp canola oil

6 spring onions, chopped

2 garlic cloves, finely diced

1 carrot, chopped

2 celery stalks, chopped

2 chicken breasts, cubed

6 cups chicken broth

1 cup quinoa

Salt and pepper to taste

Heat canola oil on Sauté. Add in celery, spring onions, garlic, and carrot. Cook for 5 minutes. Add in chicken, quinoa, salt, chicken broth, and pepper. Seal the lid, select Soup/Broth, and cook for 15 minutes on High. Do a quick release. Serve.

## Vegetable Soup with Coconut Milk

Serving Size: 5 | Total Time: 40 minutes

2 tbsp olive oil

1 leek, chopped

2 cloves garlic, minced

2 carrots, diced

1 celery stalk, chopped

4 potatoes, quartered

1 red bell pepper, diced

¼ tsp red pepper flakes

Salt and pepper to taste

1 ½ cups vegetable stock

2 tbsp parsley

½ cup coconut milk

Heat olive oil on Sauté. Add garlic and leek and cook for 5 minutes. Add in red bell pepper, carrots, salt, potatoes, pepper flakes, celery stalk, and pepper. Mix in stock. Seal the lid and cook for 15 minutes on High Pressure. Release pressure naturally for 10 minutes. Add parsley and coconut milk to the soup. Use an immersion blender to blitz the soup until smooth.

## Black Bean & Corn Chicken Soup

Serving Size: 4 | Total Time: 25 minutes

½ lb boneless, skinless chicken thighs

5 cups chicken broth

Salt and pepper to taste

14 oz can tomatoes, diced

2 jalapeño peppers, minced

2 tbsp tomato puree

3 cloves garlic, minced

1 tbsp chili powder

1 tbsp ground cumin

½ tsp dried oregano

1 (14.5-oz) can black beans

2 cups corn kernels

Crushed tortilla chips

¼ cup cheddar, shredded

2 tbsp cilantro, chopped

Add the chicken, oregano, garlic, tomato puree, broth, cumin, tomatoes, chili, and jalapeño to your Instant Pot. Seal the lid and cook on High Pressure for 10 minutes.

Once cooking is done, release the pressure quickly. Unlock the lid. Transfer the chicken to a plate. Press Sauté and cook corn and black beans. Shred the chicken with a pair of forks, and return to the pot, stirring well. Select Keep Warm and simmer the soup for 5 minutes until heated through. Adjust the seasoning and divide among serving plates. Garnish with cilantro, shredded cheese, and crushed tortilla chips to serve.

## Traditional Italian Vegetable Soup

Serving Size: 6 | Total Time: 32 minutes

2 tbsp olive oil

1 onion, diced

1 cup celery, chopped

1 carrot, diced

1 green bell pepper, chopped

2 cloves garlic, minced

3 cups chicken broth

½ tsp dried parsley

½ tsp dried thyme

½ tsp dried oregano

Salt and pepper to taste

2 bay leaves

28 oz can diced tomatoes

1 tbsp tomato paste

2 cups kale

14 oz canned navy beans

½ cup rice

¼ cup Parmesan, shredded

Warm olive oil on Sauté. Stir in carrot, celery, and onion and cook for 5 minutes until soft. Add garlic and bell pepper and cook for 2 minutes as you stir until aromatic. Stir in pepper, thyme, broth, salt, parsley, oregano, tomatoes, bay leaves, and tomato paste. Mix in rice. Seal the lid and cook on High Pressure for 15 minutes. Do a quick release. Add kale and stir. Use residual heat to slightly wilting the greens. Discard bay leaves. Stir in navy beans and serve topped with Parmesan cheese.

## Chipotle Pumpkin Soup

Serving Size: 4 | Total Time: 30 minutes

1 tbsp olive oil

1 onion, chopped

2 chipotle peppers, minced

1 tsp ground black pepper

¼ tsp grated nutmeg

¼ tsp ground cinnamon

1 butternut pumpkin, cubed

4 cups vegetable broth

1 tsp salt

1 cup half-and-half

Warm oil on Sauté and cook nutmeg, pepper, cinnamon, and onion for 3-5 minutes until translucent. Add pumpkin and cook for 5 minutes, stirring infrequently. Pour in broth and add chipotle peppers and any remaining pumpkin. Seal the lid and cook on High Pressure for 10 minutes. Release pressure quickly. Stir in half-and-half and transfer to a blender to purée until you obtain a smooth consistency. Season with salt and serve hot.

## Spicy Tomato Soup with Rice

Serving Size: 4 | Total Time: 55 minutes

1 cup tomato puree

1 onion, chopped

1 garlic clove, minced

¼ cup rice

Salt and pepper to taste

2 tbsp olive oil

4 cups vegetable broth

¼ tsp cayenne pepper

1 tsp basil, chopped

Heat oil on Sauté and cook garlic and onion 3 minutes until soft. Add in tomato puree, rice, vegetable broth, and cayenne pepper. Season with salt and black pepper. Seal the lid and cook on Soup/Broth for 30 minutes on High Pressure. Release the pressure naturally for about 10 minutes. Serve in bowls sprinkled with basil.

## Green Immune-Boosting Soup

Serving Size: 4 | Total Time: 35 minutes

1 lb Brussels sprouts, halved

6 oz baby spinach

1 tsp salt

1 tbsp whole milk

3 tbsp sour cream

¼ cup celery, chopped

3 cups water

1 tbsp butter

Add sprouts, spinach, salt, milk, sour cream, celery, water, and butter to the Instant Pot. Seal the lid and set the steam release. Press Soup/Broth and cook for 30 minutes on High. Do a quick release. Transfer to a food processor, and blend well to combine.

## Chowder with Broccoli, Carrot & Tofu

Serving Size: 4 | Total Time: 35 minutes

1 head broccoli, chopped

1 carrot, chopped

2 tbsp sesame oil

1 onion, chopped

2 garlic cloves

1 cup soy milk

2 cups vegetable broth

¼ cup tofu, crumbled

A pinch of salt

Heat oil on Sauté. Add onion and garlic and stir-fry for 2 minutes, or until translucent. Pour in broth, a cup of water, broccoli, salt, and carrot. Seal the lid and cook on Manual/Pressure Cook for 5 minutes on High. Do a quick release. Stir in the soy milk and transfer to a food processor. Pulse until creamy. Serve with crumbled tofu.

## Vegetarian Lentil Soup with Nachos

Serving Size: 6 | Total Time: 40 minutes

2 ½ cups vegetable broth

1 ½ cups tomato sauce

1 onion, chopped

1 cup dry red lentils

½ cup prepared salsa verde

2 garlic cloves, minced

1 tbsp smoked paprika

2 tsp ground cumin

1 tsp chili powder

¼ tsp cayenne pepper

Salt and pepper to taste

Crushed tortilla chips

Add in tomato sauce, broth, onion, salsa verde, cumin, cayenne pepper, chili powder, garlic, lentils, paprika, salt, and pepper. Seal the lid and cook for 20 minutes on High Pressure. Release pressure naturally for 10 minutes. Garnish with crushed tortilla chips and serve. Enjoy!

## White Cabbage & Beetroot Borscht Soup

Serving Size: 4 | Total Time: 30 minutes

1 dried habanero pepper, crushed

2 tbsp olive oil

1 cup leeks, chopped

1 tsp garlic, smashed

2 beets, peeled and diced

1 tbsp cayenne pepper

4 cups beef stock

1 lb white cabbage, grated

2 tsp apple cider vinegar

¼ tsp paprika

Greek yogurt for garnish

Warm oil on Sauté. Stir in garlic and leeks and cook for 5 minutes until soft. Mix in the beef stock, paprika, cayenne pepper, vinegar, beets, white cabbage, and crushed habanero pepper. Seal the lid and cook on High Pressure for 20 minutes. Do a quick release. Place in serving bowls and top with Greek yogurt to serve.

## Chorizo Soup with Roasted Tomatoes

Serving Size: 6 | Total Time: 25 minutes

28 oz fire-roasted diced tomatoes

3 tbsp olive oil

2 shallots, chopped

3 cloves garlic, minced

Salt and pepper to taste

4 cups beef broth

½ cup tomatoes, chopped

½ cup raw cashews

1 tbsp red wine vinegar

3 chorizo sausage, chopped

½ cup chopped basil

Warm oil on Sauté and cook chorizo until crispy Remove to a plate lined with paper towels. Add in garlic and shallots and cook for 5 minutes until soft. Season with salt. Stir in red wine vinegar, broth, fire-roasted tomatoes, cashews, tomatoes, and pepper into the cooker Seal the lid and cook on High Pressure for 8 minutes Release the pressure quickly. Pour the soup into a blender and process until smooth. Divide into bowls Top with chorizo and decorate with basil.

## Mediterranean Carrot & Chickpea Soup

Serving Size: 6 | Total Time: 15 minutes

14 oz can chickpeas

2 carrots, chopped

2 onions, chopped

2 tomatoes, chopped

3 tbsp tomato paste

2 tbsp chopped parsley

2 cups vegetable broth

2 tbsp olive oil

1 tsp salt

Add in chickpeas, oil, onions, carrots, and tomatoes. Pour in the broth and sprinkle salt. Stir in the paste and seal the lid. Cook on High Pressure for 6 minutes. Do a quick release. Carefully unlock the lid. Remove the meal to a serving place. Sprinkle with parsley and serve.

## Chili Cream of Acorn Squash Soup

Serving Size: 4 | Total Time: 25 minutes

4 cups vegetable broth

2 tbsp butter

1 onion, diced

1 lb acorn squash, chopped

2 carrots, diced

¼ tsp chili pepper

A pinch of salt

½ cup coconut milk

1/3 cup sour cream

Melt butter on Sauté. Add onion and cook for 3 minutes until soft. Add in carrots, squash, salt, and chili pepper and stir-fry for 2 minutes until fragrant. Add the broth to the vegetable mixture. Seal the lid and cook for 12 minutes on High Pressure. Quick-release the pressure. Add soup to a food processor and puree to obtain a smooth consistency. Take the soup back to the cooker, stir in coconut milk until you get a consistent color. Serve hot with a dollop of sour cream.

## Cauliflower & Potato Soup with Parsley

Serving Size: 4 | Total Time: 30 minutes

1 lb cauliflower florets

2 potatoes, chopped

4 cups chicken broth

2 tbsp parsley, chopped

Salt and pepper to taste

¼ cup heavy cream

¼ cup sour cream

1 cup milk

Add cauliflower, potatoes, broth, parsley, salt, pepper, heavy cream, sour cream, and milk to the pot. Seal the lid and set the steam release handle. Cook on High Pressure for 20 minutes. Do a quick release. Let chill and transfer to a blender. Pulse until well-combined. Serve.

## Squash Soup with Yogurt & Cilantro

Serving Size: 6 | Total Time: 50 minutes

1 lb acorn squash, peeled diced

1 tbsp olive oil

1 onion, diced

1 stalk celery, diced

1 large carrot, diced

2 garlic cloves, minced

6 cups chicken stock

Juice from 1 lemon

1 cup coconut milk

Salt and pepper to taste

2 tbsp cilantro, chopped

Yogurt for garnish

Heat oil on Sauté and stir-fry carrot, celery, garlic, salt, and onion for 4 to 5 minutes until soft. Mix acorn squash with the vegetables; cook for 1 more minute until tender. Add stock and seal the lid and cook on High Pressure for 20 minutes. Release pressure naturally for 10 minutes. Add in lemon juice and coconut milk and stir. Transfer the soup to a blender and process until smooth. Divide soup into serving plates. Garnish with cilantro, black pepper, and yogurt.

## Simple Carrot & Oregano Soup

Serving Size: 4 | Total Time: 30 minutes

2 carrots, chopped

4 cups vegetable broth

1 tbsp butter

½ tsp dried oregano

½ tsp salt

Add carrots, broth, butter, oregano, and salt to the pot. Seal the lid and cook on Manual/Pressure Cook for 12 minutes on High. Do a natural release for 10 minutes. Transfer to a food processor and pulse until creamy.

## Garam Masala Parsnip & Red Onion Soup

Serving Size: 4 | Total Time: 20 minutes

2 tbsp vegetable oil

1 red onion, finely chopped

3 parsnips, chopped

2 garlic cloves, crushed

2 tsp garam masala

½ tsp chili powder

1 tbsp plain flour

4 cups vegetable stock

1 whole lemon, juiced

Salt and pepper to taste

Strips of lemon rind

Heat oil on Sauté, and stir-fry onion, parsnips, and garlic for 5 minutes, or until soft but not changed color. Stir in garam masala and chili powder and cook for 30 seconds. Stir in the flour for another 30 seconds. Pour in the stock, lemon rind, and lemon juice, and seal the lid. Cook on Manual for 5 minutes on High. Do a quick release. Remove a third of the vegetable pieces with a slotted spoon and reserve. Process the remaining soup and vegetables in a food processor until smooth. Return to the pot and stir in the reserved vegetables. Press Sauté and heat the soup until piping hot. Season with salt and pepper. Garnish with strips of lemon and serve.

## Fall Vegetable Soup

Serving Size: 4 | Total Time: 35 minutes

2 tbsp olive oil

1 onion, chopped

2 carrots, chopped

1 cup celery, chopped

2 cloves garlic, minced

5 cups vegetable broth

2 turnips, chopped

28 oz canned tomatoes

15 oz can garbanzo beans

1 cup frozen green peas

2 bay leaves

1 sprig fresh sage

Salt and pepper to taste

¼ cup Parmesan, grated

On Sauté, warm oil, stir in celery, carrots, and onion, and cook for 4 minutes until soft. Add in garlic and cook for 30 seconds. Add in vegetable broth, turnips, garbanzo beans, bay leaves, tomatoes, pepper, salt, peas, and sage.

Seal the lid and cook on High Pressure for 12 minutes. Allow natural pressure release for 10 minutes. Carefully unlock the lid. Serve topped with Parmesan cheese.

## Farro & Vegetable Chicken Soup

Serving Size: 6 | Total Time: 45 minutes

4 boneless, skinless chicken thighs

1 tbsp olive oil

¼ cup white wine

1 cup farro

1 large onion, chopped

2 celery stalks, chopped

3 large carrots, chopped

1 tsp garlic powder

1 tsp ground cumin

1 bay leaf

6 cups chicken broth

2 tsp parsley to garnish

Warm oil on Sauté. Brown the chicken on all sides for 6 minutes. Transfer the chicken to a bowl. Into the pot, add the wine to deglaze, scraping any brown bits present at the bottom of the cooker. Mix the wine with farro, cumin, broth, onion, carrots, celery, garlic powder, and bay leaf. Seal the lid, press Meat/Stew, and cook on High for 20 minutes. Release pressure naturally for about 10 minutes. Add parsley for garnish. Serve and enjoy!.

## Chili Soup with Avocado & Corn

Serving Size: 4 | Total Time: 25 minutes

1 avocado, mashed

2 tbsp lemon juice

1 tbsp vegetable oil

4 oz canned sweet corn

2 tomatoes, chopped

1 garlic clove, crushed

1 leek, chopped

1 red chili, chopped

14 oz vegetable stock

4 oz soy milk

Chopped leeks to garnish

In a bowl, mix the avocado mash with lemon juice and reserve until required. Heat the oil on Sauté and add corn, tomatoes, garlic, leek, and chili. Stir-fry for 4-5 minutes until softened. Put half of the vegetable mixture in a food processor, add the mashed avocado and process until smooth. Transfer the contents to the Instant Pot.

Pour in the stock, soy milk, and reserved vegetables, and seal the lid. Cook on Manual/Pressure Cook for 4 minutes on High. Once ready, press Cancel and release the steam naturally for about 10 minutes. Carefully unlock the lid. Garnish with chopped leeks and serve.

## Kimchi Ramen Noodle Soup

Serving Size: 4 | Total Time: 20 minutes

1 chicken breast, cubed

2 tbsp olive oil

½ tsp ground ginger

2 tbsp garlic, minced

4 cups chicken stock

2 tbsp soy sauce

½ tbsp kimchi paste

1 cup mushrooms, chopped

10 oz ramen noodles

1 lb collard greens, trimmed

2 tbsp cilantro, chopped

1 red chili, chopped to serve

Warm the olive oil on Sauté. Add in the chicken and cook for 5-6 minutes until slightly browned. Add in the mushrooms, garlic, kimchi paste, and ginger and sauté for 4-5 minutes. Mix in chicken stock and soy sauce. Seal the lid and cook on High Pressure for 10 minutes. Release pressure quickly. Press Sauté and stir in the ramen noodles and collard greens and simmer for 2 minutes. Top with red chili and cilantro to serve.

## Quick Mushroom-Quinoa Soup

Serving Size: 4 | Total Time: 30 minutes

4 cups vegetable broth

1 carrot, chopped

1 stalk celery, diced

2 cups quinoa, rinsed

1 cup mushrooms, sliced

1 onion, chopped

2 garlic cloves, smashed

1 tsp salt

½ tsp dried thyme

3 tbsp butter

½ cup heavy cream

Melt the butter on Sauté. Add onion, garlic, celery, and carrot, and cook for 8 minutes until tender. Mix in broth, thyme, quinoa, mushrooms, and salt. Seal the lid and cook on High Pressure for 10 minutes. Release pressure quickly. Stir in heavy cream. Cook for 2 minutes to obtain a creamy consistency. Serve warm.

## Garden Vegetable Soup

Serving Size: 4 | Total Time: 25 minutes

1 carrot, finely chopped

2 spring onions, chopped

1 red bell pepper, chopped

2 celery stalks, chopped

½ cup celery, chopped

½ tsp dried thyme

2 tbsp butter

1 tsp vegetable oil

4 cups vegetable broth

1 cup milk

Salt and pepper to taste

Melt butter on Sauté. Add carrot, onions, bell pepper, and celery. Cook for 5 minutes, stirring constantly. Pour in vegetable broth, seal the lid and cook on Manual/Pressure Cook for 5 minutes on High. Do a quick release. Carefully unlock the lid. Stir in celery stalks, thyme, milk, oil, salt, and pepper and cook for 2-3 minutes on Sauté.

## Potato-Leek Soup with Tofu

Serving Size: 4 | Total Time: 25 minutes

3 large leeks

3 tbsp butter

1 onion, chopped

1 lb potatoes, chopped

5 cups vegetable stock

2 tsp lemon juice

¼ tsp nutmeg

¼ tsp ground coriander

1 bay leaf

5 oz silken tofu

Salt and pepper to taste

2 tbsp chopped chives

Remove most of the green parts of the leeks. Slice the white parts very finely. Melt butter on Sauté. Stir-fry leeks and onion for 5 minutes. Add potatoes, stock, lemon juice, nutmeg, ground coriander, and bay leaf. Season to taste with salt and white pepper, and seal the lid. Press Manual and set the timer to 10 minutes. Cook on High. Do a quick release and discard the bay leaf. Process the soup in a food processor until smooth. Season to taste and add silken tofu. Sprinkle with chives and serve.

## Delicious Chicken & Potato Soup

Serving Size: 4 | Total Time: 35 minutes

1 lb chicken breasts, cubed

1 onion, chopped

1 carrot, chopped

2 potatoes, peeled, chopped

1 tsp cayenne pepper

2 egg yolks

1 tsp salt

3 tbsp lemon juice

3 tbsp olive oil

Add chicken, onion, carrot, potatoes, cayenne pepper, egg yolks, salt, lemon juice, oil, and 4 cups of water to the pot and seal the lid. Set the steam release handle and cook on Soup/Broth for 20 minutes on High. Release the pressure naturally for 10 minutes. Serve.

## Homemade Winter Soup

Serving Size: 4 | Total Time: 40 minutes

3 sweet potatoes, chopped

1 tsp salt

2 fennel bulbs, chopped

16 oz pureed pumpkin

1 large onion, chopped

1 tbsp coconut oil

4 cups water

1 tbsp sour cream

Heat the oil on Sauté, and add onion and fennel bulbs. Cook for 3-5 minutes until tender. Add sweet potatoes, salt, pumpkin puree, and water, and seal the lid. Cook on High Pressure for 25 minutes. Do a quick release. Carefully unlock the lid. Transfer the soup to a food processor and blend for 20 seconds until creamy. Top with sour cream and serve.

## Potato & Broccoli Soup with Rosemary

Serving Size: 4 | Total Time: 30 minutes

1 lb broccoli, cut into florets

2 potatoes, peeled, chopped

4 cups vegetable broth

½ tsp dried rosemary

½ tsp salt

½ cup sour cream

Place broccoli and potatoes in the pot. Pour the broth, rosemary, and seal the lid. Cook on Soup/Broth for 20 minutes on High. Do a quick release. Carefully unlock the lid and remove the soup to a blender. Pulse to combine. Stir in sour cream and add salt. Serve.

## Traditional Cheesy Onion Soup

Serving Size: 4 | Total Time: 35 minutes

2 tbsp butter

1 thinly chopped onion

Salt and pepper to taste

½ cup dry white wine

4 cups beef stock

2 sprigs fresh thyme

2 bay leaves

4 baguette slices

1 cup Swiss cheese, grated

Melt butter on Sauté. Add in onions and cook for 3-5 minutes until soft. Add in beef stock, wine, bay leaves, thyme, salt, and pepper as you stir. Seal the lid, press Manual, and cook for 15 minutes. Do a quick release. Discard bay leaves and thyme. Preheat the oven's broiler. Divide into four soup bowls. Top with ¼ cup Swiss cheese and 1 baguette slice. Transfer the bowls to a baking sheet and cook for 2-4 minutes under broiler until golden brown. Serve.

## Parsley Noodle Soup with Chicken

Serving Size: 4 | Total Time: 35 minutes

1 lb chicken breasts, cubed

½ cup egg noodles

4 cups chicken broth

2 tbsp parsley, chopped

Salt and pepper to taste

Season the fillets with salt and place them in the pot. Pour the broth and seal the lid. Cook on Soup/Broth for 20 minutes on High. Do a quick release. Add in the noodles and seal the lid again. Press Manual/Pressure Cook and cook for 5 minutes on High Pressure. Release the pressure quickly. Carefully unlock the lid. Sprinkle with black pepper and parsley. Serve warm.

## Creamy Broccoli-Gorgonzola Soup

Serving Size: 4 | Total Time: 35 minutes

8 oz Gorgonzola cheese, crumbled

1 cup broccoli, chopped

2 tbsp olive oil

½ cup full-fat milk

1 tbsp parsley, chopped

Salt and pepper to taste

Add broccoli, oil, milk, salt, pepper, and gorgonzola cheese to the pot and 4 cups of water. Seal the lid and cook on Soup/Broth for 30 minutes on High Pressure. Do a quick release. Carefully unlock the lid. Remove the lid and sprinkle with fresh parsley. Serve.

## Rustic Soup with Turkey Balls & Carrots

Serving Size: 4 | Total Time: 45 minutes

2 tbsp olive oil

6 oz turkey balls

4 cups chicken broth

1 onion, chopped

1 garlic clove, minced

3 large carrots, chopped

Salt and pepper to taste

1 tbsp cilantro, chopped

Heat olive oil on Sauté and stir-fry onion, carrots, and garlic for 5 minutes until soft. Add turkey balls, broth, salt, and pepper to the pot. Seal the lid and press Manual. Cook for 25 minutes on HIgh. Release the pressure naturally for 10 minutes and serve sprinkled with cilantro.

## Vegetable Beef Soup

Serving Size: 4 | Total Time: 45 minutes

½ lb lean beef, cut into bite-sized pieces

1 onion, chopped

2 carrots, chopped

1 tsp cayenne pepper

Salt and pepper to taste

2 tbsp butter

Melt butter on Sauté. Add onion and stir-fry for 3 minutes. Add carrots, cayenne pepper, salt, and pepper. Cook for 2 more minutes. Add the meat and pour in 4 cups of water. Seal the lid and cook on Manual for 35 minutes. Release the pressure quickly. Serve warm.

## Modern Minestrone with Pancetta

Serving Size: 6 | Total Time: 30 minutes

2 tbsp olive oil

2 oz pancetta, chopped

1 onion, diced

1 parsnip, chopped

2 carrots, cut into rounds

2 celery stalks

2 garlic cloves, minced

1 tbsp dried basil

1 tbsp dried thyme

1 tbsp dried oregano

6 cups vegetable broth

1 lb green beans, chopped

1 (15-oz) can diced tomatoes

1 (15-oz) can chickpeas

2 cups small shaped pasta

Salt and pepper to taste

½ cup grated Parmesan

Heat oil on Sauté. Add onion, carrots, garlic, pancetta, celery, and parsnip and cook for 5 minutes until they become soft. Stir in basil, oregano, beans, broth, tomatoes, pepper, salt, thyme, chickpeas, and pasta. Seal the lid and cook for 6 minutes on High Pressure. Release pressure naturally for 10 minutes. Carefully unlock the lid. Garnished with Parmesan cheese and serve.

## Piri Piri Chicken Soup

Serving Size: 4 | Total Time: 40 minutes

2 chicken breasts, cubed

1 garlic clove, minced

1 sweet onion, diced

½ cup celery, diced

2 tbsp butter

3 cups chicken bone broth

1/3 cup Piri Piri spicy sauce

1 tsp thyme

1 tbsp lemon juice

Salt and pepper to taste

Melt butter in your Instant Pot on Sauté and cook onion, celery, and garlic for 3 minutes. Add in the chicken and Sauté for another 4-5 minutes, stirring occasionally. Pour in chicken broth, thyme, and spicy sauce and seal the lid. Select Manual and cook for 12 minutes on High pressure.

When done, allow a natural release for 10 minutes, then perform a quick pressure release. Carefully unlock the lid. Adjust the taste and drizzle with the lemon juice. Ladle into bowls and serve warm. Enjoy!

## Turmeric Butternut Squash Soup

Serving Size: 4 | Total Time: 40 minutes
1.5 lb butternut squash, peeled and chopped
1 onion, chopped
4 cups vegetable broth
1 tbsp ground turmeric
½ tbsp heavy cream
Salt and pepper to taste
2 tbsp parsley, chopped
3 tbsp olive oil

Heat oil on Sauté and stir-fry onion for 3 minutes. Add in butternut squash, turmeric, vegetable broth, salt, and pepper and stir well. Seal the lid. Press Soup/Broth and cook for 30 minutes on High. Do a quick release. With an immersion blender, blend until smooth. Stir in heavy cream and top with freshly chopped parsley. Serve warm.

## Vegetarian Soup with White Beans

Serving Size: 4 | Total Time: 30 minutes
1 cup green peas
1 carrot, chopped
2 red bell peppers, chopped
½ cup white beans, soaked
1 tomato, roughly chopped
4 cups vegetable broth
1 onion, chopped
2 tbsp olive oil
Salt and pepper to taste
¼ tsp dried oregano

Heat the olive oil on Sauté and stir-fry onion, carrot, and bell peppers for 5 minutes until tender. Stir in green peas, white beans, tomato, broth, salt, pepper, and oregano.

Seal the lid. Cook on High Pressure for 20 minutes. Do a quick release. Serve warm.

## Yellow Beef Soup

Serving Size: 4 | Total Time: 35 minutes
1 bay leaf
2 garlic cloves
½ lb beef sirloin, cubed
2 shallots
2 candlenuts
½ tsp turmeric
2 tbsp beansprouts
1 lemongrass
1 tsp vegetable oil
Salt and pepper to taste

In a blender, combine the shallots, garlic, candlenuts, and turmeric until smooth. Warm vegetable oil in your Instant Pot on Sauté. Place the shallot mixture and cook for 3-4 minutes, stirring often until aromatic. Add in the beef and lemongrass and stir-fry until the lemongrass is wilted, about 5 minutes. Put in 4 cups water, bay leaf, salt, and pepper and seal the lid. Select Manual and cook for 15 minutes on High. When done, perform a quick pressure release. Discard bay leaf. Mix in beansprouts and cook for 2-3 minutes until wilted. Serve warm.

## Spicy Red Kidney Bean Soup

Serving Size: 4 | Total Time: 45 minutes
14.5 oz can red kidney beans
14.5 oz canned tomatoes
2 tbsp oil
1 onion, chopped
2 cloves garlic, crushed
2 red chilies, chopped
1 green bell pepper, diced
½ cup tomato sauce

Heat oil on Sauté and stir-fry garlic, chilies, and onion for 3 minutes. Add tomatoes, beans, bell pepper, tomato sauce, and 4 cups of water. Seal the lid. Cook on Manual for 25 minutes on High Pressure. Release the steam naturally for 10 minutes. Carefully unlock the lid. Serve.

## Creamy Celery & Green Pea Soup

Serving Size: 4 | Total Time: 25 minutes

3 oz carrots, finely chopped

3 oz celery root, chopped

1 cup green peas

2 tbsp butter

2 tbsp parsley, chopped

1 egg yolk

2 tbsp cream cheese

Salt and pepper to taste

4 cups beef broth

Add carrots, celery, green peas, butter parsley, egg yolk, cream cheese, salt, pepper, and broth to the Instant Pot and seal the lid. Cook on High Pressure for 10 minutes. When done, release the steam naturally for 10 minutes.

## Creamy Bean & Potato Soup

Serving Size: 4 | Total Time: 35 minutes

½ cup canned beans

4 cups beef broth

1 potato, chopped

½ cup heavy cream

Salt and pepper to taste

1 tsp garlic powder

Add beans, broth, potato, heavy cream, salt, pepper, and garlic powder to the pot, seal the lid, and cook on Manual/Pressure for 10 minutes on High. Release the steam naturally for 10 minutes. Carefully unlock the lid. Transfer the ingredients to a blender. Pulse until smooth. Return the soup to the pot. Press Sauté and add a half cup of water. Cook for 5 more minutes, or until desired thickness. Let it chill for a while before serving.

## Effortless Tomato-Lentil Soup

Serving Size: 4 | Total Time: 35 minutes

1 cup red lentils

1 carrot, cut into thin slices

1 tbsp tomato paste

3 garlic cloves, crushed

4 cups vegetable broth

2 tomatoes, chopped

1 onion, diced

½ tsp dried thyme

2 tbsp olive oil

Warm oil on Sauté. Cook onion, carrot, and garlic for 5 minutes. Add in tomato paste, tomatoes, lentils, broth, and thyme. Seal the lid and cook on Soup/Broth for 15 minutes on High Pressure. Release the pressure naturally for 10 minutes. Carefully unlock the lid. Serve.

## Parsley Creamy Tomato Soup

Serving Size: 4 | Total Time: 50 minutes

2 lb tomatoes, diced

1 cup canned white beans

1 small onion, diced

2 garlic cloves, crushed

1 cup heavy cream

1 cup vegetable broth

½ tsp sugar

Salt and pepper to taste

2 tbsp olive oil

2 tbsp parsley, chopped

Warm oil on Sauté. Stir-fry onion and garlic for 2 minutes. Add tomatoes, beans, broth, 3 cups of water, parsley, salt, pepper, and a little bit of sugar to balance the bitterness. Seal the lid and cook on Soup/Broth for 30 minutes on High Pressure. Release the pressure naturally for 10 minutes. Carefully unlock the lid. Top with a dollop of heavy cream and serve.

## Tasty Asparagus Soup

Serving Size: 4 | Total Time: 35 minutes

2 lb asparagus, chopped

2 onions, chopped

1 cup heavy cream

4 cups vegetable broth

2 tbsp butter

1 tbsp vegetable oil

½ tsp salt

½ tsp dried oregano

½ tsp paprika

Melt butter on Sauté, and add 1 tbsp of oil. Stir-fry the onions for 2 minutes until translucent. Add asparagus, oregano, salt, and paprika. Stir well and cook until asparagus soften for a few minutes. Pour the broth and mix well to combine.

Seal the lid and cook on Soup/Broth for 20 minutes on High. Do a quick release and whisk in 1 cup of heavy cream. Unlock the lid. Serve.

## Gingery Squash & Leek Soup

Serving Size: 4 | Total Time: 35 minutes

2 cups butternut squash, chopped
4 leeks, chopped
Salt and pepper to taste
1 tsp ginger, grated
4 cups vegetable broth
2 tbsp olive oil
1 tsp cumin
1 tsp ginger powder

Heat the oil on Sauté, add stir-fry leeks for about 5 minutes, on Sauté. Add ginger powder and cumin. Give it a good stir and continue to cook for 1 more minute. Pour in squash, ginger, salt, pepper, and broth and seal the lid. Cook on Soup/Broth for 10 minutes on High. Release the pressure naturally for about 10 minutes.

## Lentil & Carrot Soup

Serving Size: 4 | Total Time: 40 minutes

1 cup red lentils, rinsed
1 red bell pepper, chopped
1 onion, chopped
½ cup carrot puree
Salt and pepper to taste
½ tsp cumin, ground
2 tbsp olive oil
2 tbsp parsley, chopped

Heat the oil on Sauté, add stir-fry the onion for 4 minutes. Add lentils, bell pepper, carrot puree, salt, pepper, and cumin and pour in 4 cups of water. Seal the lid and cook on Soup/Broth for 30 minutes on High. Do a quick pressure release. Sprinkle with fresh parsley and serve.

## Cabbage & Pork Soup

Serving Size: 6 | Total Time: 20 minutes

1 lb ground pork
1 onion, diced
2 lb napa cabbage, chopped
1 potato, diced
6 button mushrooms, sliced
3 scallions, sliced
2 tbsp butter
4 cups vegetable broth
Salt and pepper to taste

Melt butter on Sauté and add the pork. Cook until it browned, breaking it with a spatula. Once browned, add onion and mushrooms and cook for another 4-5 minutes. Season with salt and pepper. Pour in vegetable broth and stir in cabbage, potato, and scallions. Seal the lid, cook on Pressure Cook for 6 minutes on High. Do a quick release. Carefully unlock the lid. Serve.

## Millet & Beef Soup

Serving Size: 4 | Total Time: 35 minutes

½ lb beef stew meat, cubed
2 tbsp vegetable oil
1 celery rib, chopped
2 shallots, chopped
2 garlic cloves, minced
1 carrot, chopped
½ cup millet, rinsed
1 cup canned tomatoes, diced
12 oz spicy vegetable juice
4 cups beef bone broth
Salt and pepper to taste
½ cup frozen peas
½ tsp dried rosemary
½ tsp dried sage

Heat vegetable oil in your Instant Pot on Sauté and cook shallots, carrot, celery, and garlic for 3 minutes. Add in the beef and Sauté for another 4-5 minutes, stirring often. Pour in beef broth, tomatoes, spicy vegetable juice, millet, rosemary, and sage and seal the lid. Select Manual and cook for 15 minutes on High pressure. Once ready, perform a quick pressure release and unlock the lid. Mix in peas and let sit for 5 minutes; adjust the seasoning. Serve right away. Enjoy!

## Jalapeño Chicken Soup with Tortilla Chips

Serving Size: 6 | Total Time: 50 minutes

¾ lb chicken thighs

1 onion, chopped

2 garlic cloves, minced

1 cup tomatoes, chopped

1 tbsp ginger, minced

2 cups collard greens

2 tbsp butter, softened

1 jalapeño pepper, minced

½ tsp dried basil

½ tsp dried oregano

Salt and pepper to taste

6 oz tortilla chips

Melt the butter in your Instant Pot on Sauté. Add in the onion, ginger, garlic, and jalapeño pepper and cook for 3 minutes. Add in the chicken thighs and brown for another 5 minutes, stirring occasionally. Mix in tomatoes, 6 cups of water, oregano, basil, salt, and pepper and seal the lid. Select Manual and cook for 15 minutes on High. Once done, allow a natural release for 15 minutes. Shred the chicken and discard the bones; return it to the soup Stir in collard greens and simmer for 3 minutes on Sauté. Adjust the seasoning. Serve topped with tortilla chips.

## Dilled Salmon Soup

Serving Size: 2 | Total Time: 20 minutes

¼ cup chopped green tomatoes

½ lb salmon fillet

1 cup fresh dill

2 tsp sliced shallots

1 tsp sliced garlic

¼ tsp ginger

¼ tsp tamarind

1 tbsp lemon juice

1 cup water

1 bay leaf

½ tsp salt

Slice salmon fillet into medium dices and place them in your Instant Pot. Add in water, green tomatoes, fresh dill, shallot, garlic, ginger, bay leaf, salt, tamarind, and lemon juice. Seal the lid, select Soup, and cook for 4 minutes on High. When done, allow a natural release for 10 minutes and unlock the lid. Serve warm and enjoy!

## Spicy Sweet Potato Soup

Serving Size: 2 | Total Time: 30 minutes

2 sweet potatoes, chopped

1 carrot, chopped

1 onion, chopped

2 cups chicken broth

2 garlic cloves, chopped

Salt and pepper to taste

1 tbsp chili flakes

1 tbsp olive oil

Warm oil on Sauté, and stir-fry potatoes, onion, and garlic for 3-4 minutes. Stir in carrot, broth, salt, pepper, and chili flakes, seal the lid and cook on High Pressure for 7 minutes. Do a natural release for 10 minutes. Serve.

## Quick Beef Soup

Serving Size: 4 | Total Time: 45 minutes

2 tbsp olive oil

½ lb beef sirloin, cubed

2 shallots, chopped

2 garlic cloves, minced

¼ tsp ginger

1 tsp celery seeds

1 carrot, chopped

½ tsp dry basil

Salt and pepper to taste

4 cups bone broth

2 russet potatoes, chopped

2 bay leaves

1 tbsp soy sauce

2 tbsp parsley, chopped

Warm the olive oil in your Instant Pot on Sauté. Add and cook the beef for 5-6 minutes, stirring occasionally until slightly brown on all sides. Add the shallots, garlic, ginger, celery seeds, and carrot and sauté for 4 minutes. Season with basil, salt, and pepper.

Add the broth to deglaze the pot. Stir the remaining ingredients. Seal the lid, select Manual, and cook for 20 minutes on High pressure. When done, allow a natural release for 10 minutes; open the lid. Discard the bay leaves. Divide between plates and serve topped with parsley.

## Pork Soup with Cabbage & Beans

Serving Size: 4 | Total Time: 30 minutes

2 tbsp olive oil
1 onion, cubed
½ lb cubed pork meat
½ head cabbage, shredded
14 oz can cannellini beans
1 carrot, shredded
1 garlic clove, minced
½ tsp dried rosemary
4 cups chicken broth
Salt and pepper to taste

Warm the oil in your Instant Pot on Sauté. Place the onion, garlic, and pork and cook for 4-5 minutes. Add in cabbage, carrot, broth, rosemary, salt, pepper, and cannellini beans. Seal the lid and cook on Manual for 20 minutes on High. Perform a quick pressure release.

## Chicken & Potato Soup

Serving Size: 4 | Total Time: 45 minutes

2 tbsp olive oil
½ lb chicken thighs
2 potatoes, cut into chunks
1 carrot, cut into chunks
1 yellow onion, diced
2 garlic cloves, minced
1 celery rib, chopped
4 cups chicken bone broth
Salt and pepper to taste
2 tbsp parsley, chopped

Heat oil in your Instant Pot on Sauté and cook onion, carrot, celery, and garlic for 3 minutes. Add in chicken and Sauté for 4-5 minutes. Pour in broth and potatoes and seal the lid. Select Manual and cook for 15 minutes on High. Once ready, allow a natural release for 10 minutes. Adjust the taste and top with parsley. Serve.

## Smoked Ham & Potato Soup

Serving Size: 4 | Total Time: 20 minutes

1 lb russet potatoes, cut into small chunks
2 tbsp butter
2 garlic cloves, minced
1 onion, diced
½ tsp celery seeds
½ tsp chili powder
½ lb smoked ham, diced
4 cups chicken broth
2 tbsp parsley, chopped

Melt butter in your Instant Pot on Sauté. Add in garlic and onion and cook for 3 minutes. Stir in celery seeds, chili powder, and smoked ham for 1-2 minutes and pour in potatoes and broth. Seal the lid. Select Manual and cook for 10 minutes on High. Once done, perform a quick pressure release. Serve topped with parsley.

## Hearty Beef Soup

Serving Size: 6 | Total Time: 65 minutes

2 tbsp olive oil
2 lb beef stew meat, cubed
1 leek, finely chopped
2 garlic cloves, minced
2 carrots, chopped
1 celery stalk, chopped
½ cup pearl barley
1 bay leaf
6 cups beef bone broth
½ tsp soy sauce sauce
Salt and pepper to taste
1 tbsp Parmesan, grated

Warm the olive oil in your Instant Pot on Sauté. Season beef with salt and pepper and cook in the pot for 10 minutes, stirring frequently; set aside. Add the leek, garlic, carrots, and celery to the pot and cook for 4 minutes. Put the beef back to the pot with pearl barley, bay leaf, beef broth, and soy sauce. Seal the lid and select Manual.

Cook for 30 minutes on High pressure. When done, allow a natural release for 10 minutes, then perform a quick pressure release and unlock the lid. Discard the bay leaf. Adjust the taste and top with Parmesan cheese.

## Lentil & Pork Shank Soup

Serving Size: 6 | Total Time: 45 minutes

2 lb pork shank, trimmed of excess fat
2 carrots, cut into chunks
1 celery stalk, chopped
3 garlic cloves, sliced
2 tbsp olive oil
1 yellow onion, chopped
½ tsp paprika
½ tsp cayenne pepper
2 tomatoes, chopped
½ lb lentils, rinsed
Salt and pepper to taste

Warm the olive oil in your Instant Pot on Sauté. Place the onion, carrots, garlic, and celery and cook for 3 minutes, stirring often. Add in pork chank, paprika, cayenne pepper, tomatoes, lentils, salt, pepper, and 6 cups water.

Seal the lid, select Manual, and cook for 25 minutes on High pressure. When over, allow a natural release for 10 minutes and unlock the lid. Serve warm.

## Ukrainian-Style Borscht

Serving Size: 4 | Total Time: 40 minutes

2 tbsp grapeseed oil
½ lb beets, peeled, diced
½ lb potatoes, peeled, diced
1 parsnip, diced
1 celery stalk, diced
1 red onion, diced
2 garlic cloves, diced
3 cups grated red cabbage
4 cups vegetable stock
½ tsp ground cumin
Salt and pepper to taste

Heat the grapeseed oil in your Instant Pot on Saué and cook celery, red onion, garlic, parsnip, and red cabbage for 4-5 minutes, stirring periodically. Pour in the vegetable stock, potatoes, beets, cumin, salt, and

pepper.Seal the lid. Select Manual and cook for 15 minutes on High pressure. When over, allow a natural release for 10 minutes and unlock the lid. Serve immediately.

## Chicken & Spinach Soup

Serving Size: 6 | Total Time: 35 minutes

3 tbsp butter
1 white onion, diced
3 celery stalks, diced
2 carrots, diced
3 garlic cloves, minced
½ tsp dried rosemary
2 chicken breasts, cubed
6 cups chicken broth
1 cup orzo pasta
2 cups spinach, chopped
Salt and pepper to taste
2 tbsp fresh dill, chopped

Melt butter in your Instant Pot on Sauté. Add in onion, celery, carrot, garlic, salt, and pepper and cook for 5 minutes. Stir in chicken breasts, and rosemary and Sauté for 5 minutes. Pour in chicken broth and orzo and seal the lid. Select Manual and cook for 12 minutes on High.Once ready, perform a quick pressure release and unlock the lid. Mix in spinach and let sit covered for 5 minutes until the spinach wilts. Scatter with dill to serve.

## Mom's Meatball Soup

Serving Size: 4 | Total Time: 25 minutes

2 Yukon Gold potatoes, peeled and diced
2 tbsp canola oil
1 onion, diced
1 garlic clove, minced
½ lb ground pork
14 oz can diced tomatoes
4 cups vegetable broth
½ tsp dried oregano
½ tsp dried thyme
Salt and pepper to taste
2 tbsp parsley, chopped

Place the ground pork in a bowl and season with oregano, thyme, salt, and pepper. Mix well with your hands and form form the mixture into small balls. Warm the canola oil in your Instant Pot on Sauté. Add in the onion and garlic and cook for 3 minutes. Pour in vegetable broth, tomatoes, potatoes, and meatballs and seal the lid. Select Manual and cook for 10 minutes on High pressure. Once ready, perform a quick pressure release and unlock the lid. Sprinkle with par and serve warm.

## Coconut Chicken Soup

Serving Size: 4 | Total Time: 30 minutes

2 green onions, sliced diagonally

2 tbsp ghee

1 sweet onion, chopped

1 cup celery, chopped

1 cup carrots, chopped

6 oz rice noodles

½ lb chicken breasts, cubed

1 tbsp parsley

3 cups chicken stock

1 tsp red pepper flakes

Salt and pepper to taste

1 cup coconut milk

1 cup green peas

Melt ghee in your Instant Pot on Sauté. Add in onion, celery, and carrots and cook for 3 minutes. Stir in chicken, parsley, stock, pepper flakes, salt, and pepper. Seal the lid and select Manual. Cook for 15 minutes on High. When done, perform a quick pressure release. Stir in coconut milk, green peas, and rice noodles and cook for 3 minutes on Sauté. Serve topped with green onions.

## Cilantro & Coconut Chicken Soup

Serving Size: 4 | Total Time: 20 minutes

1 tsp ground nutmeg

2 cups diced tomatoes

4 chicken breasts, cubed

1 tbsp olive oil

1 onion, chopped

1 tsp garlic powder

1 tsp ginger powder

1 tsp turmeric

1 tsp paprika

1 tsp Cayenne Powder

2 tbsp Tomato Puree

1 cup Coconut Milk Whey

1 cup Coconut Cream

¼ cup Almonds, sliced

¼ cup Chopped Cilantro

Salt to taste

Warm olive oil in your Instant Pot on Sauté. Place the onions and salt and cook for 3 minutes. Add in nutmeg garlic powder, ginger powder, turmeric, paprika, and cayenne pepper and cook for 2 minutes, stirring often.

Mix in diced tomatoes, coconut milk, and chicken breasts and seal the lid. Select Manual and cook for 10 minutes on High pressure. When done, perform a quick pressure release. Stir in tomato puree, coconut cream and cilantro. Adjust seasoning to taste. Serve topped with almond.

## Spring Chicken Vermicelli Soup

Serving Size: 6 | Total Time: 50 minutes

2 tbsp olive oil

½ cup vermicelli

¾ lb chicken breasts, cubed

2 carrots, diced

3 waxy potatoes, diced

3 green onions, sliced

1 green garlic stalk, sliced

1 celery stalk, chopped

4 cups chicken stock

½ tsp oregano

1 bay leaf

Salt and pepper to taste

2 tbsp cilantro, chopped

Warm the olive oil in your Instant Pot on Sauté. Add in the green onion, carrots, green garlic, and celery and cook for 3 minutes. Add in chicken and Sauté for 5 minutes, stirring often. Mix in potatoes, chicken stock, 2 cups of water, oregano, salt, pepper, and bay leaf and seal the lid. Select Manual, and cook for 20 minutes on High pressure. When over, allow a natural release for 10 minutes, then perform a quick pressure release. Discard the bay leaf, stir in vermicelli, and press Sauté. Cook for 5 minutes. Serve topped with cilantro.

## Veggie & Elbow Pasta Soup

Serving Size: 2 | Total Time: 25 minutes

1 cup canned chickpeas

1 carrot, diced

14 oz can tomatoes, diced

½ cup elbow pasta

2 cups chicken broth

1 tsp dried basil

1 tbsp olive oil

1 tsp dried oregano

2 garlic cloves, minced

1 onion, diced

¼ cup fresh spinach

Salt and pepper to taste

Place the olive oil, carrot, onion, and garlic in your Instant Pot and cook until tender and soft on Sauté. Stir in oregano, basil, black pepper, salt, tomatoes, spinach, pasta, and chicken broth. Seal the lid, select Manual, and cook for 6 minutes on High. When done, allow a natural release for 10 minutes. Mix in chickpeas and serve.

## Kale, Bean & Pancetta Soup

Serving Size: 6 | Total Time: 35 minutes

1 can (15-oz) pinto beans

1 tbsp olive oil

4 slices pancetta, chopped

1 onion, chopped

1 carrot, chopped

1 celery stalk, chopped

2 tbsp tomato paste

1 sprig fresh rosemary

2 bay leaves

4 cups chicken broth

3 cups baby kale

Salt and pepper to taste

Press the Sauté on your Instant Pot and heat the olive oil. Add in the pancetta and cook until it becomes crispy, about 4-5 minutes. Remove to a lined with paper towel plate. Put the onion, carrot, and celery in the pot and

cook for 3 minutes. Stir in tomato paste, pinto beans, rosemary, bay leaves, and chicken broth.

Seal the lid, select Manual, and cook for 10 minutes on High. When done, allow a natural release for 10 minutes, then perform a quick pressure release and unlock the lid. Discard rosemary and bay leaves. Mix in the kale and adjust the seasoning. Serve topped with pancetta. Enjoy!

## Navy Bean & Zucchini Soup

Serving Size: 4 | Total Time: 25 minutes

2 tbsp olive oil

1 onion, chopped

2 garlic cloves, minced

1 zucchini, chopped

1 carrot, chopped

1 celery stalk, chopped

1 cup canned navy beans

1 tsp fresh thyme

1 bay leaf

4 cups vegetable stock

Salt and pepper to taste

2 tbsp parsley, chopped

Warm the olive oil in your Instant Pot on Sauté. Add in onion and garlic and sweat for 4-5 minutes. Add in zucchini, carrot, and celery and cook for 5 more minutes. Stir in beans, thyme, bay leaf, stock, salt, and pepper and seal the lid. Select Manual and cook for 8 minutes on High. When over, perform a quick pressure release. Discard bay leaf. Top with parsley and serve. Enjoy!

## Turkish-Inspired Lentil Soup

Serving Size: 6 | Total Time: 30 minutes

2 tbsp olive oil

1 white onion, chopped

1 celery stalk, diced

4 garlic cloves, minced

1 carrot, chopped

1 tsp paprika

½ tsp ground cumin

½ tsp ground coriander

1 tbsp red pepper paste

¼ cup bulgur

1 cup red lentils

14 oz can diced tomatoes

6 cups vegetable broth

Salt and pepper to taste

2 tbsp parsley, chopped

Warm the olive oil in your Instant Pot on Sauté. Add in onion, carrot, and celery and cook for 4-5 minutes. Stir in garlic, paprika, cumin, coriander, and red pepper paste and cook for another 1-2 minutes. Pour in vegetable broth, lentils, tomatoes, and bulgur and seal the lid. Select Manual and cook for 12 minutes on High. Once ready, perform a quick pressure release. Unlock the lid and adjust the seasoning. Top with parsley and serve.

## Mexican Bean Soup

Serving Size: 6 | Total Time: 40 minutes

2 tbsp olive oil

2 garlic cloves, minced

1 onion, chopped

1 red bell pepper, chopped

½ tsp dried oregano

1 tsp ground cumin

1 bay leaf

1 lb black beans, soaked

4 cups vegetable broth

14 oz can diced tomatoes

2 hot cherry peppers, sliced

Salt and pepper to taste

1 lime, cut into wedges

3 tbsp cilantro, chopped

Chili oil to serve

Warm the olive oil in your Instant Pot on Sauté. Add in garlic and onion and cook for 3 minutes. Stir in bell pepper, oregano, cumin, cherry peppers, and bay leaf and cook for another minute.

Pour in black beans, vegetable broth, tomatoes, salt, and pepper and seal the lid. Select Manual and cook for 30 minutes. Once done, perform a quick pressure release and unlock the lid. Discard the bay leaf. Drizzle with chili oil and sprinkle with cilantro. Serve with lime wedges.

## Black-Eyed Pea Soup

Serving Size: 4 | Total Time: 40 minutes

2 tbsp canola oil

2 shallots, diced

2 garlic cloves, minced

1 celery stalk, sliced

1 carrot, chopped

1 lb dry black-eyed peas

¼ tsp cayenne pepper

¼ tsp dried dill

¼ tsp dried oregano

¼ tsp dried sage

1 cup spinach, torn

4 cups vegetable broth

Warm the canola oil in your Instant Pot on Sauté. Add in shallots, garlic, celery, and carrot and cook for 4 minutes. Add in black-eyed peas, cayenne pepper, dill, oregano, sage, and vegetable broth and stir well.

Seal the lid, select Manual, and cook for 10 minutes on High pressure. Once over, allow a natural release for 10 minutes, then perform a quick pressure release and unlock the lid. Stir in spinach, cover with the lid, and leave to sit in the residual heat for 5 minutes. Serve warm.

## Greek-Style Fish Soup

Serving Size: 4 | Total Time: 20 minutes

1 lb codfish, cut into bite-sized pieces

2 tbsp olive oil

1 onion, chopped

1 carrot, chopped

2 garlic cloves, minced

2 tomatoes, chopped

½ tsp dill weed

½ tsp Greek oregano

½ tsp hot sauce

4 cups seafood stock

10 Kalamata olives, chopped

Warm olive oil in your Instant Pot on Sauté. Add in onion, garlic, and carrot and cook for 4 minutes. Stir in dill weed, oregano, hot sauce, and fish and cook for 3-4 minutes. Pour in stock and tomatoes and seal the lid. Select Manual and cook for 5 minutes on High. When eady, perform a quick pressure release. Carefully unlock the lid. Sprinkle with Kalamata olives and serve.

## Chicken & Lima Bean Soup

Serving Size: 6 | Total Time: 45 minutes

2 tbsp sesame oil

1 cup lima beans, soaked

¾ lb chicken breasts, cubed

1 serrano pepper, minced

½ tsp cayenne pepper

1 sweet onion, sliced

2 garlic cloves, minced

2 tomatoes, chopped

2 tbsp rosemary, chopped

6 cups vegetable broth

4 tbsp salsa

1 tsp soy sauce

Salt and pepper to taste

Press Sauté and heat the sesame oil in your Instant Pot. Cook the onion and garlic until tender and fragrant. Add the chicken, serrano pepper, cayenne pepper, salt, and black pepper and sauté for 4-5 minutes. Pour in salsa, tomatoes, vegetable broth, soy sauce, and lima beans.

Seal the lid, select Manual, and cook for 30 minutes on High pressure. Once ready, perform a quick pressure release. Sprinkle with rosemary and serve warm. Enjoy!

## Zuppa Toscana

Serving Size: 4 | Total Time: 40 minutes

2 tbsp olive oil

1 white onion, diced

2 garlic cloves, minced

1 lb Italian sausages, chopped

4 oz bacon, chopped

2 potatoes, sliced

14 oz can cannellini beans

1 red pepper, crushed

4 cups chicken broth

Salt and pepper to taste

1 tsp Italian seasoning

2 cups kale, chopped

½ cup grated Parmesan

Warm the olive oil in your Instant Pot on Sauté. Add in onion, garlic, bacon, and Italian sausages and cook for 4-5 minutes. Stir in potatoes, cannellini beans, Italian seasoning, chicken broth, and red pepper and seal the lid. Select Manual and cook for 20 minutes on High pressure. Once done, perform a quick pressure release and unlock the lid. Stir in kale and simmer for 3-4 minutes on Sauté. Adjust the seasoning and top with Parmesan to serve.

## Moroccan Lentil Soup

Serving Size: 4 | Total Time: 30 minutes

2 tsp olive oil

2 garlic cloves, minced

1 onion, chopped

1 cup red lentils

2 tbsp tomato purée

1 potato, chopped

1 carrot, chopped

½ cup celery

½ tsp ground coriander

½ tsp ground cumin

½ tsp cinnamon

1 red chili pepper, chopped

4 cups water

Salt and pepper to taste

2 tbsp fresh mint, chopped

Warm olive oil in your Instant Pot on Sauté. Add in garlic, celery, carrot, and onion and cook for 3 minutes. Stir in chili pepper, tomato puree, ground coriander, cumin, salt, pepper, and cinnamon and cook for 1 minute. Pour in lentils, potato, and 4 cups of water and stir.

Seal the lid, select Manual, and cook for 10 minutes on High pressure. When done, allow a natural release for 10 minutes and unlock the lid. Sprinkle with mint and serve.

## Green Soup

Serving Size: 4 | Total Time: 20 minutes

2 tbsp olive oil

1 onion, chopped

1 celery rib, chopped

10 oz broccoli florets

2 cups kale

4 cups chicken broth

Salt and pepper to taste

2 tbsp peanut butter

¼ cup heavy cream

Warm the olive oil in your Instant Pot on Sauté. Place the onion and cook for 3 minutes until translucent. Add in celery and broccoli and cook for another 2 minutes. Pour in chicken broth and kale and seal the lid. Select Manual and cook for 5 minutes on High pressure. Once done, perform a quick pressure release and unlock the lid. Let chill, then blend it. Stir in peanut butter and heavy cream and adjust the seasonings. Serve right away.

## Harvest Vegetable Soup with Pesto

Serving Size: 6 | Total Time: 30 minutes

10 oz spinach

½ cup canned white beans

2 tbsp olive oil

1 onion, chopped

2 garlic cloves, minced

1 carrot, chopped

1 celery stalk, chopped

1 can crushed tomatoes

2 tbsp parsley

6 cups chicken bone broth

Salt and pepper to taste

2 tbsp pesto

Warm the olive oil in your Instant Pot on Sauté. Add in onion, garlic, carrot, and celery and cook for 3 minutes until tender. Pour in chicken broth, white beans, parsley, and tomatoes and seal the lid. Select Manual and cook for 10 minutes on High pressure.

When done, allow a natural release for 10 minutes and unlock the lid. Stir in spinach, seal the lid, and let sit in the residual heat until the spinach wilts. Adjust the seasonings and top with pesto. Serve immediately.

## Mediterranean Soup with Tortellini

Serving Size: 4 | Total Time: 40 minutes

1 cup cream of mushroom soup

½ cup mushrooms, chopped

9 oz refrigerated tortellini

1 cup green peas

2 carrots, chopped

2 tbsp olive oil

2 shallots, chopped

2 garlic cloves, minced

½ tsp oregano

3 cups vegetable broth

Salt and pepper to taste

2 tbsp Parmesan, shredded

Heat the olive oil in your Instant Pot on Sauté. Add in shallots and garlic and cook for 3 minutes until translucent. Add in the carrots and mushrooms and continue sautéing for 3-4 minutes. Pour in broth, mushroom soup, and oregano, and tomatoes and seal the lid. Select Manual and cook for 7 minutes on High.

Once over, allow a natural release for 10 minutes, then perform a quick pressure release and unlock the lid. Stir in green peas and tortellini and cook for 3-5 minutes on Sauté. Sprinkle with Parmesan cheese and serve.

## Creamed Butternut Squash Soup

Serving Size: 4 | Total Time: 30 minutes

1 lb butternut squash, cut into chunks

1 tbsp pumpkin seeds, toasted

2 tbsp grapeseed oil

1 onion, chopped

1 turnip, diced

½ tsp nutmeg

½ tsp ground cinnamon

4 cups vegetable stock

1 cup heavy cream

Salt and pepper to taste

Heat the grapeseed oil in your Instant Pot on Sauté. Add in onion and cook for 3 minutes until softened. Stir in vegetable stock, butternut squash, turnip, nutmeg, and cinnamon and seal the lid. Select Manual and cook for 10 minutes on High pressure.

When over, allow a natural release for 10 minutes and unlock the lid. Blend the soup using an immersion blender and stir in heavy cream; adjust the seasonings. Sprinkle with pumpkin seeds and serve immediately.

# French Onion Soup

Serving Size: 4 | Total Time: 45 minutes

1 cup cream of mushroom soup

2 tbsp olive oil

2 tbsp butter

2 lb onions, chopped

2 sprigs fresh thyme

½ cup Gruyere, grated

4 cups chicken stock

Salt and pepper to taste

1 baguette, sliced

1 tbsp chives, chopped

Heat butter and olive oil in your Instant Pot on Sauté. Add in onion and cook for 10 minutes, stirring occasionally until caramelized. Pour in the chicken stock, thyme, mushroom soup, salt, and pepper and seal the lid. Select Manual and cook for 10 minutes on High. When ready, allow a natural release for 10 minutes. Discard the thyme sprigs.

Divide the soup between four oven-safe bowls and top each one with bread slices and cheese. Cook under the broiler for 4-5 minutes until the cheese has melted and bubbly. Serve topped with chives.

# Peasant Bean Soup

Serving Size: 6 | Total Time: 45 minutes

1 cup cipollini onions, chopped

2 tbsp olive oil

1 garlic clove, minced

1 chopped celery rib

1 cup chopped carrots

1 cup ham, chopped

1 cup great northern beans

1 potato, peeled, diced

1 cup stewed tomatoes, diced

5 cups vegetable broth

Salt and pepper to taste

2 tbsp parsley, chopped

Warm the olive oil in your Instant Pot on Sauté. Place the garlic, cipollini onions, celery, and carrots and cook for 5 minutes. Pour in vegetable broth, tomatoes, ham, great northern beans, and potato and stir. Seal the lid,

select Manual, and cook for 20 minutes on High pressure. When ready, allow a natural release for 10 minutes. Adjust the seasoning. Serve topped with parsley.

# Pea & Garbanzo Bean Soup

Serving Size: 4 | Total Time: 30 minutes

2 tbsp olive oil

½ cup shallots, sliced

14 oz can garbanzo beans

½ cup green peas

2 Roma chopped tomatoes

4 cups vegetable broth

Salt and pepper to taste

1 lemon, zested and juiced

Warm the olive oil in your Instant Pot on Sauté. Add in shallots and cook for 3 minutes until tender and fragrant. Pour in vegetable broth, tomatoes, lemon zest, and garbanzo beans and stir.

Seal the lid, select Manual, and cook for 10 minutes on High pressure. Once over, allow a natural release for 10 minutes, then perform a quick pressure release and unlock the lid. Stir in green peas and let it sit covered in the residual heat until warmed through. Season with salt and pepper and drizzle with lemon juice. Serve.

# Cauliflower Cheese Soup

Serving Size: 4 | Total Time: 30 minutes

2 tbsp butter

1 onion, diced

2 garlic cloves, minced

2 russet potatoes, chopped

5 oz cauliflower florets

4 cups vegetable broth

1 cup heavy cream

1 tsp mustard powder

1 cup cheddar, shredded

1 green onion, chopped

Salt and pepper to taste

Melt the butter in your Instant Pot on Sauté. Add in onion and garlic and cook for 2-3 minutes until lightly golden. Add in potato, cauliflower, mustard powder, vegetable broth, and give it a good stir.

Seal the lid, select Manual, and cook for 8 minutes on High. Once over, allow a natural release for 10 minutes and unlock the lid. Stir in heavy cream and half of the cheddar cheese and whizz until smooth, using a stick blender. Adjust the seasoning. Scatter the remaining cheddar on top and sprinkle with green onion to serve.

## Minestrone with Fresh Herbs

Serving Size: 4 | Total Time: 25 minutes

2 tbsp olive oil
1 large onion, diced
3 garlic cloves, minced
2 celery stalks, diced
1 carrot, diced
2 tsp basil, chopped
1 tsp oregano, chopped
1 tsp rosemary, chopped
Salt and pepper to taste
14 oz can tomatoes, diced
5 curly kale, chopped
½ cup elbow macaroni
4 cups vegetable broth
14 oz can cannellini beans

Warm the olive oil in your Instant Pot on Sauté. Add in onion, garlic, celery, and carrot and cook for 5 minutes until tender. Stir in basil, oregano, rosemary, tomatoes, elbow macaroni, cannellini beans, and vegetable broth.

Seal the lid, select Manual, and cook for 6 minutes on High. Once done, perform a quick pressure release. Unlock the lid. Stir in kale and press Sauté. Cook for 4-5 minutes until it's wilted. Taste and adjust the seasoning.

## Spicy Pumpkin Soup

Serving Size: 4 | Total Time: 25 minutes

2 tbsp butter
1 Vidalia onion, chopped
2 garlic cloves, chopped
2 carrots, diced
1 lb pumpkin, peeled, diced
½ tsp thyme
1 tsp cumin seeds
1 tbsp hot curry paste
4 cups vegetable broth
Salt and pepper to taste
1 cup heavy cream

2 tbsp cilantro, chopped

Melt the butter in your Instant Pot on Sauté. Add in onion, garlic, carrots, salt, and pepper and cook for 3 minutes. Stir in cumin seeds, thyme, hot curry paste, and pumpkin for 2 minutes and pour in vegetable broth.

Seal the lid, select Manual, and cook for 10 minutes on High. When ready, perform a quick pressure release. Blend the soup using an immersion blender and stir in heavy cream. Top with cilantro to serve.

## Corn Soup with Chicken & Egg

Serving Size: 2 | Total Time: 25 minutes

1 tbsp cilantro, chopped
1 egg
½ lb chicken breasts
1 leek, chopped
1 tbsp sliced shallots
¼ tsp nutmeg
2 cups water
¼ cup corn kernels
¼ cup diced carrots
Salt and pepper to taste

Slice the chicken breasts into small cubes and place them in your Instant Pot. Add in corn kernels, water, shallots, salt, nutmeg, and black pepper. Seal the lid, select Pressure Cook, and cook for 15 minutes on High.

When done, allow a natural release and unlock the lid. Mix in carrots and leek and bring to a boil on Sauté. Beat the egg in a bowl. Once the Soup boil, pour in the beaten egg and toss until well combined and done. Divide between bowls, sprinkle with cilantro, and serve.

# Mustard Carrot Soup

Serving Size: 4 | Total Time: 25 minutes

1 green bell pepper, diced

¼ cup butter

1 lb quartered carrots

3 cups chicken stock

1 tsp paprika

1 tsp ground cumin

2 tsp minced garlic

2 tbsp Dijon mustard

Salt and pepper to taste

Pour 1 cup of water into your Instant Pot; fit in a trivet. Place the carrots on the trivet and seal the lid. Select Manual and cook for 1 minute on High. When done, perform a quick pressure release; unlock the lid. Remove the carrots and pat dry the pot with a paper towel.

Melt butter in your Instant Pot on Sauté. Place the chicken stock, paprika, bell pepper, cumin, garlic, mustard, salt, black pepper, and cooked carrots. Seal the lid, select Manual, and cook for 4 minutes on High pressure.

When done, allow a natural release for 10 minutes and unlock the lid. Using an immersion blender, blend the soup until smooth and creamy. Serve right away.

# Easy Veggie Soup

Serving Size: 4 | Total Time: 35 minutes

1 cup okra, trimmed

1 Carrot, sliced

1 cup Broccoli florets

1 green Bell Pepper, sliced

1 red Bell Pepper, sliced

1 Onion, sliced

2 cups vegetable broth

1 tbsp Lemon juice

4 Garlic cloves, minced

Salt and pepper to taste

2 tbsp Olive oil

Warm olive oil in your Instant Pot on Sauté. Place the onion and garlic and cook for 1 minute. Add in carrot, okra, broccoli florets, green bell pepper, and red bell pepper and cook for 5-10 minutes.

Stir in vegetable broth, salt, and black pepper and seal the lid. Select Meat/Stew and cook for 15 minutes on High pressure. When done, perform a quick pressure release and unlock the lid. Sprinkle with lemon juice and divide between bowls before serving.

# Cheesy & Creamy Broccoli Soup

Serving Size: 4 | Total Time: 25 minutes

1 ½ cups grated Cheddar Cheese + extra for topping

2 tbsp cilantro, chopped

1 lb chopped Broccoli

3 cups Heavy Cream

3 cups Chicken Broth

4 tbsp Butter

4 tbsp Almond flour

1 red onion, chopped

3 garlic cloves, minced

1 tsp Italian Seasoning

Salt and pepper to taste

4 oz Cream Cheese

Melt butter in your Instant Pot on Sauté. Place the almond flour and stir until it clumps up. Slowly pour in heavy cream and stir until it gets a sauce. Remove to a bowl. Put the onions, garlic, chicken broth, broccoli, Italian seasoning, and cream cheese in the pot and stir.

Seal the lid, select Soup, and cook for 15 minutes on High pressure. When done, perform a quick pressure release and unlock the lid. Mix in butter sauce and cheddar cheese until the cheese melts. Divide between bowls and top with cheddar cheese. Serve topped with cilantro.

# Gingery Carrot Soup

Serving Size: 2 | Total Time: 30 minutes

½ tsp red pepper flakes

2 cups chicken broth

½ lb carrots, chopped

½ tbsp Sriracha sauce

1 cup canned coconut milk

1 tbsp cilantro, chopped

1 tbsp unsalted butter
½ tsp fresh ginger, minced
1 garlic clove, minced
1 small onion, chopped

Place the butter and onion in your Instant Pot and cook for 2-3 minutes until soft on Sauté. Add in ginger and garlic and cook for 1 minute. Stir in carrots and cook for 2 minutes. Mix in coconut milk, chicken broth, red pepper flakes, and Sriracha and seal the lid.

Select Manual and cook for 6 minutes on High. When done, allow a natural release for 10 minutes; unlock the lid. Using an immersion blender, pulse the soup until purée. Serve topped with cilantro. Enjoy!

## Carrot & Cabbage Soup

Serving Size: 4 | Total Time: 25 minutes
1 cup canned white beans
14 oz can diced tomatoes
1 head cabbage, chopped
3 tbsp Apple cider vinegar
4 minced garlic cloves
4 cup chicken broth
1 chopped celery stalk
3 chopped carrots
1 tbsp lemon juice
1 chopped onion

Place the chopped tomatoes, cabbage, apple cider vinegar, garlic, chicken broth, celery, carrots, lemon juice, and onion in your Instant Pot. Seal the lid, select Manual, and cook for 15 minutes on High pressure. When done, perform a quick pressure release and unlock the lid. Mix in white beans and cook for 2 minutes on Sauté. Serve.

## Scallion Chicken & Lentil Soup

Serving Size: 4 | Total Time: 45 minutes
4 garlic cloves, sliced
6 oz skinless chicken thighs
½ lb dried lentils
½ chopped onion
4 cups water
¼ tsp paprika
½ tsp garlic powder

1 diced tomato
2 tbsp chopped cilantro
¼ tsp oregano
½ tsp cumin
1 chopped scallion
¼ tsp salt

Place the chicken thighs, dried lentils, onion, water, paprika, garlic powder, sliced garlic, tomato, cilantro, oregano, cumin, scallion, and salt in your Instant Pot. Seal the lid, select Soup, and cook for 30 minutes. When done, allow a natural release for 10 minutes and unlock the lid. Using a fork, shred the chicken before serving.

## Tomato Shrimp Soup

Serving Size: 4 | Total Time: 40 minutes
½ cup coconut Cream
2 Tomatoes, sliced
2 oz Shrimp
4 cups Chicken broth
¼ cup Apple Cider Vinegar
2 Garlic cloves, minced
Salt and pepper to taste
1 tbsp Olive oil

Warm olive oil in your Instant Pot on Sauté. Place the garlic and cook for 1 minute. Add in shrimp and cook for 10 minutes. Stir in salt, black pepper, chicken broth, tomatoes, and apple cider vinegar.

Seal the lid, select Manual, and cook for 10 minutes on High pressure. When done, allow a natural release for 10 minutes and unlock the lid. Divide between 4 bowls and top each with coconut cream. Serve warm.

## Mustard Potato Soup with Crispy Bacon

Serving Size: 4 | Total Time: 30 minutes
2 Yukon gold potatoes, chopped
2 tbsp olive oil
2 garlic cloves, minced
1 leek, diced
1 tbsp onion powder
1 green bell pepper, diced
4 cups chicken stock
Salt and pepper to taste

1 tbsp Dijon mustard

4 dashes hot pepper sauce

4 oz bacon, chopped

2 cups shredded mozzarella

1 cup milk

Warm olive oil in your Instant Pot on Sauté and cook the bacon for 5 minutes until crispy; set aside. Place garlic and leek in the pot and sauté for 3 minutes. Add in onion powder, potatoes, bell pepper, stock, salt, and pepper. Seal the lid, select Manual, and cook for 15 minutes.

When done, perform a quick pressure release. Mix in Dijon mustard, hot sauce, mozzarella cheese, and milk until thoroughly heated. Top with bacon and serve.

## Curried Pumpkin Soup

Serving Size: 4 | Total Time: 20 minutes

1 tsp chili powder

2 tbsp Pumpkin seeds

2 tbsp Olive oil

1 onion, chopped

1 Carrot, chopped

2 garlic cloves, minced

2 tsp Curry powder

4 cups vegetable broth

Warm olive oil in your Instant Pot on Sauté. Place the onion and garlic and cook for 3 minutes until tender. Add in vegetable broth, pumpkin seeds, chili powder, curry powder, and carrots. Seal the lid, select Manual, and cook for 10 minutes on High. When done, allow a natural release for 10 minutes. Serve.

## Nutmeg Broccoli Soup with Cheddar

Serving Size: 4 | Total Time: 25 minutes

2 garlic cloves, minced

1 tbsp butter

½ lb broccoli florets

¼ tsp nutmeg

½ tsp garlic powder

1 cup vegetable broth

¼ cup grated cheddar

¼ cup chopped onion

¼ tsp paprika

Salt and pepper to taste

Melt butter in your Instant Pot on Sauté. Place the onion and garlic and cook until wilted and aromatic. Put in vegetable broth, broccoli, black pepper, paprika, salt, nutmeg, and garlic powder. Seal the lid, select Manual, and cook for 5 minutes on High pressure.

When done, allow a natural release for 10 minutes and unlock the lid. Using an immersion blender, pulse the soup until smooth. Divide between bowls and serve.

## Kielbasa Sausage Soup

Serving Size: 4 | Total Time: 60 minutes

12 oz Kielbasa smoked sausage, sliced

2 tbsp olive oil

1 yellow onion, chopped

1 celery stalk, chopped

1 carrot, chopped

2 tbsp parsley, chopped

3 garlic cloves, pressed

1 ripe tomato, pureed

1 cup pinto beans, soaked

Salt and pepper to taste

6 oz baby kale

Warm the olive oil in your Instant Pot on Sauté. Add in onion, garlic, celery, and carrot and cook for 4 minutes. Stir in smoked sausage for another 2 minutes and pour in pinto beans, salt, pepper, and 4 cups of water. Seal the lid, select Manual, and cook for 30 minutes on High.

When over, allow a natural release for 10 minutes and unlock the lid. Stir in baby kale and tomato and let it sit covered for 5 minutes. Serve sprinkled with parsley.

## Chorizo & Bean Soup

Serving Size: 6 | Total Time: 55 minutes

2 tbsp olive oil

¾ lb chorizo sausage, sliced

1 cup white beans, soaked

1 sweet pepper, sliced

14 oz can diced tomatoes

1 clove garlic, minced

1 onion, diced

½ tsp dried oregano

1 tsp chili powder

6 cups chicken broth

Warm the olive oil in your Instant Pot on Sauté. Add in onion, garlic, chorizo, sweet pepper, chili powder, and oregano and cook for 4-5 minutes. Stir in chicken broth, tomatoes, and white bean and seal the lid. Select Manual and cook for 30 minutes. Once ready, perform a quick pressure release and let sit for 10 minutes. Serve warm.

## Beet & Potato Soup

Serving Size: 4 | Total Time: 45 minutes

2 tbsp olive oil

2 garlic cloves, minced

1 carrot, chopped

3 potatoes, chopped

¾ lb beets, peeled, chopped

4 cups vegetable broth

1 onion, chopped

Salt and pepper to taste

¼ cup basil leaves, chopped

Heat the olive oil in your Instant Pot on Sauté. Place the onion, carrot, and garlic paste and cook for 3 minutes. Stir in vegetable broth, beets, and potatoes and seal the lid. Select Manual and cook for 25 minutes.

Once ready, allow a natural release for 10 minutes, then perform a quick pressure release and unlock the lid. Blend the soup using an immersion blender and adjust the seasoning. Serve topped with basil.

## Vegan Tomato Soup

Serving Size: 4 | Total Time: 20 minutes

2 tbsp olive oil

2 (14-oz) cans tomatoes

1 tsp caraway seeds

1 cup vegetable broth

½ tsp thyme

1 large onion, diced

2 garlic cloves, sliced

Salt and pepper to taste

¾ cup almond milk

Warm the olive oil in your Instant Pot on Sauté. Add in onion, and garlic and cook for 5-6 minutes until lightly golden. Stir in caraway seeds for 1 minute and pour in tomatoes, thyme, and vegetable broth.

Seal the lid, select Manual, and cook for 8 minutes on High. Once ready, perform a quick pressure release and unlock the lid. Stir in almond milk and adjust the seasonings. Purée the soup with an immersion blender.

## Asian Tomato Soup

Serving Size: 8 | Total Time: 20 minutes

2 tbsp coconut oil

1 onion, diced

1 tbsp garlic-ginger puree

3 lb tomatoes, quartered

½ tsp ground cumin

1 tsp red pepper flakes

Pink salt to taste

3 ½ cups vegetable broth

1 cup coconut cream

2 tbsp cilantro, chopped

Heat the coconut oil in your Instant Pot on Sauté. Place the onion and garlic-ginger paste and cook for 3 minutes. Stir in tomatoes and cumin and Sauté for 3 more minutes.

Pour in the broth and salt and seal the lid. Select Manual and cook for 6 minutes. When done, perform a quick pressure release. Mix in coconut cream. Puree the soup with a stick blender until smooth. Serve topped with red pepper flakes and cilantro.

## Tangy Pumpkin Soup

Serving Size: 4 | Total Time: 30 minutes

2 tbsp sesame oil

1 yellow onion, chopped

2 garlic cloves, minced

½ tbsp ginger, grated

1 lb pumpkin, cubed

Salt to taste

1 tbsp curry powder

1 tsp cayenne pepper

½ cup coconut milk

2 tbsp cilantro, chopped

Warm the sesame oil in your Instant Pot on Sauté. Add in onion and cook for 5 minutes. Stir in garlic and ginger and Sauté for 1 more minute. Stir in pumpkin, cayenne pepper, salt, and curry powder and 4 cups of water and seal the lid. Select Manual and cook for 20 minutes. Once ready, perform a quick pressure release and unlock the lid. Blend the soup using a stick blender and mix in coconut milk. Garnish with cilantro and serve.

## Chicken Soup with Vegetables

Serving Size: 4 | Total Time: 35 minutes

½ lb chicken breasts, cubed
1 beet, chopped
1 carrot, diced
½ celery, diced
1 onion, chopped
1 cup mushrooms, sliced
5 cups chicken stock
2 garlic cloves, chopped
1 tsp thyme
1 tsp rosemary
2 bay leaves
2 tbsp olive oil
Salt and pepper to taste

Warm olive oil in your Instant Pot on Sauté. Place the carrots, beet, and onion and cook for 2-3 minutes. Add in garlic, celery, and mushrooms and cook for 3 minutes. Put in chicken breasts, chicken stock, thyme, rosemary, bay leaves, salt, and. black pepper. Seal the lid, select Soup, and cook on Low pressure for 20 minutes. When done, perform a quick pressure release. Serve warm.

## Celery & Oxtail Soup

Serving Size: 4 | Total Time: 30 minutes

4 cups vegetable broth
2 tbsp chopped' carrots
1 lb oxtails
1 tbsp chopped' celeries
¼ tsp nutmeg
Salt and pepper to taste

Place the oxtails, nutmeg, salt, and black pepper in your Instant Pot. Pour in vegetable broth and seal the lid. Select Pressure Cook and cook for 20 minutes on High. When done, perform a quick pressure release and unlock the lid. Stir in chopped carrots and celeries and cook for 3 minutes until the carrots are tender on Sauté. Divide between bowls and serve.

# STEWS

## Pea & Beef Stew

Serving Size: 6 | Total Time: 35 minutes

1 cup mixed wild mushrooms

1 cup green peas

1 cup diced potatoes

1 lb cubed beef

3 sliced carrots

1 tsp red pepper flakes

2 sliced garlic cloves

½ cup dry red wine

2 tbsp butter

1 diced onion

2 cups beef broth

14 oz can diced tomatoes

Melt the butter in your Instant Pot on Sauté. Place the onion and cook for 3 minutes until soft. Add in beef cubes and cook for 5-7 minutes until the meat browns. Add in garlic and cook for 1 minute until fragrant. Pour in red wine and scrape any brown bits from the bottom. Put in potatoes, carrots, red pepper flakes, mushrooms, beef broth, diced tomatoes, and green peas. Seal the lid, select Manual, and cook for 15 minutes on High pressure. When done, perform a quick pressure release and unlock the lid. Serve immediately.

## Cauliflower Beef Stew

Serving Size: 4 | Total Time: 60 minutes

½ head cauliflower, chopped

1 lb Beef stew meat

1 large quartered Onion

½ cup Beef or Bone broth

¼ cup Coconut aminos

2 tbsp Fish sauce

2 Garlic cloves, minced

1 tsp ground Ginger

½ tsp Salt

1 tbsp Coconut oil

Place the beef meat, onion, beef broth, coconut aminos, fish sauce, garlic, ginger, salt, and coconut oil in your Instant Pot. Seal the lid, select Manual, and cook for 35 minutes on High pressure. When done, perform a quick pressure release and unlock the lid. Put in cauliflower and simmer covered for 15 minutes on Sauté. Serve.

## Rosemary Pork Belly Stew

Serving Size: 6 | Total Time: 50 minutes

3 lb sirloin pork roast

1 tbsp honey

1 tsp chili powder

1 tbsp rosemary

1 tbsp olive oil

Salt and pepper to taste

Combine chili powder, rosemary, salt, and pepper in a bowl and rub them onto the pork. Heat oil on Sauté and sear the pork on all sides. Stir in honey and seal the lid. Cook for 30 minutes on Meat/Stew. Do a natural pressure release for 10 minutes. Carefully unlock the lid.

## Seafood Stew with Sausage

Serving Size: 4 | Total Time: 35 minutes

1 lb Andouille Sausages, sliced

1 lb halibut fillets, skinless and cut into 1-inch pieces

2 lb Mussels, debearded and scrubbed

1 lb Shrimp, peeled and deveined

1 tsp turmeric

2 (16 oz) cans Clam Juice

1 cup White Wine

Salt and pepper to taste

4 tbsp Olive oil

4 garlic cloves, minced

2 Fennel Bulb, chopped

4 Leeks, sliced

2 Bay Leaves

28 oz can Diced Tomatoes

2 tbsp chopped Parsley

Warm olive oil in your Instant Pot on Sauté. Place sausage, fennel, and leeks and cook for 5 minutes. Stir in garlic, turmeric, and bay leaves and cook for 30 seconds. Pour in white wine and cook for 2 minutes. Add in tomatoes, clam juice, and 3 cups of water; stir. Put in mussels, fish, and shrimp and slightly cover them with the sauce.

Seal the lid, select Meat/Stew, and cook for 15 minutes on High pressure. When done, perform a quick pressure release and unlock the lid. Discard bay leaves and sprinkle with parsley, salt, and black pepper. Serve right away.

## Mushroom & Spinach Chicken Stew

Serving Size: 4 | Total Time: 40 minutes

1 ¼ lb White Button Mushrooms, halved

1 celery stalk, chopped

3 tbsp Olive oil

4 Chicken Breasts, diced

1 Onion, sliced

5 garlic cloves, minced

Salt and pepper to taste

1 ¼ tsp Arrowroot Starch

½ cup spinach, chopped

1 bay leaf

1 ½ cup Chicken Stock

1 tsp Dijon Mustard

1 ½ cup Sour Cream

3 tbsp Chopped Parsley

Warm olive oil in your Instant Pot on Sauté. Place the onion and cook for 3 minutes. Stir in mushrooms, chicken, celery, garlic, bay leaf, salt, black pepper, Dijon mustard, and chicken broth. Seal the lid, select Meat/Stew, and cook for 15 minutes on High. When done, allow a natural release for 10 minutes and unlock the lid.

Discard bay leaf. In a bowl, combine some cooking liquid with arrowroot starch until any lump left. Pour it into the pot and stir until the sauce thickens. Add in sour cream and spinach and let sit for 4 minutes. Divide between bowls and sprinkle with parsley. Serve with squash mash.

## Green Pork Chili

Serving Size: 4 | Total Time: 90 minutes

1 lb Tomatillos, husks removed

1 tsp ground nutmeg

2 Green Chilies

1 onion, sliced

1 ½ lb Pork Roast, cubed

2 tbsp Olive oil, divided into

1 bulb Garlic, tail sliced off

½ cup Chicken Broth

1 Green Bell pepper, diced

Salt and pepper to taste

½ tsp Cumin Powder

1 tsp dried Oregano

1 Bay Leaf

2 tbsp Cilantro, chopped

Preheat oven to 360°F. Place the garlic bulb, green bell peppers, onion, green chilies, and tomatillos on a baking tray and sprinkle with olive oil. Place the tray in the oven and roast for 25 minutes. Let cool the garlic before peeling. Place it in a blender with bell peppers, tomatillos, onion, and green chilies and pulse until slightly chunky.

Warm olive oil in your Instant Pot on Sauté. Sprinkle pork with salt and pepper and place it in the pot. Cook for 5 minutes until brown. Stir in oregano, nutmeg, cumin, bay leaf, green sauce, and broth. Seal the lid, select Manual, and cook for 35 minutes on High. When done, let sit for 10 minutes and allow a natural release for 5 minutes Stir in salt and pepper. Top with cilantro. Serve immediately.

## Cheesy Turkey Stew

Serving Size: 4 | Total Time: 20 minutes

1 tbsp soy Sauce

1 lb Turkey Breast

1 ½ cups Chicken Broth

1 cup Sour Cream

¼ cup grated Parmesan

1 tsp Dijon Mustard

¼ tsp Garlic Powder

Salt and pepper to taste

Place the turkey breast and chicken broth in your Instant Pot. Seal the lid, select Manual, and cook for 10 minutes on High pressure. When done, perform a quick pressure release. Transfer the turkey onto a cutting board and cut it into cubes. Discard the broth and wipe the pot out.

Mix in soy sauce, sour cream, Parmesan cheese, Dijon mustard, garlic powder, salt, black pepper, and cubed chicken and cook for 2 minutes on Sauté. Serve.

## Chicken Stew with Potatoes & Broccoli

Serving Size: 4 | Total Time: 25 minutes

1 lb potatoes, chopped

2 tbsp Butter

3 Chicken Breasts, cubed

2 Onions, chopped

2 cups Chicken Broth

Salt and pepper to taste

¼ tsp Red Chili Flakes

2 tbsp Dried Parsley

10 oz broccoli florets

1 cup cheddar cheese, grated

Sprinkle chicken breast with salt and pepper. Melt butter in your Instant Pot on Sauté. Place the chicken and cook for 8 minutes on both sides until browns. Add in onion and cook for 5 minutes, stirring often.

Put chicken broth, black pepper, salt, red pepper flakes, potatoes, chicken, and parsley and seal the lid. Select Manual and cook for 4 minutes on High pressure.

When done, perform a quick pressure release and unlock the lid. Min in broccoli and cook until tender on Sauté. Serve right away topped with cheddar cheese.

## Taco-Style Chicken Stew

Serving Size: 4 | Total Time: 25 minutes

2 tbsp butter

1 lb Chicken Breasts

1 Carrot, chopped

1 Celery stalk, chopped

1 Onion, chopped

3 garlic cloves, minced

3 tbsp Taco Seasoning

Salt and pepper to taste

1 ½ cups Diced Tomatoes

1 lb cubed Butternut Squash

2 cups Chicken Broth

1 tsp Lime Juice

4 Lime Wedges

2 tbsp Chopped Cilantro

Melt butter in your Instant Pot on Sauté. Place the celery, onion, carrots, garlic, taco seasoning, black pepper, and salt and cook for 5 minutes, stirring often. Mix in chicken breast, tomatoes, butternut squash, broth, and lime juice. Seal the lid, select Soup and cook for 10 minutes.

When done, perform a quick pressure release. Transfer the chicken onto a cutting board and shred it. Put the chicken back in the pot and divide between bowls. Serve topped with cilantro and lime wedges.

## One-Pot Sausages with Peppers & Onions

Serving Size: 4 | Total Time: 20 minutes

2 red bell peppers, cut into strips

4 pork sausages

1 sweet onion, sliced

1 tbsp olive oil

½ cup beef broth

¼ cup white wine

1 tsp garlic, minced

Salt and pepper to taste

On Sauté, add the sausages and brown them for a few minutes. Remove to a plate and discard the liquid. Press Cancel. Wipe clean the cooker and heat the oil on Sauté. Stir in onion and bell peppers. Stir-fry them for 5 minutes until soft. Add garlic and cook for a minute. Add the sausages and pour in broth and wine. Season with salt and pepper. Seal the lid and cook for 5 minutes on High pressure. Once done, do a quick pressure release. Serve.

## Cheesy Duck & Spinach Stew

Serving Size: 4 | Total Time: 25 minutes

1 onion, chopped

2 cups Spinach

1 lb Duck Breasts

¼ cup grated Parmesan

1 cup Heavy Cream

8 oz Cream Cheese

¼ cup Chicken Broth

1 tbsp Olive oil

1 tsp minced Garlic

Salt and pepper to taste

Warm olive oil in your Instant Pot on Sauté. Place the garlic and onion and cook for 1 minute. Add in duck breasts and cook for 6-8 minutes on both sides until golden brown. Remove to a plate and slice thinly. Mix the spinach, Parmesan cheese, heavy cream, cream cheese, broth, garlic, salt, and pepper in the pot and top with the sliced duck. Seal the lid, select Manual, and cook for 5 minutes on High pressure. When done, perform a quick pressure release and unlock the lid. Serve warm.

## Sausage & Cannellini Bean Stew

Serving Size: 6 | Total Time: 35 minutes

1 cup cannellini beans

2 tbsp olive oil

1 lb Italian sausages, halved

1 celery stalk, chopped

1 carrot, chopped

1 onion, chopped

1 sprig fresh sage

1 sprig fresh rosemary

1 bay leaf

2 cups vegetable stock

3 cups fresh spinach

1 tsp salt

Warm oil on Sauté in your Instant pot. Add in sausage pieces and sear for 5 minutes until browned; set aside on a plate. To the pot, add celery, onion, bay leaf, sage, carrot, salt, and rosemary; cook for 3 minutes to soften slightly. Stir in vegetable stock and beans. Arrange seared sausage on top of the beans. Seal the lid, press Bean/Chili, and cook on High for 10 minutes. Release pressure naturally for 10 minutes. Get rid of bay leaf, rosemary, and sage. Mix in spinach and serve.

## Tuscan Chicken Thighs

Serving Size: 4 | Total Time: 35 minutes

3 cups kale

6 Chicken Thighs

6 oz Cream Cheese

½ cup Sundried Tomatoes

2 tbsp Chicken Seasoning

½ cup Parmesan, grated

4 garlic cloves, minced

2 tsp Olive oil

2 cups Chicken Broth

1 ½ cups Milk

3 tbsp Heavy Cream

3 tsp Italian Seasoning

Salt and pepper to taste

2 tbsp chopped parsley

Sprinkle chicken thighs with salt, black pepper, and Italian seasoning. Warm olive oil in your Instant Pot on Sauté. Place the chicken and cook for 6 minutes. Add in milk, chicken stock, and chicken seasoning. Seal the lid, select Manual, and cook for 15 minutes on High.

When done, perform a quick pressure release. Remove the chicken to a plate. Put the tomatoes, heavy cream, cheese cream, Parmesan, kale, and garlic in the pot and cook for 5 minutes on Sauté. Put the chicken back to the pot and toss to combine. Serve topped with parsley.

## Spicy Pumpkin Curry

Serving Size: 4 | Total Time: 30 minutes

4 spring onions, chopped into lengths

1 ½ lb pumpkin, chopped

4 cups chicken stock

½ cup buttermilk

2 tbsp curry powder

1 tsp ground turmeric

½ tsp ground cumin

¼ tsp cayenne pepper

2 bay leaves

Salt and pepper to taste

2 tbsp cilantro, chopped

In the pot, stir in pumpkin, buttermilk, curry, turmeric, spring onions, stock, cumin, and cayenne. Season with pepper and salt. Add bay leaves to the liquid and ensure they are submerged. Seal the lid, press Soup/Broth and cook for 10 minutes on High.

Naturally release the pressure for 10 minutes. Discard bay leaves. Transfer the soup to a blender and process until smooth. Use a fine-mesh strainer to strain the soup. Garnish with cilantro before serving.

## Vegetables with Veal & Pork

Serving Size: 4 | Total Time: 25 minutes

12 oz button mushrooms, sliced

1 lb veal cuts, cut into bite-sized pieces

1 lb pork tenderloin, cubed

3 carrots, chopped

2 tbsp butter, softened

2 tbsp olive oil

1 tbsp cayenne pepper

Salt and pepper to taste

3 oz celery root, chopped

Heat the olive oil and butter in the Instant Pot on Sauté. Add in veal, pork, mushrooms, carrots, salt, pepper, cayenne pepper, and celery, and cook for 5 minutes. Stir in 2 cups of water. Seal the lid and cook on High Pressure for 15 minutes. Do a quick release Open the lid and adjust the seasoning. Serve warm.

## Aromatic Lamb Stew

Serving Size: 4 | Total Time: 60 minutes

1 ½ lb lamb stew meat, cubed

2 tbsp olive oil

3 garlic cloves, chopped

1 onion, chopped

3 cups mushrooms, sliced

1 celery stalk, chopped

1 carrot, chopped

28-oz can tomatoes, diced

3 cups chicken broth

½ cup pomegranate juice

½ tsp allspice

1 tsp ground cumin

½ tsp ground bay leaf

½ tsp curry powder

1 tsp ground coriander

Salt and pepper to taste

In a bowl, mix the allspice, ground cumin, ground bay leaf, curry powder, ground coriander, salt, and pepper and add in the lamb; toss to coat. Warm the olive oil in your Instant Pot on Sauté. Add in the lamb and cook for 5-6 minutes until browned. Add in garlic, onion, celery, carrot, and mushrooms and sauté for 5 minutes. Pour in tomatoes, pomegranate juice, and chicken broth.

Seal the lid, select Manual, and cook for 30 minutes on High pressure. When over, allow a natural release for 10 minutes, then perform a quick pressure release. Serve.

# VEGAN & VEGETARIAN

## Mashed Potato Balls with Tomato Sauce

Serving Size: 4 | Total Time: 55 minutes

2 potatoes, peeled
1 onion, peeled, chopped
1 lb spinach, torn
¼ cup mozzarella, shredded
2 eggs, beaten
Salt and pepper to taste
1 tsp dried oregano
1 cup whole milk
¼ cup flour
¼ cup cornflour
2 garlic cloves

TOMATO SAUCE:

1 lb tomatoes, chopped
1 onion, chopped
2 garlic cloves, minced
3 tsp olive oil
¼ cup white wine
1 tsp sugar
1 tsp dried rosemary
½ tsp salt
1 tsp tomato paste

Place the potatoes in your Instant Pot and add enough water to cover. Seal the lid and cook on High Pressure for 13 minutes. Do a quick release. Add 1 cup of milk and mash with a potato masher. Whisk in eggs, add onion, spinach, mozzarella, salt, pepper, oregano, flour, cornflour, and garlic, and mix with hands. Shape into balls and set aside. Press Sauté, warm olive oil, and stir-fry onion and garlic until translucent.

Stir in tomatoes and cook until tender, about 10 minutes. Pour in the wine and add sugar, rosemary, and salt. Stir in 1 tsp of tomato paste and mix well. Cook for five more minutes. Place the potato balls in the cooker and seal with the lid. Cook on High Pressure for 5 minutes. Do a natural release for 10 minutes. Ser

## Weekend Burrito Bowls

Serving Size: 4 | Total Time: 30 minutes

2 tbsp olive oil
1 onion, chopped
2 garlic cloves, minced
1 tbsp chili powder
2 tbsp ground cumin
2 tbsp paprika
Salt and pepper to taste
¼ tbsp cayenne pepper
1 cup quinoa, rinsed
14.5-oz can diced tomatoes
1 (14.5-oz) can black beans
1 ½ cups vegetable stock
1 cup frozen corn kernels
2 tbsp chopped cilantro
2 tbsp cheddar, grated
1 avocado, chopped

Warm oil on Sauté. Add in onion and stir-fry for 3-5 minutes until fragrant. Add garlic and Sauté for 2 more minutes until soft and golden brown. Add in chili powder, paprika, cayenne pepper, salt, cumin, and black pepper and cook for 1 minute until spices are soft. Pour quinoa into onion and spice mixture and stir to coat quinoa thoroughly in spices. Add tomatoes, black beans, vegetable stock, and corn; stir to combine.

Seal the lid and cook for 7 minutes on High Pressure. Release the pressure quickly. Open the lid and let sit for 6 minutes until flavors combine. Use a fork to fluff quinoa and season with pepper and salt. Stir in cilantro and divide into plates. Top with cheese and avocado slices and serve.

## Plant-Based Indian Curry

Serving Size: 4 | Total Time: 20 minutes

1 tsp butter
1 onion, chopped
2 cloves garlic, minced
1 tsp ginger, grated
1 tsp ground cumin
1 tsp red chili powder
1 tsp salt
½ tsp ground turmeric
1 (15-oz) can chickpeas
1 tomato, diced
1/3 cup water
2 lb collard greens, chopped
½ tsp garam masala
1 tsp lemon juice

Melt butter on Sauté. Add in the onion, ginger, cumin, turmeric, red chili powder, garlic, and salt and cook for 30 seconds until crispy. Stir in tomato. Pour in ⅓ cup of water and chickpeas. Seal the lid and cook on High Pressure for 4 minutes. Release the pressure quickly. Press Sauté. Into the chickpea mixture, stir in lemon juice, collard greens, and garam masala until well coated. Cook for 2 to 3 minutes until collard greens wilt on Sauté. Serve over rice or naan.

## Spicy Vegetable Pilaf

Serving Size: 4 | Total Time: 40 minutes

3 tbsp olive oil
1 tbsp ginger, minced
1 cup onion, chopped
1 cup green peas
1 cup carrots, chopped
1 cup mushrooms, chopped
1 cup broccoli, chopped
1 tbsp chili powder
½ tbsp ground cumin
1 tbsp garam masala
½ tbsp turmeric
1 cup basmati rice
2 cups vegetable broth

1 tbsp lemon juice
Salt and pepper to taste

Warm 1 tbsp olive oil on Sauté. Add in onion and ginger and cook for 3 minutes. Stir in broccoli, green peas, mushrooms, and carrots and cook for 5 minutes. Stir in the turmeric, chili powder, garam masala, salt, pepper, and cumin for 1 minute. Add ¼ cup broth and scrape the bottom to get rid of any browned bits. Add the remaining broth and rice. Seal the lid and cook for 20 minutes on High Pressure. Release the pressure quickly. Drizzle with lemon juice and serve.

## Quick Farro with Greens & Pine Nuts

Serving Size: 6 | Total Time: 20 minutes

6 oz spinach, chopped
6 oz collard greens, torn
3 oz Swiss chard, chopped
3 tbsp parsley, chopped
1 leek, chopped
1 ½ cups farro
2 tbsp olive oil
2 ¼ cups vegetable broth
1 tbsp salt
½ cup toasted pine nuts

Add farro and vegetable broth to the Instant Pot. Season with salt and seal the lid. Cook on Manual for 9 minutes on High. Do a quick release and open the lid. Fluff the farro with a fork and set aside. Wipe the pot clean.

Warm the olive oil in the pot on Sauté. Add the leek and stir-fry for 4-5 minutes until slightly caramelized. Add in the spinach, Swiss chard, and salt and sauté for another 4-5 minutes until the greens are wilted. Toss in the farro, sprinkle with pine nuts, and serve.

## Quinoa with Brussels Sprouts & Broccoli

Serving Size: 2 | Total Time: 25 minutes

1 cup quinoa, rinsed
Salt and pepper to taste
1 beet, peeled, cubed
1 cup broccoli florets
1 carrot, chopped
½ lb Brussels sprouts

2 eggs

1 avocado, chopped

¼ cup pesto sauce

Lemon wedges, for serving

In the pot, mix 2 cups of water, salt, quinoa and pepper. Set trivet over quinoa and set steamer basket on top. To the steamer basket, add eggs, Brussels sprouts, broccoli, beet cubes, carrots, pepper, and salt. Seal the lid and cook for 1 minute on High Pressure. Release pressure naturally for 10 minutes. Remove the steamer basket and trivet from the pot and set the eggs in a bowl of ice water. Peel and halve the eggs. Use a fork to fluff the quinoa. Divide quinoa, broccoli, avocado, carrots, beet, Brussels sprouts, eggs between two bowls, and top with a pesto dollop. Serve with lemon wedges.

## Vegetarian Green Dip

Serving Size: 4 | Total Time: 15 minutes

10 oz canned green chiles, drained, liquid reserved

2 cups broccoli florets

1 green bell pepper, diced

¼ cup raw cashews

¼ cup soy sauce

½ tsp sea salt

¼ tsp chili powder

¼ tsp garlic powder

¼ tsp cumin

In the pot, add cashews, broccoli, green bell pepper, and 1 cup water. Seal the lid and cook for 5 minutes on High Pressure. Release the pressure quickly. Carefully unlock the lid. Drain water from the pot. Add reserved liquid from canned green chiles, salt, garlic powder, chili powder, soy sauce, and cumin. Use an immersion blender to blitz the mixture until smooth. Stir in chiles and serve.

## Cauliflower & Potato Curry with Cilantro

Serving Size: 4 | Total Time: 40 minutes

1 tbsp vegetable oil

10 oz cauliflower florets

1 potato, peeled and diced

1 tbsp ghee

2 tbsp cumin seeds

1 onion, minced

4 garlic cloves, minced

1 tomato, chopped

1 jalapeño pepper, minced

1 tbsp curry paste

1 tbsp ground turmeric

½ tsp chili pepper

Salt and pepper to taste

2 tbsp cilantro, chopped

Warm oil on Sauté. Add in potato and cauliflower and cook for 8 to 10 minutes until lightly browned; season with salt. Set the vegetables in a bowl. Add ghee to the pot. Mix in cumin seeds and cook for 10 seconds until they start to pop; add onion and cook for 3 minutes until softened. Mix in garlic and pepper; cook for 30 seconds. Add in tomato, curry paste, chili pepper, jalapeño pepper, and turmeric; cook for 4 to 6 minutes. Return potato and cauliflower to the pot. Stir in 1 cup water. Seal the lid and cook on High Pressure for 4 minutes. Quick-release the pressure. Unlock the lid. Top with cilantro and serve.

## Parmesan Topped Vegetable Mash

Serving Size: 6 | Total Time: 15 minutes

3 lb Yukon gold potatoes, chopped

2 cups cauliflower florets

1 carrot, chopped

1 cup Parmesan, shredded

¼ cup butter, melted

¼ cup milk

1 tsp salt

1 garlic clove, minced

2 tbsp parsley, chopped

Into the pot, add potatoes, cauliflower, carrot and salt; cover with enough water. Seal the lid and cook on High Pressure for 10 minutes. Release the pressure quickly. Drain the vegetables and mash them with a potato masher. Add garlic, butter, and milk. Whisk until well incorporated. Top with Parmesan cheese and parsley.

## Steamed Artichokes with Lime Aioli

Serving Size: 4 | Total Time: 20 minutes

2 large artichokes

2 garlic cloves, smashed

½ cup mayonnaise

Salt and pepper to taste

Juice of 1 lime

Using a serrated knife, trim about 1 inch from the top of the artichokes. Into the pot, add 1 cup of water and set trivet over. Lay the artichokes on the trivet. Seal lid and cook for 14 minutes on High Pressure. Release the pressure quickly. Mix the mayonnaise, garlic, and lime juice. Season with salt and pepper. Serve artichokes on a platter with garlic mayo on the side.

## Buttery Mashed Cauliflower

Serving Size: 4 | Total Time: 15 minutes

2 cups water

1 head cauliflower

1 tbsp butter

Salt and pepper to taste

¼ cup heavy cream

1 tbsp parsley, chopped

Into the pot, add water and set trivet on top. Lay cauliflower head onto the trivet. Seal the lid and cook for 8 minutes on High Pressure. Release the pressure quickly. Remove trivet and drain the liquid from the pot. Take back the cauliflower to the pot. Add heavy cream, butter, salt, and pepper. Use an immersion blender to blend until smooth. Top with parsley and serve.

## Vegetarian Chili with Lentils & Quinoa

Serving Size: 4 | Total Time: 45 minutes

28-oz can diced tomatoes

1 cups cashew, chopped

1 cup onion, chopped

½ cup red lentils

½ cup red quinoa

2 chipotle peppers, minced

2 garlic cloves, minced

1 tsp chili powder

1 tsp salt

1 cup carrots, chopped

1 (15-oz) can black beans

¼ cup parsley, chopped

In the pot, mix tomatoes, onion, chipotle peppers, chil powder, lentils, cashew, carrot, quinoa, garlic, and salt Cover with water. Seal the lid, Press Soup/Stew, and cook for 30 minutes on High Pressure. Release the pressure quickly. Add in black beans. Simmer on Sauté until heated through. Top with parsley and serve.

## Minestrone Soup with Green Vegetables

Serving Size: 4 | Total Time: 15 minutes

2 tbsp olive oil

10 oz broccoli florets

4 celery stalks, chopped

1 leek, chopped thinly

1 zucchini, chopped

1 cup green beans

2 cups vegetable broth

2 cups chopped kale

Add broccoli, leek, beans, zucchini, and celery. Mix in vegetable broth, oil, and enough water to cover. Seal the lid and cook on High Pressure for 4 minutes. Release pressure naturally for 5 minutes, then release the remaining pressure quickly. Stir in kale on Sauté and cook until tender. Serve.

## Homemade Gazpacho Soup

Serving Size: 4 | Total Time: 2 hours 20 minutes

1 lb trimmed carrots

1 lb tomatoes, chopped

1 cucumber, peeled, cubed

¼ cup olive oil

2 tbsp lemon juice

1 red onion, chopped

2 cloves garlic

2 tbsp white wine vinegar

Salt and pepper to taste

Add carrots, salt, and enough water to cover the carrots. Seal the lid and cook for 10 minutes on High Pressure. Do a quick release. In a blender, add carrots, cucumber, red onion, pepper, garlic, oil, tomatoes, lemon juice, vinegar, 4 cups of water, and salt. Blend until very smooth. Place gazpacho into a serving bowl, chill while covered for 2 hours. Serve and enjoy!

## Easy Tahini Sweet Potato Mash

Serving Size: 4 | Total Time: 15 minutes

1 cup water

2 lb sweet potatoes, cubed

2 tbsp tahini

¼ tsp ground nutmeg

2 tbsp chopped chives

Salt and pepper to taste

Into the cooker, add 1 cup water and insert a steamer basket. Put potato cubes into the steamer basket. Seal the lid and cook for 8 minutes at High Pressure. Release the pressure quickly. In a bowl, add cooked sweet potatoes and slightly mash. Using a hand mixer, whip in nutmeg and tahini until the sweet potatoes attain desired consistency. Add salt and pepper and top with chives.

## Parsley Lentil Soup with Vegetables

Serving Size: 4 | Total Time: 20 minutes

1 tbsp olive oil

1 onion, chopped

1 cup celery, chopped

2 garlic cloves, chopped

3 cups vegetable stock

1 ½ cups lentils, rinsed

4 carrots, halved lengthwise

½ tsp salt

2 tbsp parsley, chopped

Warm olive oil on Sauté. Add in onion, garlic, and celery and sauté for 5 minutes until soft. Mix in lentils, carrots, salt, and stock. Seal the lid and cook on High Pressure for 10 minutes. Release the pressure quickly. Serve topped with parsley.

## Simple Cheese Spinach Dip

Serving Size: 6 | Total Time: 20 minutes

2 cups cream cheese

1 cup baby spinach

1 cup mozzarella, grated

Salt and pepper to taste

½ cup scallions

1 cup vegetable broth

Place cream cheese, spinach, mozzarella cheese, salt, pepper, scallions, and broth in a mixing bowl. Stir well and transfer to your Instant Pot. Seal the lid and cook on High Pressure for 5 minutes. Release the steam naturally for 10 minutes. Serve with celery sticks or chips.

## Savory Spinach with Mashed Potatoes

Serving Size: 6 | Total Time: 20 minutes

3 lb potatoes, peeled

½ cup milk

⅓ cup butter

2 tbsp chopped chives

Salt and pepper to taste

2 cups spinach, chopped

Cover the potatoes with salted water in your Instant Pot. Seal the lid and cook on High Pressure for 8 minutes. Release the pressure quickly. Drain the potatoes, and reserve the liquid in a bowl. Mash the potatoes. Mix with butter and milk; season with pepper and salt. With reserved cooking liquid, thin the potatoes to attain the desired consistency. Put the spinach in the remaining potato liquid and stir until wilted; Season to taste. Drain and serve with potato mash. Garnish with chives.

## Coconut Milk Yogurt with Honey

Serving Size: 6 | Total Time: 15 hours

2 cans coconut milk

1 tbsp gelatin

1 tbsp honey

1 tbsp probiotic powder

Zest from 1 lime

Into the pot, stir in gelatin and coconut milk until well dissolved. Seal the lid, Press Yogurt until the display is reading "Boil". Once done, the screen will then display "Yogurt". Ensure milk temperature is at 180°F. Remove steel pot from Pressure cooker base and place into a large ice bath to cool milk for 5 minutes to reach 112°F.

Remove the pot from the ice bath and wipe the outside dry. Into the coconut milk mixture, add probiotic powder, honey, and Lime zest, and stir to combine.

Return steel pot to the base of the Instant Pot. Seal the lid, press Yogurt, and cook for 10 hours. Once complete, spoon yogurt into glass jars with rings and lids; place in the refrigerator to chill for 4 hours to thicken.

## Tofu with Noodles & Peanuts

Serving Size: 4 | Total Time: 15 minutes

1 package tofu, cubed

8 oz egg noodles

2 bell peppers, chopped

¼ cup soy sauce

¼ cup orange juice

1 tbsp fresh ginger, minced

2 tbsp vinegar

1 tbsp sesame oil

1 tbsp sriracha

¼ cup roasted peanuts

3 scallions, chopped

In the Instant Pot, mix tofu, bell peppers, orange juice, sesame oil, ginger, egg noodles, soy sauce, vinegar, and sriracha. Cover with enough water. Seal the lid and cook for 2 minutes on High Pressure. Release the pressure quickly. Divide the meal between 4 plates and top with scallions and peanuts to serve.

## Mushroom & Gouda Cheese Pizza

Serving Size: 4 | Total Time: 30 minutes

4 oz button mushrooms, chopped

½ cup grated gouda cheese

1 pizza crust

½ cup tomato paste

1 tbsp sugar

1 tbsp dried oregano

2 tbsp olive oil

12 olives

1 cup arugula

Grease the bottom of a baking dish with one tbsp of olive oil. Line some parchment paper. Flour the working surface and roll out the pizza crust to the approximate size of your Instant Pot. Gently fit the dough in the previously prepared baking dish.

In a bowl, combine tomato paste, ¼ cup water, sugar and oregano. Spread the mixture over the crust, make a layer with button mushrooms and grated gouda. Add a trivet inside the pot and pour in 1 cup water. Seal the lid and cook for 15 minutes on High Pressure. Do a quick release. Sprinkle the pizza with the remaining oil and top with olives and arugula. Serve.

## Chickpea Stew with Onion & Tomatoes

Serving Size: 4 | Total Time: 40 minutes

6 oz chickpeas, soaked

2 tomatoes, chopped

1 red onion, chopped

1 tbsp cumin seeds

2 cups vegetable broth

2 tbsp olive oil

2 tbsp butter

2 tbsp parsley, chopped

Salt and pepper to taste

To the Instant Pot, add olive oil, tomatoes, onion, cumin seeds, chickpeas, and pour in the broth. Seal the lid and set the steam handle. Cook on Manual for 30 minutes on High. Do a quick release and set aside to cool for a while.

Transfer the soup to a food processor and season with salt and pepper. Process until pureed and spoon onto a serving bowl. Stir in 2 tbsp of butter. Top with freshly chopped parsley and serve.

## Parsnip & Cauliflower Mash with Chives

Serving Size: 8 | Total Time: 15 minutes

1 ½ lb parsnips, cubed

10 oz cauliflower florets

2 garlic cloves

Salt and pepper to taste

¼ cup sour cream

¼ cup grated Parmesan

1 tbsp butter

2 tbsp minced chives

In the pot, mix parsnips, garlic, 2 cups water, salt, cauliflower, and pepper. Seal the lid and cook on High Pressure for 4 minutes. Release the pressure quickly.

Drain parsnips and cauliflower and return to pot. Add Parmesan, butter, and sour cream. Use a potato masher to mash until the desired consistency is attained. Top with chives and place to a serving plate. Serve.

## Traditional Italian Pesto

Serving Size: 4 | Total Time: 20 minutes

3 zucchini, peeled, chopped

1 eggplant, peeled, chopped

3 red bell peppers, chopped

½ cup basil-tomato juice

½ tbsp salt

2 tbsp olive oil

Add zucchini, eggplant, bell peppers, basil-tomato juice, salt, and olive oil to the pot and give it a good stir. Pour 1 cup of water. Seal the lid and cook on High Pressure for 15 minutes. Do a quick release. Set aside to cool completely. Serve as a cold salad or a side dish.

## Mozzarella & Eggplant Lasagna

Serving Size: 2 | Total Time: 30 minutes

1 large eggplant, chopped

4 oz mozzarella, chopped

3 oz mascarpone cheese

2 tomatoes, sliced

¼ cup olive oil

Salt and pepper to taste

Grease a baking dish with olive oil. Slice the eggplant and make a layer in the dish. Cover with mozzarella and tomato slices. Top with mascarpone cheese. Repeat the process until you run out of ingredients.

In a bowl, mix olive oil, salt, and pepper. Pour the mixture over the lasagna, and add ½ cup of water. In your pot, pour 1 cup of water and insert a trivet. Lower the baking dish on the trivet, seal the lid and cook on High Pressure for 4 minutes. Do a natural release for 10 minutes.

## Mushroom & Ricotta Cheese Manicotti

Serving Size: 4 | Total Time: 35 minutes

6 oz button mushrooms, chopped

8 oz pack manicotti pasta

12 oz spinach, torn

3 oz ricotta cheese

¼ cup milk

3 oz butter

¼ tbsp salt

1 tbsp sour cream

Melt butter on Sauté and add mushrooms. Cook until soft, 5 minutes. Add spinach and milk and continue to cook for 6 minutes. Stir in cheese and season with salt. Line a baking dish with parchment paper. Fill manicotti with spinach mixture. Transfer them on the baking sheet. Pour 1 cup water into the Instant Pot and insert a trivet. Lay the baking sheet on the trivet. Seal the lid and cook on High Pressure for 15 minutes. Do a quick release. Top with sour cream and serve.

## Mixed Vegetables Medley

Serving Size: 4 | Total Time: 20 minutes

10 oz broccoli florets

16 asparagus, trimmed

10 oz cauliflower florets

5 oz green beans

2 carrots, cut on bias

Salt to taste

Add 1 cup of water and set trivet on top. Place a steamer basket over the water. In an even layer, spread green beans, broccoli, cauliflower, asparagus, and carrots in the steamer basket. Seal the lid and cook on Steam for 3 minutes on High. Release the pressure quickly. Remove basket from the pot and season with salt.

## Carrot & Chickpea Boil with Tomatoes

Serving Size: 4 | Total Time: 25 minutes

½ cup button mushrooms, chopped

1 cup canned chickpeas

1 onion, peeled, chopped

1 lb string beans, trimmed

1 apple, cubed

½ cup raisins

2 carrots, chopped

2 garlic cloves, crushed

4 cherry tomatoes

1 tbsp grated ginger

½ cup orange juice

Place mushrooms, chickpeas, onion, beans, apple, raisins, carrots, garlic, cherry tomatoes, ginger, and orange juice in the Instant Pot. Pour enough water to cover. Cook on High Pressure for 8 minutes. Do a natural release for 10 minutes. Serve warm.

## Amazing Vegetable Paella

Serving Size: 4 | Total Time: 25 minutes

½ cup green peas

2 carrots, chopped

1 cup fire-roasted tomatoes

1 cup zucchini, chopped

3 oz celery root, chopped

1 tbsp turmeric

2 cup vegetable broth

1 cup long-grain rice

Place green peas, carrots, tomatoes, zucchini, celery, turmeric, and broth in the Instant Pot. Stir well and seal the lid. Cook on Manual for 15 minutes on High. Do a quick release, open the lid, and stir in the rice. Seal the lid and cook on High pressure for 3 minutes. When ready, release the pressure naturally for about 10 minutes.

## Delicious Mushroom Goulash

Serving Size: 4 | Total Time: 50 minutes

6 oz portobello mushrooms, sliced

1 cup green peas

1 cup pearl onions, minced

2 carrots, chopped

1 celery stalk, chopped

2 garlic cloves, crushed

2 potatoes, chopped

1 tbsp apple cider vinegar

1 tbsp rosemary

Salt and pepper to taste

2 tbsp butter

4 cups vegetable stock

Melt butter on Sauté and stir-fry onions, carrots, celery stalks, and garlic for 2-3 minutes. Season with salt, pepper, and rosemary. Add mushrooms, peas, potatoes,

vinegar, and stock and seal the lid. Cook on High Pressure for 30 minutes. When ready, release the pressure naturally.

## Stuffed Peppers with Rice & Mushrooms

Serving Size: 4 | Total Time: 40 minutes

4 bell peppers, seeds and stems removed

6 oz button mushrooms, chopped

1 onion, peeled, chopped

2 garlic cloves, minced

2 tbsp olive oil

½ cup rice

½ tbsp paprika

2 cups vegetable stock

Warm the olive oil on Sauté. Add onion, garlic, and mushrooms, and stir-fry until tender for about 5 minutes. Press Cancel and set aside. In a bowl, combine rice with the mixture from the pot. Sprinkle with paprika.

Stuff each bell pepper with this mixture. Place them in the Instant Pot, filled side up, and pour in the stock. Seal the lid and cook on High Pressure for 15 minutes. Release the pressure naturally for about 10 minutes.

## Celery & Red Bean Stew

Serving Size: 4 | Total Time: 25 minutes

6 oz red beans, cooked

2 carrots, chopped

2 celery stalks, chopped

1 onion, chopped

2 tbsp tomato paste

1 bay leaf

2 cups vegetable broth

3 tbsp olive oil

1 tbsp salt

2 tbsp parsley, chopped

1 tbsp flour

Warm olive oil on Sauté and stir-fry the onion for 3 minutes. Add celery and carrots. Cook for 5 more minutes. Add red beans, bay leaf, salt, and tomato paste. Stir in 1 tbsp of flour and pour in the vegetable broth. Seal the lid and cook on High Pressure for 5 minutes.

Do a natural release for about 10 minutes. Sprinkle with some fresh parsley and serve warm.

## Penne Pasta with Shiitake & Vegetables

Serving Size: 4 | Total Time: 20 minutes

6 oz shiitake mushrooms, chopped

6 oz penne pasta

2 garlic cloves, crushed

1 carrot, chopped into strips

6 oz zucchini cut into strips

6 oz finely chopped leek

4 oz baby spinach

3 tbsp oil

2 tbsp soy sauce

1 tbsp ground ginger

½ tbsp salt

Heat oil on Sauté and stir-fry carrot and garlic for 3-4 minutes. Add mushrooms, penne, zucchini, leek, spinach, soy sauce, ginger, and salt and pour in 2 cups of water. Cook on High Pressure for 4 minutes. Quick-release the pressure and serve.

## Thyme Asparagus Soup

Serving Size: 4 | Total Time: 15 minutes

1 carrot, chopped

2 cups sour cream

½ lb Asparagus, chopped

1 sliced Onion

3 Garlic cloves, minced

3 tbsp Coconut oil

½ tsp dried Thyme

5 cups Bone broth

1 Lemon, juiced, zested

Melt coconut oil in your Instant Pot on Sauté. Place the onions and garlic and cook for 2 minutes, stirring often. Add in thyme and cook for 1 minute. Put in bone broth, asparagus, carrot, and lemon zest and seal the lid. Select Manual and cook for 5 minutes on High pressure. When done, perform a quick pressure release and unlock the lid. Mix in sour cream and serve.

## Gingery Butternut Squash Soup

Serving Size: 6 | Total Time: 25 minutes

1 lb peeled and diced Butternut Squash

2 garlic cloves, minced

1 tbsp Ginger powder

4 cups Chicken broth

1 cup Heavy cream

2 tbsp vegetable oil

Salt and pepper to taste

Place the vegetable oil and half of the butternut squash cubes and cook for 5 minutes until browns on Sauté. Add in the remaining cubes, garlic, ginger powder, chicken broth, heavy cream, salt, and black pepper. Seal the lid, select Manual, and cook for 10 minutes on High pressure. When done, perform a quick pressure release and unlock the lid. Using an immersion blender, pulse until purée. Serve immediately.

## Vegan Lentil & Quinoa Stew

Serving Size: 4 | Total Time: 35 minutes

10 sun-dried tomatoes, chopped

1 cup quinoa

1 cup tomatoes, diced

1 cup lentils

1 tsp garlic, minced

4 cups vegetable broth

1 tsp salt

1 tsp red pepper flakes

Add sun-dried tomatoes, quinoa, tomatoes, lentils, garlic, broth, salt, and red pepper flakes to your Instant Pot. Seal the lid and adjust the steam release handle. Cook on High Pressure for 20 minutes. Release the steam naturally for about 10 minutes. Carefully unlock the lid.

## Spinach Tagliatelle with Mushrooms

Serving Size: 4 | Total Time: 25 minutes

8 oz spinach tagliatelle
6 oz mixed mushrooms
3 tbsp butter
¼ cup feta cheese
¼ cup grated Parmesan
2 garlic cloves, crushed
¼ cup heavy cream
1 tbsp Italian seasoning

Melt butter on Sauté and stir-fry the garlic for a minute. Stir in feta, Italian seasoning, and mushrooms. Add the tagliatelle, 2 cups water, and heavy cream. Cook on High Pressure for 4 minutes. Quick-release the pressure. Top with Parmesan cheese. Serve and enjoy!

## Pasta Orecchiette with Broccoli & Tofu

Serving Size: 4 | Total Time: 25 minutes

1 (9 oz) pack orecchiette
16 oz broccoli, chopped
2 garlic cloves
3 tbsp olive oil
1 tbsp grated tofu
Salt and pepper to taste

Place the orecchiette and broccoli in your Instant Pot. Cover with water and seal the lid. Cook on High Pressure for 10 minutes. Do a quick release. Drain the broccoli and orecchiette. Set aside. Heat the olive oil on Sauté. Stir-fry garlic for 2 minutes. Stir in broccoli, orecchiette, salt, and pepper. Cook for 2 minutes. Stir in tofu to serve.

## English Vegetable Potage

Serving Size: 4 | Total Time: 50 minutes

1 lb potatoes, cut into bite-sized pieces
2 carrots, peeled, chopped
3 celery stalks, chopped
2 onions, peeled, chopped
1 zucchini, sliced
A handful of celery leaves
2 tbsp butter, unsalted

3 tbsp olive oil
2 cups vegetable broth
1 tbsp paprika
Salt and pepper to taste
2 bay leaves

Warm olive oil on Sauté and stir-fry the onions for 3-4 minutes until translucent. Add carrots, celery, zucchini, and ¼ cup of broth. Continue to cook for 10 more minutes, stirring constantly. Stir in potatoes, paprika, salt, pepper, bay leaves, remaining broth, and celery leaves. Seal the lid and cook on Meat/Stew for 30 minutes on High. Do a quick release and stir in butter.

## Spicy Split Pea Stew

Serving Size: 4 | Total Time: 40 minutes

2 cups split yellow peas
1 cup onion, chopped
1 carrot, chopped
2 potatoes, chopped
2 tbsp butter
2 garlic cloves, crushed
1 tbsp chili pepper
4 cups vegetable stock

Melt butter on Sauté and stir-fry the onion for 3 minutes. Add peas, carrot, potatoes, and garlic and cook for 5-6 minutes until tender. Stir in chili pepper. Pour in the stock and seal the lid. Cook on Meat/Stew for 25 minutes. Do a quick release. Serve.

## Speedy Mac & Goat Cheese

Serving Size: 4 | Total Time: 20 minutes

1 lb elbow macaroni
2 oz goat's cheese, crumbled
½ cup skim milk
1 tsp Dijon mustard
1 tsp dried oregano
1 tsp Italian seasoning
2 tbsp olive oil
5 oz olives, sliced

Add macaroni in the Instant Pot and cover with water. Seal the lid and cook on High Pressure for 4 minutes. Do a quick release. Drain the macaroni and set aside.

Press Sauté on the pot and add the olive oil, mustard, milk, oregano, and Italian seasoning. Cook for 3 minutes. Stir in macaroni and cook for 2 minutes. Top with fresh goat's cheese and olives and serve.

## Two-Cheese Carrot Sauce

Serving Size: 4 | Total Time: 25 minutes

1 carrot, shredded
1 cup cream cheese
½ cup Gorgonzola cheese
3 cups vegetable broth
1 cup Gruyere, crumbled
Salt and pepper to taste
1 tsp garlic powder
1 tbsp parsley, chopped

Combine carrot, cream cheese, gorgonzola cheese, broth, gruyere, salt, pepper, garlic powder, and parsley in a large bowl. Pour in the Instant Pot, seal the lid and cook on High Pressure for 8 minutes. Do a natural release for 10 minutes. Store for up to 5 days.

## Curly Kale Soup

Serving Size: 4 | Total Time: 20 minutes

4 cups curly kale
2 tbsp Ginger, minced
4 Garlic cloves, minced
1 tbsp Mustard seeds
1 tbsp Olive oil
1 cup Heavy cream
2 cups vegetable broth
1 tbsp Cumin powder

Warm olive oil in your Instant Pot on Sauté. Place the mustard seeds, garlic, ginger, cumin powder, vegetable broth, curly kale, and heavy cream. Seal the lid, select Manual, and cook for 10 minutes on High pressure. When done, perform a quick pressure release and unlock the lid. Serve warm.

## Cauliflower Rice with Peas & Chili

Serving Size: 2 | Total Time: 20 minutes

10 oz cauliflower florets
2 tbsp olive oil

Salt to taste
1 tsp chili powder
¼ cup green peas
1 tbsp chopped parsley

Add 1 cup water, set rack over water and place the steamer basket onto the rack. Add cauliflower into the steamer basket. Seal the lid and cook on High Pressure for 1 minute. Release the pressure quickly. Remove rack and steamer basket. Drain water from the pot. Set it to Sauté and warm oil. Add in cauliflower and stir to break into smaller pieces like rice. Stir in chili powder, peas and salt. Serve the cauliflower topped with parsley.

## Sweet Potato Medallions with Garlic

Serving Size: 4 | Total Time: 25 minutes

1 tbsp fresh rosemary
1 tbsp garlic powder
4 sweet potatoes
2 tbsp butter
Salt to taste

Add 1 cup water and place a steamer rack over the water. Use a fork to prick sweet potatoes all over and set onto the steamer rack. Seal the lid and cook on High Pressure for 12 minutes. Release the pressure quickly. Transfer sweet potatoes to a cutting board. Peel and slice them into ½-inch medallions. Melt butter in the on Sauté. Add in the medallions and cook each side for 2 to 3 minutes until browned. Season with salt and garlic powder. Serve topped with rosemary.

## Steamed Artichokes & Green Beans

Serving Size: 4 | Total Time: 20 minutes

4 artichokes, trimmed
½ lb green beans, trimmed
1 lemon, halved
1 tbsp lemon zest
1 tbsp lemon juice
3 cloves garlic, crushed
½ cup mayonnaise
Salt to taste
2 tbsp parsley, chopped

Rub the artichokes and green beans with lemon. Add 1 cup water into the pot. Set steamer rack over water and set steamer basket on top. Add in artichokes and green beans and sprinkle with salt. Seal lid and cook on High Pressure for 10 minutes.

Release the pressure quickly. In a mixing bowl, combine mayonnaise, garlic, lemon juice, and lemon zest. Season to taste with salt. Serve with warm steamed artichokes and green beans sprinkled with parsley.

## Stuffed Potatoes with Feta & Rosemary

Serving Size: 4 | Total Time: 50 minutes

1 cup button mushrooms, chopped
6 whole potatoes
¼ cup olive oil
3 garlic cloves, minced
¼ cup feta cheese
1 tsp rosemary, chopped
½ tsp dried thyme
1 tsp salt

Rub the potatoes with salt and place them in the Instant Pot. Add enough water to cover and seal the lid. Cook on High Pressure for 30 minutes. Do a quick release and remove the potatoes. Let chill for a while.

In the pot, mix oil, garlic, rosemary, thyme, and mushrooms. Sauté until the mushrooms soften, 5 minutes on Sauté. Stir in feta. Cut the top of each potato and spoon out the middle. Fill with cheese mixture and serve.

## Grandma's Asparagus with Feta & Lemon

Serving Size: 4 | Total Time: 20 minutes

1 lb asparagus spears
1 tbsp olive oil
Salt and pepper to taste
1 lemon, cut into wedges
1 cup feta cheese, cubed

Into the pot, add 1 cup of water and set trivet over the water. Place steamer basket on the trivet. Place the asparagus into the steamer basket. Seal the lid and cook on High Pressure for 1 minute. Release the Pressure quickly. Add olive oil in a bowl and toss in asparagus

until well coated. Season with pepper and salt. Serve with feta and lemon wedges.

## Turmeric Stew with Green Peas

Serving Size: 4 | Total Time: 35 minutes

2 cups green peas
1 onion, chopped
4 cloves garlic, minced
3 oz of olives, pitted
1 tbsp ginger, shredded
1 tbsp turmeric
1 tbsp salt
4 cups vegetable stock
3 tbsp olive oil

Heat olive oil on Sauté. Stir-fry the onion and garlic for 2-3 minutes, stirring a few times. Add peas, olives, ginger, turmeric, salt, and stock and press Cancel. Seal the lid, select Manual, and cook on High Pressure for 20 minutes. Once the timer goes off, do a quick release before opening the lid. Serve with a dollop of yogurt.

## Spicy Shiitake Mushrooms with Potatoes

Serving Size: 4 | Total Time: 45 minutes

1 lb shiitake mushrooms
2 potatoes, chopped
3 garlic cloves, crushed
2 tbsp olive oil
1 tsp garlic powder
1 tbsp cumin seeds
½ tbsp chili powder
1 large zucchini, chopped
1 cup onions
2 cups vegetable stock
1 cup tomato sauce

Warm olive oil on Sauté. Stir-fry cumin seeds for one minute. Add onions, chili powder, garlic, and garlic powder. Cook for 3 minutes, stirring constantly. Add mushrooms and continue to cook on Sauté for 3 more minutes. Add potatoes, zucchini, stock, and tomato sauce and seal the lid. Cook on High Pressure for 20 minutes. When done, release the pressure naturally. Serve warm.

## Creamy Turnips Stuffed with Cheese

Serving Size: 4 | Total Time: 20 minutes

½ cup chopped roasted red bell pepper

4 small turnips

¼ cup whipping cream

¼ cup sour cream

1 tsp Italian seasoning

1 ½ cups grated mozzarella

4 green onions, chopped

1/3 cup grated Parmesan

Pour 1 cup of water into the pot and insert a trivet. Place the turnips on top. Seal the lid and cook on High for 10 minutes. Do a quick pressure release. Remove the turnips to a cutting board and allow cooling. Cut the turnips in half. Scoop out the pulp into a bowl and mash it with a potato mash. Mix in the whipping and sour cream until smooth. Stir in the roasted bell pepper.

Add in Italian seasoning and mozzarella cheese. Fetch out 2 tbsp of green onions and put into the turnips. Fill the turnip skins with the mashed mixture and sprinkle with Parmesan cheese. Arrange on a greased baking dish and place on the trivet. Seal the lid and cook on High pressure for 3 minutes. Do a quick pressure release. Top with the remaining onions to serve.

## Sautéed Spinach with Roquefort Cheese

Serving Size: 2 | Total Time: 10 minutes

½ cup Roquefort cheese, crumbled

9 oz fresh spinach

2 leeks, chopped

2 red onions, chopped

2 garlic cloves, crushed

3 tbsp olive oil

Grease the inner pot with oil. Stir-fry leeks, garlic, and onions for about 5 minutes on Sauté. Add spinach and give it a good stir. Press Cancel, transfer to a serving dish, and sprinkle with Roquefort cheese. Serve right away.

# DESSERTS & DRINKS

## Vanilla Cheesecake with Cranberry Filling

Serving Size: 8 | Total Time: 1 hour + chilling time

1 cup coarsely crumbled cookies

2 tbsp butter, melted

1 cup mascarpone cheese

½ cup sugar

2 tbsp sour cream

½ tsp vanilla extract

2 eggs

1/3 cup dried cranberries

Fold a 20-inch piece of aluminum foil in half lengthwise twice and set on the Instant Pot. In a bowl, combine butter and crumbled cookies. Press firmly to the bottom and about 1/3 of the way up the sides of a cake pan. Freeze the crust. In a separate bowl, beat mascarpone cheese and sugar to obtain a smooth consistency. Stir in vanilla and sour cream. Beat one egg and add into the cheese mixture to combine well. Do the same with the second egg.

Stir cranberries into the filling. Transfer the filling into the crust. Into the pot, add 1 cup water and set the steam rack. Center the springform pan onto the prepared foil sling. Use the sling to lower the pan onto the rack.

Fold foil strips out of the way of the lid. Seal the lid, press Manual, and cook on High Pressure for 40 minutes. Release the pressure quickly. Transfer the cheesecake to a refrigerator for 3 hours. Use a paring knife to run along the edges between the pan and cheesecake to remove the cheesecake and set to the plate.

## Orange New York Cheesecake

Serving Size: 6 | Total Time: 1 hour + freezing time

FOR THE CRUST

1 cup graham crackers crumbs

2 tbsp butter, melted

1 tsp sugar

FOR THE FILLING

2 cups cream cheese

½ cup sugar

1 tsp vanilla extract

Zest from 1 orange

A pinch of salt

2 eggs

Fold a 20-inch piece of aluminum foil in half lengthwise twice and set on the Instant Pot. Grease a parchment paper and line it to a cake pan. In a bowl, combine melted butter, sugar, and graham crackers. Press into the bottom and about ⅓ up the sides of the pan. Transfer the pan to the freezer as you prepare the filling.

In a separate bowl, beat sugar, cream cheese, salt, orange zest, and vanilla until smooth. Beat eggs into the filling, one at a time. Stir until combined. Add the filling over the chilled crust in the pan. Add 1 cup water and set a trivet into the pot. Put the pan on the trivet.

Seal the lid, press Cake, and cook for 40 minutes on High. Release the pressure quickly. Cool the cheesecake and then transfer it to the refrigerator for 3 hours. Use a paring knife to run along the edges between the pan and cheesecake to remove the cheesecake and set to the plate.

## Pie Cups with Fruit Filling

Serving Size: 6 | Total Time: 40 minutes + chilling time

FOR THE CRUST:

2 cups flour

¾ tsp salt

¾ cup butter, softened

1 tbsp sugar

½ cup ice water

FOR THE FILLING:

½ fresh peach

½ cup apples, chopped

¼ cup cranberries

2 tbsp flour

1 tbsp sugar

½ tsp cinnamon

1 egg yolk, for brushing

Place flour, salt, butter, sugar, and water in a food processor and pulse until dough becomes crumbly. Remove to a lightly floured work surface. Divide among

4 equal pieces and wrap in plastic foil. Refrigerate for an hour. Place apples, peach, cranberries, flour, sugar, and cinnamon in a bowl. Toss to combine and set aside. Roll each piece into 6-inch round discs. Add 2 tablespoons of the apple mixture at the center of each disc and wrap to form small bowls. Brush each bowl with egg yolk and gently Transfer to an oiled baking dish. Pour 1 cup of water into the pot and insert the trivet. Place the pan on top. Seal the lid, and cook for 25 minutes on High Pressure. Release the pressure naturally. Serve cool.

# Homemade Lemon Cheesecake

Serving Size: 6 | Total Time: 1 hour + chilling time

CRUST:

4 oz graham crackers

1 tsp ground cinnamon

3 tbsp butter, melted

FILLING:

1 lb mascarpone cheese, softened

¾ cup sugar

¼ cup sour cream, at room temperature

2 eggs

1 tsp vanilla extract

1 tsp lemon zest

1 tbsp lemon juice

A pinch of salt

1 cup strawberries, halved

In a food processor, beat cinnamon and graham crackers to attain a texture almost same as sand; mix in melted butter. Press the crumbs into the bottom of a 7-inch springform pan in an even layer. In a stand mixer, beat sugar, mascarpone cheese, and sour cream for 3 minutes to combine well and have a fluffy and smooth mixture. Scrape the bowl's sides and add eggs, lemon zest, salt, lemon juice, and vanilla. Carry on to beat the mixture until you obtain a consistent color and all ingredients are completely combined. Pour filling over crust.

Into the inner pot, add 1 cup water and set in a trivet. Place the springform pan on the trivet. Seal the lid, press Cake, and cook for 40 minutes on High. Release the pressure quickly. Remove the cheesecake and let it cool. Garnish with strawberry halves on top. Use a paring knife to run along the edges between the pan and cheesecake to remove it and set it to a plate. Serve.

# Classic French Squash Tart

Serving Size: 6 | Total Time: 35 minutes

15 oz mashed squash

6 fl oz milk

½ tsp cinnamon, ground

½ tsp nutmeg

½ tsp salt

3 large eggs

½ cup granulated sugar

1 pack pate brisee

Place squash puree in a large bowl. Add milk, cinnamon, eggs, nutmeg, salt, and sugar. Whisk together until well incorporated. Grease a baking dish with oil. Gently place pate brisee creating the edges with hands. Pour the squash mixture over and flatten the surface with a spatula. Pour 1 cup of water into the pot and insert the trivet. Lay the baking dish on the trivet. Seal the lid, and cook for 25 minutes on High Pressure. Do a quick release. Transfer the pie to a serving platter. Refrigerate.

# Walnut & Pumpkin Tart

Serving Size: 6 | Total Time: 70 minutes

1 cup packed shredded pumpkin

3 eggs

½ cup sugar

1 cup flour

½ cup half-and-half

¼ cup olive oil

1 tsp baking powder

1 tsp vanilla extract

1 tsp ground cinnamon

½ tsp ground nutmeg

½ cup chopped walnuts

2 cups water

FROSTING:

4 oz cream cheese, room temperature

8 tbsp butter

½ cup confectioners sugar

½ tsp vanilla extract

½ tsp salt

In a bowl, beat eggs and sugar to get a smooth mixture. Mix in oil, flour, vanilla extract, cinnamon, half-and-half, baking powder, and nutmeg. Stir well to obtain a fluffy batter. Fold walnuts and pumpkin through the batter. Add batter into a cake pan and cover with aluminum foil. Into the pot, add 1 cup water and set a trivet. Lay cake pan onto the trivet.

Seal the lid, select Manual, and cook on High Pressure for 40 minutes. Release pressure naturally for 10 minutes. Beat cream cheese, confectioners' sugar, salt, vanilla, and butter in a bowl until smooth. Place in the refrigerator until needed. Remove cake from the pan and transfer to a wire rack to cool. Over the cake, spread frosting and apply a topping of shredded carrots.

## Cottage Cheesecake with Strawberries

Serving Size: 6 | Total Time: 35 minutes +cooling time
10 oz cream cheese
¼ cup sugar
½ cup cottage cheese
1 lemon, zested and juiced
2 eggs, cracked into a bowl
1 tsp lemon extract
3 tbsp sour cream
1 cup water
10 strawberries, halved to decorate

Blend with an electric mixer, the cream cheese, quarter cup of sugar, cottage cheese, lemon zest, lemon juice, and lemon extract until a smooth consistency is formed. Adjust the sweet taste to liking with more sugar. Add the eggs. Fold in at low speed until incorporated. Spoon the mixture into a greased baking pan. Level the top with a spatula and cover with foil. Fit a trivet in the pot and pour in water. Place the cake pan on the trivet.

Seal the lid. Select Manual and cook for 15 minutes. Mix the sour cream and 1 tbsp of sugar. Set aside. Once the timer has gone off, do a natural pressure release for 10 minutes. Use a spatula to spread the sour cream mixture on the warm cake. Let cool. Top with strawberries.

## Yogurt Cheesecake with Cranberries

Serving Size: 6 | Total Time: 45 minutes + chilling time
2 lb Greek yogurt
2 cups sugar
4 eggs
2 tsp lemon zest
1 tsp lemon extract
1 cheesecake crust
FOR TOPPING:
7 oz dried cranberries
2 tbsp cranberry jam
2 tsp lemon zest
1 tsp vanilla sugar
1 tsp cranberry extract
¾ cup lukewarm water

In a bowl, combine yogurt, sugar, eggs, lemon zest, and lemon extract. With a mixer, beat well until well-combined. Place the crust in a greased cake pan and pour in the filling. Flatten the surface with a spatula. Leave in the fridge for 30 minutes. Combine cranberries, jam, lemon zest, vanilla sugar, cranberry extract, and water in the pot. Simmer for 15 minutes on Sauté. Remove and wipe the pot clean. Fill in 1 cup water and insert a trivet. Set the pan on top of the trivet and pour cranberry topping. Seal the lid and cook for 20 minutes on High Pressure. Do a quick release. Run a sharp knife around the edge of the cheesecake. Refrigerate. Serve and enjoy!

## Lemon-Apricot Compote

Serving Size: 6 | Total Time: 20 minutes
2 lb fresh apricots, sliced
1 lb sugar
2 tbsp lemon zest
1 tsp ground nutmeg
10 cups water

Add apricots, sugar, water, nutmeg, and lemon zest. Cook, stirring occasionally until half of the water evaporates, on Sauté. Press Cancel and transfer the apricots and the remaining liquid into glass jars. Let cool. Refrigerate.

## Banana Chocolate Bars

Serving Size: 6 | Total Time: 25 minutes

½ cup almond butter

3 bananas

2 tbsp cocoa powder

Place the bananas and almond butter in a bowl and mash finely with a fork. Add the cocoa powder and stir until well combined. Grease a baking dish. Pour the banana and almond butter into the dish. Pour 1 cup water into the cooker and lower a trivet. Place the baking dish on the trivet and seal the lid. Select Pressure Cook for 15 minutes on High. When it goes off, do a quick release. Let cool for a few minutes before cutting into squares.

# RECIPE INDEX

Cheesy Turkey Stew 125
Chicken & Bacon Cacciatore 27
Chicken & Broccoli Rice 88
Chicken & Lima Bean Soup 115
Chicken & Pepper Cacciatore 22
Chicken & Potato Soup 110
Chicken & Spinach Soup 111
Chicken & Tomato Curry 22
Chicken Fricassee 20
Chicken Gumbo 25
Chicken in Creamy Mushroom Sauce 27
Chicken Soup with Vegetables 123
Chicken Stew with Potatoes & Broccoli 126
Chicken Wings in Yogurt-Garlic Sauce 20
Chicken with Chili & Lime 26
Chicken with Port Wine Sauce 28
Chickpea Stew with Onion & Tomatoes 134
Chili & Lemon Chicken Wings 21
Chili Cream of Acorn Squash Soup 100
Chili Deviled Eggs 91
Chili Soup with Avocado & Corn 102
Chili Squid 82
Chili Steamed Catfish 73
Chili-Braised Pork Chops with Tomatoes 38
Chinese Beef with Bok Choy 54
Chinese Shrimp with Green Beans 79
Chipotle Pumpkin Soup 99
Chipotle Shredded Beef 64
Chorizo & Bean Soup 121
Chorizo & Tomato Pork Chops 41
Chorizo Soup with Roasted Tomatoes 100
Chorizo with Macaroni & Cheddar Cheese 38
Chowder with Broccoli, Carrot & Tofu 99
Cilantro & Coconut Chicken Soup 112
Cilantro Pork with Avocado 46
Cinnamon BBQ Pork Ribs 40
Classic Beef Stroganoff 57
Classic French Squash Tart 143
Classic Mushroom Beef Stroganoff 52
Coconut Chicken Soup 112
Coconut Milk Yogurt with Honey 133
Coconut Pumpkin Chili 14
Corn & Mackerel Chowder 73

Corn Soup with Chicken & Egg 118
Cottage Cheesecake with Strawberries 144
Country Chicken with Vegetables 19
Crab Pilaf with Broccoli & Asparagus 81
Cranberry Millet Pilaf 89
Cranberry Orange Sauce 95
Cranberry Turkey with Hazelnuts 30
Creamed Butternut Squash Soup 116
Creamy Bean & Potato Soup 107
Creamy Broccoli-Gorgonzola Soup 105
Creamy Celery & Green Pea Soup 107
Creamy Mascarpone Chicken 23
Creamy Turnips Stuffed with Cheese 140
Creole Chicken with Rice 26
Creole Seafood Gumbo 76
Creole Shrimp with Okra 78
Cuban Mojo Chicken Tortillas 26
Cumin Chicken with Capers 28
Curly Kale Soup 139
Curried Chicken with Mushrooms 21
Curried Pumpkin Soup 121
Curried Tofu with Vegetables 17

## D

Date & Apple Risotto 87
Delicious Chicken & Potato Soup 104
Delicious Mushroom Goulash 136
Delicious Pork & Vegetables Soup 48
Delicious Turkey Burgers 29
Dijon Catfish Fillets with White Wine 72
Dilled Salmon Soup 109
Duck Breasts with Honey-Mustard Glaze 36

## E

Easy Camembert Cakes 91
Easy Seafood Paella 75
Easy Tahini Sweet Potato Mash 133
Easy Veggie Soup 119
Effortless Tomato-Lentil Soup 107
Egg Bites with Mushrooms & Arugula 92
Eggplant & Beef Stew with Parmesan 53
English Vegetable Potage 138

## F

Fall Beef Steak with Vegetables 55
Fall Vegetable Mash 13
Fall Vegetable Soup 102
Famous Chicken Adobo 23
Farro & Vegetable Chicken Soup 102
Fennel & Rosemary Pork Belly 44
Fennel Chicken with Tomato Sauce 25
Fennel Lamb Ribs 68
Feta & Vegetable Faro 89
Feta Cheese Turkey Balls 28
Filipino-Style Chicken Congee 23
French Onion Soup 117
Friday Night BBQ Pork Butt 37
Fruity Pork Steaks 41

## G

Garam Masala Parsnip & Red Onion Soup 101
Garden Vegetable Soup 103
Garlic & Thyme Pork 49
Garlic Chicken 19
Garlic Eggplants with Parmesan 15
Garlic Lamb with Thyme 67
Garlicky Herb-Rubbed Beef Brisket 61
Garlic-Spicy Ground Pork with Peas 38
German Pork with Sauerkraut 44
German-Style Red Cabbage with Apples 49
Ginger & Garlic Crab 80
Ginger & Vegetable Beef Broth 94
Gingered Beef Pot Roast 51
Gingery Butternut Squash Soup 137
Gingery Carrot Soup 119
Gingery Squash & Leek Soup 108
Gluten-Free Porridge 90
Grandma's Asparagus with Feta & Lemon 140
Greek Chicken with Potatoes & Okra 23
Greek-Style Fish Soup 114
Greek-Style Stuffed Peppers 64
Green Immune-Boosting Soup 99
Green Pea & Beef Ragout 52
Green Pork Chili 125
Green Soup 115
Green Vegetables with Tomatoes 17
Gruyere Mushroom & Mortadella Cups 50

## H

Haddock with Edamame Soybeans 71
Hard-Boiled Eggs with Paprika 91
Harissa Chicken Thighs 23
Harissa Chicken with Fruity Farro 90
Harvest Vegetable Soup with Pesto 116
Hawaiian Rice 88
Hearty Beef Soup 110
Herby Chicken Stock 94
Herby Chicken with Peach Gravy 19
Herby Crab Legs with Lemon 80
Hoisin Spare Pork Ribs 40
Homemade Chicken & Quinoa Soup 97
Homemade Chicken Puttanesca 24
Homemade Chicken Stock 95
Homemade Gazpacho Soup 132
Homemade Lemon Cheesecake 143
Homemade Turkey Pepperoni Pizza 30
Homemade Vichyssoise Soup with Chives 96
Homemade Winter Soup 104
Honey-Glazed Turkey 35
Hot Paprika & Oregano Lamb 65
Hot Pork Chops with Cheddar Cheese 43
Hot Shrimp & Potato Chowder 77
Hungarian-Style Turkey Stew 33

## I

Indian Prawn Curry 79
Indian-Style Chicken 26
Italian Roast Beef 56
Italian Steamed Sea Bream with Lemon 71

## J

Jalapeño Chicken Soup with Tortilla Chips 109
Jalapeño Shrimp with Herbs & Lemon 78
Jamaican Chicken with Pineapple Sauce 24
Japanese-Style Pork Tenderloin 43
Juicy Hot Chicken Wings 92
Juicy Pork Butt Steaks 43

## K

Kale & Artichoke Cheese Bites 92
Kale, Bean & Pancetta Soup 113
Kielbasa Sausage Soup 121

Kimchi Ramen Noodle Soup 102
Korean-Style Chicken 22

# L

Lamb Chops with Mashed Potatoes 69
Lamb Chorba 70
Lamb Shanks with Garlic & Thyme 65
Lamb Stew with Lemon & Parsley 66
Lamb with Tomato & Green Peas 65
Leftover Beef Sandwiches 59
Leg of Lamb with Garlic and Pancetta 67
Lemon & Leek Tilapia 72
Lemon & Thyme Chicken 28
Lemon-Apricot Compote 144
Lentil & Carrot Soup 108
Lentil & Pork Shank Soup 111

# M

Mackerel with Potatoes & Spinach 73
Mango & Pumpkin Porridge 13
Maple Beef Teriyaki 56
Mascarpone Mashed Turnips 14
Mashed Potato Balls with Tomato Sauce 129
Mediterranean Beef Stew with Olives 59
Mediterranean Carrot & Chickpea Soup 100
Mediterranean Duck with Olives 35
Mediterranean Lamb 66
Mediterranean Soup with Tortellini 116
Merlot Pork Chops 37
Mexican Bean Soup 114
Mexican Pork Chili Verde 42
Millet & Beef Soup 108
Minestrone Soup with Green Vegetables 132
Minestrone with Fresh Herbs 118
Minty Lamb 65
Mixed Vegetables Medley 135
Modern Minestrone with Pancetta 105
Mom's Meatball Soup 111
Moroccan Lentil Soup 115
Moroccan-Style Chicken 27
Mozzarella & Eggplant Lasagna 135
Mushroom & Bell Pepper Casserole 17
Mushroom & Gouda Cheese Pizza 134
Mushroom & Pork Stroganoff 45

Mushroom & Ricotta Cheese Manicotti 135
Mushroom & Spinach Chicken Stew 125
Mushroom-Spinach Cream Soup 96
Mussels With Lemon & White Wine 81
Mustard Carrot Soup 119
Mustard Potato Soup with Crispy Bacon 120

# N

Navy Bean & Zucchini Soup 113
North African Turkey Stew 34
Nutmeg Broccoli Soup with Cheddar 121

# O

Old-Fashioned Apple Pie 91
One-Pot Sausages with Peppers & Onions 126
Orange & Thyme Beet Wedges 16
Orange Glazed Carrots 15
Orange New York Cheesecake 142

# P

Paprika Chicken Wings 93
Paprika Pulled Pork Fajitas 42
Parmesan Topped Vegetable Mash 131
Parsley & Lemon Turkey Risotto 31
Parsley Creamy Tomato Soup 107
Parsley Lentil Soup with Vegetables 133
Parsley Noodle Soup with Chicken 104
Parsley Pork with Savoy Cabbage 46
Parsnip & Cauliflower Mash 13
Parsnip & Cauliflower Mash with Chives 134
Party Shrimp with & Rice Veggies 77
Pasta Orecchiette with Broccoli & Tofu 138
Pea & Beef Stew 124
Pea & Garbanzo Bean Soup 117
Pear & Cider Pork Tenderloin 42
Peasant Bean Soup 117
Penne Pasta with Shiitake & Vegetables 137
Peppered Chicken with Chunky Salsa 27
Picante Chicken Wings 93
Pie Cups with Fruit Filling 142
Pino Noir Beef Pot Roast 55
Piri Piri Chicken Soup 105
Plant-Based Indian Curry 130
Pollock & Tomato Stew 72

Pork Chops & Mushrooms with Tomato Sauce 38
Pork Medallions with Porcini Sauce 43
Pork Sirloin Chili 41
Pork Soup with Cabbage & Beans 110
Potato & Broccoli Soup with Rosemary 104
Potato & Cauliflower Turkey Soup 34
Potato Skins with Shredded Turkey 32
Potato-Leek Soup with Tofu 103
Prune & Shallot Pork Tenderloin 45
Pulled BBQ Beef 63
Pulled Pork Tacos 47

## Q

Quick Beef Soup 109
Quick Farro with Greens & Pine Nuts 130
Quick French-Style Lamb with Sesame 66
Quick Mushroom-Quinoa Soup 103
Quick Pork & Vegetable Rice 45
Quick Shrimp Gumbo with Sausage 77
Quinoa with Brussels Sprouts & Broccoli 130

## R

Ranch Potatoes with Ham 50
Red Soup with Cheesy Croutons 96
Red Wine Beef & Vegetable Hotpot 53
Red Wine Squid 81
Rich Beef & Vegetable Casserole 60
Rich Millet with Herbs & Cherry Tomatoes 89
Rich Shrimp Risotto 78
Rigatoni with Turkey & Tomato Sauce 29
Risotto with Broccoli & Grana Padano 86
Risotto with Spring Vegetables & Shrimp 85
Roast Goose with White Wine 36
Rosemary Braised Beef in Red Wine 60
Rosemary Pork Belly Stew 124
Rustic Soup with Turkey Balls & Carrots 105

## S

Sage Turkey & Red Wine Casserole 31
Salmon & Tomato Farfalle 85
Sambal Beef Noodles 57
Saucy Chicken Marsala 19
Saucy Clams with Herbs 82
Sausage & Cannellini Bean Stew 127

Sautéed Spinach with Roquefort Cheese 141
Savory Herb Meatloaf 58
Savory Irish Lamb Stew 67
Savory Spinach with Mashed Potatoes 133
Scallion Chicken & Lentil Soup 120
Seafood & Fish Stew 73
Seafood Chowder with Oyster Crackers 74
Seafood Hot Pot with Rice 75
Seafood Medley with Rosemary Rice 74
Seafood Pilaf 75
Seafood Stew with Sausage 124
Seafood Traditional Spanish Paella 74
Shrimp Boil with Chorizo Sausages 76
Shrimp with Chickpeas & Olives 76
Shrimp with Okra & Brussels Sprouts 77
Sicilian Seafood Linguine 84
Simple Beef Bolognese Sauce 95
Simple Beef with Rice & Cheese 54
Simple Carrot & Oregano Soup 101
Simple Cheese Spinach Dip 133
Simple Chicken Soup with Fennel 97
Simple Roast Lamb 67
Smoked Ham & Potato Soup 110
Smoky Chipotle Beef Brisket 59
Smoky Shredded Pork with White Beans 47
Speedy Mac & Goat Cheese 138
Spiced Mexican Pork 47
Spiced Pork with Garbanzo Beans 46
Spicy Ground Turkey Chili with Vegetables 31
Spicy Honey Chicken 22
Spicy Lamb & Bean Chili 68
Spicy Mussels & Anchovies with Rice 82
Spicy Okra & Eggplant Dish 15
Spicy Pasta with Seafood 76
Spicy Pork Sausage Ragu 44
Spicy Pumpkin Curry 127
Spicy Pumpkin Soup 118
Spicy Red Kidney Bean Soup 106
Spicy Rice Noodles with Tofu & Chives 84
Spicy Shiitake Mushrooms with Potatoes 140
Spicy Split Pea Stew 138
Spicy Sweet Potato Soup 109
Spicy Tomato Soup with Rice 99

Spicy Turkey Casserole with Tomatoes 30
Spicy Vegetable Pilaf 130
Spinach & Shrimp Fusilli 78
Spinach Chicken Thighs 20
Spinach Tagliatelle with Mushrooms 138
Spinach, Garlic & Mushroom Pilaf 85
Spring Chicken Vermicelli Soup 112
Spring Onion Buffalo Wings 21
Spring Risotto 87
Squash Soup with Yogurt & Cilantro 101
Steamed Artichokes & Green Beans 139
Steamed Artichokes with Lime Aioli 131
Steamed Artichokes with Salsa Roquefort 14
Steamed Asparagus with Salsa Verde 14
Steamed Halibut Packets 73
Stewed Beef with Potatoes 51
Sticky Chicken Wings 21
Sticky Teriyaki Chicken 25
Stuffed Mushrooms with Rice & Cheese 85
Stuffed Peppers with Rice & Mushrooms 136
Stuffed Potatoes with Feta & Rosemary 140
Stuffed Tench with Herbs & Lemon 72
Sunday Turkey Lettuce Wraps 29
Sweet & Spicy BBQ Chicken 24
Sweet & Spicy Pork Ribs 39
Sweet Mustard Pork Chops with Piccalilli 38
Sweet Potato Medallions with Garlic 139

# T

Taco-Style Chicken Stew 126
Tandoori Pork Butt 44
Tangy Pumpkin Soup 122
Tangy Shrimp Curry 79
Tarragon Apple Pork Chops 42
Tarragon Baby Carrots with Parsnips 14
Tasty Asparagus Soup 107
Tasty Beef Neck Bone Stock 94
Tasty Spicy Beef 53
T-Bone Steaks with Basil & Mustard 51
Thai Beef Short Ribs 58
Thai Chicken 20
Thai-Style Chili Pork 39
Thyme Asparagus Soup 137

Thyme Ground Beef Roll 55
Thyme Sea Bass with Turnips 72
Tilapia Fillets with Hazelnut Crust 71
Tilapia with Basil Pesto & Rice 71
Tofu with Noodles & Peanuts 134
Tomato & Feta Pearl Barley 89
Tomato Shrimp Soup 120
Traditional American Beef Meatloaf 57
Traditional Cheesy Onion Soup 104
Traditional Italian Pesto 135
Traditional Italian Rice & Cheese Balls 91
Traditional Italian Vegetable Soup 98
Traditional Lamb with Vegetables 67
Turkey & Black Bean Chili 32
Turkey Cakes with Ginger Gravy 29
Turkey Meatball Soup with Rice 33
Turkey Sausage with Brussels Sprouts 34
Turkey Soup with Noodle 32
Turkey Stew with Salsa Verde 32
Turkey with Rice & Peas 35
Turkish-Inspired Lentil Soup 113
Turkish-Style Roasted Turkey 30
Turmeric Butternut Squash Soup 106
Turmeric Stew with Green Peas 140
Tuscan Chicken Thighs 127
Two-Cheese Carrot Sauce 139

# U

Ukrainian-Style Borscht 111

# V

Vanilla Cheesecake with Cranberry Filling 142
Veal Chops with Greek Yogurt 64
Vegan Lentil & Quinoa Stew 137
Vegan Tomato Soup 122
Vegetable & Lamb Casserole 69
Vegetable Beef Soup 105
Vegetable Soup with Coconut Milk 98
Vegetables with Veal & Pork 128
Vegetarian Chili with Lentils & Quinoa 132
Vegetarian Green Dip 131
Vegetarian Lentil Soup with Nachos 99
Vegetarian Soup with White Beans 106
Vegetarian Wild Rice with Carrots 85

CPSIA information can be obtained
at www.ICGtesting.com
Printed in the USA
LVHW061314060721
691747LV00005B/160